■ The Arkansas State Constitution

The Oxford Commentaries on the State Constitutions of the United States
G. Alan Tarr, Series Editor

Professor G. Alan Tarr, Director of the Center on State Constitutional Studies at Rutgers University, serves as General Editor for this important new series which in its entirety will cover each of the 50 states. Each volume of The Oxford Commentaries on the State Constitutions of the United States contains a historical overview of the state's constitutional development, plus a section-by-section analysis of the state's current constitution. Other features included in the volumes are the text of the state's constitution, a bibliographic essay, table of cases, and index. This series provides essential reference tools for those investigating state constitutional development and constitutional law.

The Arkansas State Constitution

Kay Collett Goss

Foreword by The Honorable Wilbur D. Mills

THE OXFORD COMMENTARIES ON THE STATE CONSTITUTIONS OF THE UNITED STATES
G. Alan Tarr, Series Editor

OXFORD
UNIVERSITY PRESS

OXFORD
UNIVERSITY PRESS

Oxford University Press, Inc., publishes works that further Oxford University's objective of excellence in research, scholarship, and education.

Oxford New York
Auckland Cape Town Dar es Salaam Hong Kong Karachi Kuala Lumpur Madrid Melbourne
Mexico City Nairobi New Delhi Shanghai Taipei Toronto

With offices in
Argentina Austria Brazil Chile Czech Republic France Greece Guatemala Hungary Italy
Japan Poland Portugal Singapore South Korea Switzerland Thailand Turkey Ukraine
Vietnam

Published by Oxford University Press, Inc.
198 Madison Avenue, New York, New York 10016

Library of Congress Cataloging-in-Publication Data

Goss, Kay Collett.
The Arkansas State Constitution / Kay Collett Goss ; foreword by Wilbur D. Mills.
p. cm. — (The Oxford commentaries on the state constitutions of the United States)
Includes bibliographical references and index.
ISBN 978-0-19-977896-6 (hardback)
1. Constitutions—Arkansas. 2. Constitutional law—Arkansas.
3. Constitutional history—Arkansas. I. Arkansas. Constitution (1874) II. Title.
KFA40011874.A6 G667 2011
342.76702—dc22 2011002850

Note to Readers
This publication is designed to provide accurate and authoritative information in regard to the subject matter covered. It is based upon sources believed to be accurate and reliable and is intended to be current as of the time it was written. It is sold with the understanding that the publisher is not engaged in rendering legal, accounting, or other professional services. If legal advice or other expert assistance is required, the services of a competent professional person should be sought. Also, to confirm that the information has not been affected or changed by recent developments, traditional legal research techniques should be used, including checking primary sources where appropriate.

(Based on the Declaration of Principles jointly adopted by a Committee of the American Bar Association and a Committee of Publishers and Associations.)

Dedicated to **The Honorable Wilbur D. Mills** who inspired me
to choose public service as a career, while being a
legendary congressional leader and
my political hero, and who inspired me throughout
the writing of this book, while being my personal confidant
and my professional adviser.

CONTENTS

Series Foreword by G. Alan Tarr *xi*
Foreword by Wilbur D. Mills *xiii*

Introduction 1

PART ONE The History of the Arkansas Constitution

The 1836 Constitution for the New State 5
The 1861 Constitution to Leave the Union 8
The 1864 Constitution to Return to the Union 9
The 1868 Constitution for Reconstruction 11
The 1874 Constitution to Recover from Reconstruction 13
The World War I Convention 16
The Rockefeller-Young Turks Convention 16
The Pryor-Clinton Convention 18
Proposed Amendments to the Arkansas Constitution, 1874 to 1992 21

PART TWO The Arkansas Constitution and Commentary

Preamble 29

Article I: Boundaries **31**

Article II: Declaration of Rights **33**

Article III: Franchise and Elections **45**

Article IV: Departments **49**

Article V: Legislative **51**

Article VI: Executive Department **63**

Article VII: Judicial Department **71**

Article VIII: Apportionment **89**

Article IX: Exemptions **91**

Article X: Agriculture, Mining and Manufacture **95**

Article XI: Militia **97**

Article XII: Municipal and Private Corporations **99**

Article XIII: Counties, County Seats and County Lines 105

Article XIV: Education 107

Article XV: Impeachment and Address 109

Article XVI: Finance and Taxation 111

Article XVII: Railroads, Canals and Turnpikes 117

Article XVIII: Judicial Circuits 123

Article XIX: Miscellaneous Provisions 125

Schedule 135

Amendments to the Constitution of 1874 145

1. "Holford" Bonds (Article 20) 145
2. Regulation of Transportation Rates 146
3. Three-Mill County Road Tax 146
4. Sureties on Official Bonds by Bonding Companies 146
5. Sixty-Day Session of the Legislature 147
6. Governor and Lieutenant Governor 147
7. Initiative and Referendum 149
8. Equal Suffrage 158
9. State Supreme Court 158
10. Local Bond Issues for Debts Only 159
11. Eighteen-Mill District School Tax 160
12. Cotton Mills Tax Exempt for Seven Years 160
13. Municipal Improvement Bonds 161
14. Local Acts by Legislature Prohibited 163
15. Salaries of State Officials 163
16. Trial by Jury 164
17. Construction and Building Tax 164
18. Tax to Aid Industries 165
19. Tax Increase Restrictions? Passage of Laws 166
20. Issuance of Bonds 167
21. Criminal Prosecutions-Salaries of Prosecuting Attorneys 168
22. Exemption of Homesteads from Certain State Taxes 169
23. The Board of Apportionment 170
24. Probate Courts 172
25. County Construction Tax 173
26. Workmens' Compensation 174
27. Industry Tax Exemption 174
28. Rules for Law Practice 175
29. Vacancies 175

30. Municipal Library Tax 177
31. Municipal Retirement Tax 178
32. County or City Hospital Tax 179
33. Boards and Commissions 181
34. Labor Union Membership 182
35. Game and Fish Commission 183
36. Votes of Military Personnel 187
37. State Officers; Compensation 187
38. County Library Tax 188
39. Voter Registration 190
40. School Tax Millage 190
41. County Clerk 191
42. Highway Commission 191
43. Judges' Salaries 194
44. Interposition 194
45. Senatorial Districts 196
46. Hot Springs Horse Racing 197
47. State Ad Valorem Tax Prohibition 198
48. Compensation of Members of General Assembly 198
49. Industrial Development Bonds Authority 199
50. The Permissive Voting Machine Amendment 201
51. Voter Registration without Poll Tax Payment 202
52. Community College Enabling Act 215
53. Kindergarten 216
54. State Printing Contracts 216
55. Revision of County Government 217
56. Establish and Limit Salaries of Governor and Other State Constitutional Officers, Members of the General Assembly and Municipal Officers 220
57. Exemption or Lowering of Intangible Personal Property Tax 221
58. Creation of a State Court of Appeals 222
59. Property Tax Relief and Rollback 223
60. Interest Rate Control 227
61. Three-Mill County Road Tax 228
62. Local Capital Improvement Bond 229
63. Four-Year Terms for State Constitutional Officers 234
64. Municipal Court Jurisdiction Amendment 234
65. Revenue Bonds 235
66. Judicial Discipline and Disability Commission 237
67. Jurisdiction of Matters Relating to Juveniles and Bastardy 239
68. Prevent Abortion Funding and to Restrict Abortion 239
69. Repeal Amendment 44 to the Constitution 239

70. An Amendment to Prohibit Public Relations Funds for State Executive and Legislative Officials and to Govern Compensation and Expense Reimbursement for Such Officials 240
71. Personal Property Tax Amendment 243
72. City and County Library Amendment 244
73. Arkansas Term Limitation Amendment 249

Bibliographical Essay 251
Table of Cases 261
Index 277
About the Author 281

■ SERIES FOREWORD

In 1776, following the declaration of independence from England, the former colonies began to draft their own constitutions. Their handiwork attracted widespread interest, and draft constitutions circulated up and down the Atlantic seaboard, as constitution-makers sought to benefit from the insights of their counterparts in sister states. In Europe, the new constitutions found a ready audience seeking enlightenment from the American experiments in self government. Even the delegates to the Constitutional Convention of 1787, despite their reservations about the course of political developments in the states during the decade after independence, found much that was useful in the newly adopted constitutions. And when James Madison, fulfilling a pledge given during the ratification debates, drafted the federal Bill of Rights, he found his model in the famous Declaration of Rights of the Virginia Constitution.

By the 1900s, however, few people would have looked to state constitutions for enlightenment. Instead, a familiar litany of complaints was heard whenever state constitutions were mentioned. State constitutions were too long and too detailed, combining basic principles with policy prescriptions and prohibitions that had no place in the fundamental law of a state. By including such provisions, it was argued, state constitutions deprived state governments of the flexibility they needed to respond effectively to changing circumstances. This—among other factors—encouraged political reformers to look to the federal government, which was not plagued by such constitutional constraints, thereby shifting the locus of political initiative away from the states. Meanwhile, civil libertarians concluded that state bills of rights, at least as interpreted by state courts, did not adequately protect rights and therefore looked to the federal courts and the federal Bill of Rights for redress. As power and responsibility shifted from the states to Washington, so too did the attention of scholars, the legal community, and the general public.

During the early 1970s, however, state constitutions were "rediscovered." The immediate impetus for this rediscovery was former President Richard Nixon's appointment of Warren Burger to succeed Earl Warren as Chief Justice of the United States Supreme Court. To civil libertarians, this appointment seemed to signal a decisive shift in the Supreme Court's jurisprudence, because Burger was expected to lead the Court away from the liberal activism that had characterized the Warren Court. They therefore sought ways to safeguard the gains they had achieved for defendants, racial minorities, and the poor during Warren's tenure from erosion by the Burger Court. In particular, they began to look to state bills of rights to secure the rights of defendants and to support other civilliberties claims that they advanced in state courts.

The "new judicial federalism," as it came to be called, quite quickly advanced beyond its initial concern to evade the mandates of the Burger Court. Indeed, less than two decades after it originated, it has become a nationwide phenomenon. For when judges and scholars turned their attention to state constitutions, they discovered an unsuspected richness. They found not only provisions that paralleled the federal Bill of Rights but also constitutional guarantees of the right to privacy and of gender equality, for example, that had no analogue in the U.S. Constitution. Careful examination of the text and history of state guarantees revealed important differences between even those provisions that most resembled federal guarantees and their federal counterparts. Looking beyond state declarations of rights, jurists and scholars discovered affirmative constitutional mandates to state governments to address such important policy concerns as education and housing. Taken altogether, these discoveries underlined the importance for the legal community of developing a better understanding of state constitutions.

Yet the renewed interest in state constitutions has not been limited to judges and lawyers. State constitutional reformers have renewed their efforts with notable success: since 1960, ten states have adopted new constitutions and several others have undertaken major constitutional revisions. These changes have usually resulted in more streamlined constitutions and more effective state governments. Also, in recent years political activists on both the left and the right have pursued their goals through state constitutional amendments, often enacted through the initiative process, under which policy proposals can be placed directly on the ballot for voters to endorse or reject. Scholars too have begun to rediscover how state constitutional history can illuminate changes in political thought and practice, providing a basis for theories about the dynamics of political change in America.

Kay Collett Goss's excellent study of the Arkansas Constitution is part of the series, The Oxford Commentaries on the State Constitutions of the United States, which reflects this renewed interest in state constitutions and will contribute to our knowledge about them. Because the constitutional tradition of each state is distinctive, the volume begins with the history and development of the Arkansas Constitution. It then provides the complete text of Arkansas's current constitution, with each section accompanied by commentary that explains the provision and traces its origins and its interpretation by the courts and by other governmental bodies. For readers with a particular interest in a specific aspect of Arkansas's constitutional experience, the book offers a bibliography of the most important sources dealing with the constitutional history and constitutional law of the state. Finally, the book concludes with a table of cases cited in the history and the constitutional commentary, as well as a subject index.

G. Alan Tarr

■ FOREWORD

State constitutions provide the primary framework for state and local governments and are grounded firmly in the basic need to prescribe governmental powers and to preserve individual liberty.

The Arkansas Constitution is the frequent subject of public discussion and debate in academic classrooms, political campaigns, professional meetings, and partisan platforms. However, the published writing on the subject is quite limited. Thus, this volume is especially a warmly welcomed addition to the literature, as well as a well-written document.

In writing on the development of the U.S. Constitution, Alexis de Toqueville wrote, in *Democracy in America*, "It is new in the history of society to see a great people turn a calm and scrutinizing eye upon itself when apprised . . . that the wheels of its government are stopped, to see it carefully examine the extent of the evil and patiently wait . . . until a remedy is discovered, to which it voluntarily submitted without its costing a tear or a drop of blood."

I congratulate Rutgers University and Greenwood Press for following in this historic tradition of constitutionalism in promoting the scholarly study and the public examination of the nation's state constitutions through this much-needed fifty-volume series. I congratulate Kay Goss for a thorough and thoughtful examination of the Arkansas Constitution: the history, the document, and the associated problems. She has presented a definitive reference guide that will be instructive to students of political science, public leaders, government employees, and private citizens who seek to know and improve their state's constitution. Deliberations of future constitutional conventions and discussions in future classrooms will be enhanced by reference to this enormously helpful work.

Wilbur D. Mills

Introduction

Americans refer frequently to the U.S. Constitution, and hardly a newscast goes by without a mention of a constitutional provision, issue, discussion, or ruling. Gradually, in this manner, we all become fairly familiar with our basic national document. William Munro has called the United States a "land of constitutions," and Thomas Jefferson even advocated that every generation should have a chance to have input into constitution making.

In contrast, very few people make or hear references to their own state constitution. Nonetheless, a state constitution serves as the fundamental law for the state government, just as the U.S. Constitution does for the national government. For example, a state charter sets forth basic human rights; prescribes state legislative, executive, and judicial powers; establishes election procedures; structures and empowers local governments; and provides methods for state constitutional revision, both overall by convention and piecemeal by amendments. The new attention to the state constitutional tradition is therefore welcome, if for no other reason than it that has been neglected for so long.

The author of this book intends to examine fully the Constitution of the state of Arkansas, setting it in its historical and political context, exploring all research and reference resources for purposes of encouraging further study, and discussing the legal development of the document, including a section-by-section commentary on the present Constitution.

I have relied most heavily upon Volume 1 of the *Arkansas Code of 1987 Annotated* (official edition) for the commentary sections and references, and I especially want to thank Senator Mike Beebe of Searcy and Representative John Upton of Warren for their leadership on the Arkansas Code Revision Commission, which put together this work.

Deep personal appreciation for invaluable assistance in this monumental undertaking goes to the Honorable Wilbur D. Mills for his profound encouragement and enormous support, including his treasured contribution of the Foreword; to Devonalu White Robinson for her extraordinarily able assistance in general for more than seven years and in editing this text, and for her loyal and cherished friendship; to Sheryl Milam Dahlstrom for her outstanding research assistance and her collegial companionship over nearly three decades; and to Susan Laura Goss for her daughterly understanding of my work schedule, her daily instruction, and her unconditional love for me.

PART ONE

The History of the Arkansas Constitution

The present Arkansas Constitution, which was drafted and adopted in 1874 as a formal part of the fundamental process of ending the carpetbagger era, was written by the fifth of eight state constitutional conventions and is Arkansas's fifth constitution.

As with all state constitutions, each of the five Arkansas constitutions has been not only a tangible expression of basic organic law but also a political response to a specific historical situation.

THE 1836 CONSTITUTION FOR THE NEW STATE

In 1833, Ambrose Sevier, a delegate to Congress from the Arkansas Territory, submitted a bill providing for a census throughout his territory to determine if there were enough people to qualify for statehood.[1] However, opposition was strong because the Missouri compromise of 1821 had left two factions with an equal number of states and senators.[2]

[1] Marie Cash, "Arkansas Achieves Statehood," *Arkansas Historical Quarterly*, 2, no. 4 (December 1943): 292.

[2] Marie Cash, "Arkansas Achieves Statehood," *Arkansas Historical Quarterly*, 2, no. 4 (December 1943): 292.

As time went by, frustration in Arkansas Territory grew equally strong and the territorial legislature passed a bill providing for the election of delegates to a constitutional convention.[3] Thus, Arkansas began the process of drafting its first state constitution even before Congress acted to begin its statehood process.[4]

Elections were held in all the counties to choose delegates, but Governor William Fulton, the territorial governor, refused to sign the legislative act authorizing the convention; however, the U.S. attorney general then ruled that the convention was a legitimate exercise of the people's right to assemble and to petition the government.[5]

On January 4, 1836, the first Arkansas Constitutional Convention began meeting in Little Rock, with fifty-one delegates evincing an enormous determination to achieve statehood.[6]

A month later, U.S. Secretary of State John Forsyth had forwarded a copy of their product to President Andrew Jackson. By summer, Arkansas had been admitted to the Union by the U.S. Congress, as a twin state with Michigan (to preserve the slave-nonslave balance) in the U.S. Senate, and among the states through legislation sponsored by Senator James Buchanan of Pennsylvania and endorsed by Senators John C. Calhoun of South Carolina, Henry Clay of Kentucky, and Thomas Hart Benton of Missouri.[7]

This initial constitution-making effort divided the state along political lines that have remained profoundly powerful over time, resulting in the mountain-delta dichotomy:

> Large numbers of non-slaveholding settlers in the Northern and Western parts of Arkansas distrusted the big plantation owners from the delta and the river bottoms who controlled the politics of the state at the time and feared that the statehood plan would be manipulated primarily to keep them in power.[8]

These divisive concerns diminished during the convention's deliberations because statehood was widely and well accepted and the only real major difference was the apportionment of legislative seats for the first General Assembly. The non-slaveholding counties in the West and Northwest sought to have only

---

[3] Marie Cash, "Arkansas Achieves Statehood," *Arkansas Historical Quarterly*, 2, no. 4 (December 1943): 292.

[4] Marie Cash, "Arkansas Achieves Statehood," *Arkansas Historical Quarterly*, 2, no. 4 (December 1943): 292., p. 295.

[5] John L. Ferguson and J. H. Atkinson, *Historic Arkansas* (Little Rock: Arkansas History Commission, 1966), p. 30.

[6] Cash, "Arkansas Achieves Statehood," p. 292.

[7] Ralph C. Bamhart, "A New Constitution for Arkansas?" *Arkansas Law Review and Bar Association Journal*, 17 (Winter 1962–63): 2.

[8] Fay Hemstead, *A Pictorial History of Arkansas* (St. Louis: N. D. Thompson Publishing Co., 1890), p. 256.

the white population to count, while the Delta sought to have male slaves count as well. The resulting compromise was modeled after the U.S. Constitution, with each slave counting as three-fifths of a person.[9]

The 1836 Constitution, which was an effective document for governing, was very brief, flexible, and more nearly modeled after the U.S. Constitution than were later Arkansas constitutions.[10] No salaries were set in the Constitution. Slavery was recognized and emancipation required the consent of the owner. The governor, legislators, and county officials were elected by the people, and the secretary of state, auditor, treasurer. Supreme Court and Circuit Court judges, and prosecuting attorneys were selected by joint legislative session.

Members of the State House of Representatives had to be twenty-five years of age, while members of the State Senate had to be thirty. Both had to be free white males who had been residents of the state for at least one year. The General Assembly met every two years on the first Monday in November. Elections were every two years on the first Monday in October and by viva voce.

Governors had to be at least thirty years of age and a state resident for at least ten years. The state auditor and state treasurer were elected at joint sessions of the General Assembly, as were members of the Supreme Court, which was composed of three judges. Property was to be taxed according to value. Poll taxes were per capita and were levied for county purposes.

Amendments were ratified in 1846 to prohibit any additional banks from being incorporated, to allow the legislature to interchange circuits under the judicial system, to confer jurisdiction of justices of the peace, and to provide that incumbent officials would hold their offices until their successors were duly elected and qualified.

Amendments were ratified in 1848 to provide for election of circuit judges by the qualified voters in their districts, as well as prosecuting attorneys and county and probate judges; to prohibit legislators from serving in any other office; and to provide that General Assembly is not restricted in its ability to ascertain the number of counties that would compose a judicial circuit. The final amendment was adopted in 1850 to strike the words, "except Washington County, which may be reduced to six hundred square miles."

Much of Arkansas was still wilderness when it became a state. Most of the Arkansas settlers had come down from Missouri and the Midwest, over from Tennessee, or up from Mississippi and Alabama, and they hacked out new homesites at scattered farming setdements along the state's major rivers. There were only a few settlements in the territorial period that were big enough to be called river towns—Batesville, Camden, Helena, Van Buren, and Fulton, and only

---

[9] Cash, *Arkansas Achieves Statehood*, p. 301.

[10] Robert A. Leflar, "Arkansas—A Survey of Her Constitutions," *Arkansas Gazette*, October 19, 1969, p. 1E.

Little Rock, with about 700 people, was an incorporated city on the eve of statehood. The more mountainous areas of the state were, as yet, approachable only on foot or horseback, and East Arkansas was still largely hardwood forest, although a vast clearing by would-be cotton farmers was under way. There were a few rough roads and trails, which were suitable for mules, horses, wagons, and oxcarts, but most transportation was by water: by hand-pulled keelboats or steamers trying to dodge the deadly and omnipresent snags. Arkansas officials campaigned hard to get the nation's first transcontinental railroad routed through Arkansas, but the state gained no railroads to speak of until after the Civil War. With the coming of statehood, and the opening of Texas at about the same time, Arkansas developed quickly, doubling in population in the first five years and making a place for itself among the cotton states of the agricultural South. Frontier life in Arkansas, with civilized touches in such towns as Washington, Fayetteville, Helena, and Camden, was tough, which caused the state's leaders to worry inordinately about its image.

Under this document, the population grew at an astounding rate, agriculture production blossomed, and industries flourished. Little progress, however, was made in education and infrastructure. Unfortunately, moreover, the economy became increasingly reliant on slavery.

THE 1861 CONSTITUTION TO LEAVE THE UNION

With the outbreak of the Civil War, a new constitutional document became a legal prerequisite for entrance into the Confederacy, so, in January 1861, Governor Henry Keeton set an election for February on the question of whether to hold a state convention on the issue of secession and for the election of delegates.[11]

The so-called secessionist convention, the second Arkansas Constitutional Convention, was called for March 1861. Its first votes were opposed to leaving the Union to join the Confederate States of America. David Walker of Fayetteville, the present home of the University of Arkansas, was president of the convention and a pro-Union leader. The convention recessed and did not reconvene until after the Confederacy won the battle at Fort Sumter, when, in four days, it finally voted by 65–5 to secede on May 6, 1861, in the face of President Abraham Lincoln's call for troops to put down the rebellion.[12]

The new Constitution contained the basic provisions of the 1836 Constitution with small revisions to further safeguard slavery and to substitute the words "Confederate States of America" for "United States of America." Being declared

[11] Clyde Cathery, "Slavery in Arkansas," *Arkansas Historical Quarterly*, 3 (Spring 1944): 68.

[12] Arkansas Constitutional Revision Study Commission, *Revising the Arkansas Constitution* (Little Rock: Arkansas Constitutional Revision Study Commission, 1968), p. 1.

as in effect by the convention, this new document was not submitted to a vote of the people."[13]

Arkansas became the ninth state to secede, following South Carolina, Mississippi, Florida, Alabama, Georgia, Louisiana, Texas, and Virginia, in that order. Tennessee seceded the following day, and North Carolina joined the Confederacy later the same month.

THE 1864 CONSTITUTION TO RETURN TO THE UNION

By September 10, 1863, federal troops, under the command of General Frederick Steele, had occupied Little Rock, the capital city, forcing the state government to move south to Washington in Hempstead County and causing a sharp political division in the state, which divided roughly from northwest to southeast along the Arkansas River. With those north of the river seeking to form a state government in harmony with the Union by writing President Lincoln to request the acceptance of Arkansas, conventions were held in Fort Smith and Van Buren to adopt resolutions calling for a constitutional convention for this purpose.[14]

President Lincoln's response was encouraging to the state's substantial number of Union supporters, especially when he issued an Amnesty Proclamation of December 1863 granting amnesty to all who had been a part of efforts to establish a southern confederacy and who would take an oath of allegiance to the United States.[15] Once 10 percent of a state's population had taken such a loyalty oath, federal recognition and financial support would be extended.

In response, twenty-four counties elected delegates to the third Arkansas constitutional convention, with each county selecting as many delegates as it deemed appropriate.[16] Newspaper accounts were said to have run the gamut, calling the delegates "traitorous sons of Arkansas" in one case and, in another, "the most respectable men of the state."[17] In yet another case, mixed sentiment ruled the day.

On a cold, snowy January 8, 1864, David O. Dodd, a teenager from Pulaski County, was accused of being a Confederate spy and was hanged by General Frederick Steele on a gallows at what is now the eastern end of the General Douglas MacArthur Park in Little Rock. A crowd of 5,000–6,000 watched the

---

[13] Dallas T. Hemdon, *Annals of Arkansas, 1947* vol. 1 (Little Rock, Ark.: Historical Record Association, 1947), p. 165.

[14] Dallas T. Hemdon, *Annals of Arkansas, 1947* vol. 1 (Little Rock, Ark.: Historical Record Association, 1947), p. 165.

[15] David Y. Thomas, *Arkansas and Its People* (Little Rock., Ark.: American Historical Society, 1930), p. 125.

[16] Dallas T. Hemdon, *Centennial History of Arkansas* (Little Rock, Ark.: S.J. Clarke Publishing Co., 1922), p. 286.

[17] *Arkansas Democrat*, Arkansas Centennial Edition, Little Rock, 1936, p. 19.

execution of a youngster who would become a legendary folk hero and stir new levels of emotional fervor and confederate sympathy.

As with the other conventions, the delegates assembled in Little Rock. The session lasted a month, included forty-five delegates, and spent much time on procedural details. Some of the delegates had been elected, some self-appointed, and some designated by the military.[18]

During the second week of the convention, a Committee of 13 was appointed to rewrite the Constitution and, within twenty-four hours, the Committee reported a preamble, a constitution, and a schedule. (The chair admitted immediately that the pre-Confederate Constitution had been adopted almost in its entirety.) Their product, as finally reported, thus contained few changes, except for the abolition of slavery and the expansion of the electorate to include all males, not just white males.[19]

President Lincoln was pleased and endorsed the convention's efforts in a letter to General Steele.[20] In March 1864, the new Constitution was approved by an incredible vote of 12,177 to 266.[21]

State and county officers were also on the ballot, which helped arouse considerable interest in the election. The lines were clearly drawn between Union and Confederate tickets, and there was much hostility over the constitutional issue. The Confederates claimed that there were enough southern soldiers in the state to meet Lincoln's 10 percent amnesty requirement. By approving the proposed Constitution while also electing their own slate of officers, the Confederates hoped to restore Arkansas to the Union while controlling the state government.

The election was a source of much confusion, and accusations of fraud were made by both factions. Counties conducted their own elections, with varying rules on eligibility and enforcement. The fact that the Constitution was approved by 98 percent of the voters seemed suspicious in itself, and many reports of improper election procedures were made by respected citizens on both sides.[22]

The Confederates had hoped to restore Arkansas to the Union and to control the state government by electing its own officials. However, the pro-Union supporters swept the election, with Isaac Murphy of Huntsville, who had been appointed as Provisional Governor by President Lincoln, elected Governor in his own right.[23]

---

[18] Hemdon, *Centennial History*, p. 287.

[19] T. S. Staples, *Reconstruction in Arkansas* (New York: Columbia University Press, 1921), p. 25.

[20] T. S. Staples, *Reconstruction in Arkansas* (New York: Columbia University Press, 1921), p. 33.

[21] T. S. Staples, *Reconstruction in Arkansas* (New York: Columbia University Press, 1921), p. 33.

[22] Leflar, "Arkansas," p. 1E.

[23] Staples, *Reconstruction*, p. 42.

In a postwar message influenced by President Lincoln's conciliatory stance toward the defeated secessionists, Governor Isaac Murphy of Madison County said:

> We have all done wrong. No one can say that his heart is altogether clean, and his hands pure. Then, as we wish to be forgiven, let us forgive those who have sinned against us, and ours. The land is steeped in blood—innocent blood—and defiled with crime. Let us wash it out with tears of sorrow and repentance, works of love, kindness and charity, that peace, goodwill and confidence may return and dwell among us. Let our last conquest be the conquest of the hearts of our enemies by kindness—then peace will be lasting.[24]

The state government appeared ethically honest and fiscally responsible. Business began to revive as hostilities ceased. Thus, Presidential Reconstruction was a relatively peaceful and productive time in Arkansas, but the state lost a strong advocate with the assassination of President Lincoln.[25]

However, President Andrew Johnson (of neighboring Tennessee) and Congress could not come to terms on the readmission of the southern states. National dissension inspired increased state dissension.

Then, on March 2, 1867, Congress passed the Reconstruction Act, dividing the South into five military districts, declaring that "no legal state government or adequate protection for life and property" existed in the southern states, and establishing the federal enforcement of law and order until acceptable governments could be formed.[26] Under this latest act, Arkansas and Mississippi comprised the fourth military district. All blacks were enfranchised and all ex-Confederates were disfranchised.

Major General E. O. C. Ord was appointed commander of Arkansas and Mississippi, with Colonel M. C. Smith in charge of Arkansas. Governor Murphy remained in office. The legislature was not permitted to meet and the courts were virtually nonexistent.[27]

By the end of August 1867, a rather hectic and controversial process of voter registration had been completed, resulting in 66,316 citizens qualifying to vote (43,170 whites and 23,146 blacks).[28]

THE 1868 CONSTITUTION FOR RECONSTRUCTION

When the election was held in November to determine whether to call a constitutional convention and elect delegates, the convention was approved by a

[24] John Gould Fletcher, *Arkansas* (Chapel Hill: University of North Carolina Press, 1947), p. 198.

[25] John Gould Fletcher, *Arkansas* (Chapel Hill: University of North Carolina Press, 1947), p. 198.

[26] John Gould Fletcher, *Arkansas* (Chapel Hill: University of North Carolina Press, 1947), p. 198.

[27] Staples, Reconstruction, p. 124.

[28] Staples, Reconstruction, p. 124.

two-to-one margin. Seventy-five delegates were elected. Sixty were Republicans, eight of whom were black.[29]

The fourth Arkansas Constitutional Convention aimed to destroy white supremacy and to weaken political leaders with Confederate ties. Public schools were to be established by the legislature. Many new offices were created, and the Governor was given broad appointive power.[30]

The General Assembly was to meet on the first Monday of January in oddnumbered years. House members had to be twenty-one years of age; Senate members, twenty-five. There were twenty-six Senators and eighty-two Representatives. An enumeration of inhabitants was established for 1875 and every ten years thereafter and apportionment was to be based on the results.

The legislature was given power over state printing. Each house was directed to keep a journal of its proceedings. Legislative sessions and meetings were to be open, "unless public welfare requires secrecy." Bills raising revenue would have to be originated in each of the houses. The legislature was given the power to provide for the organization of cities through general laws and to restrict their power of taxation, assessment, borrowing money, contracting debts, and loaning their credit. The secrecy of the ballot was mandated.

The legislature was to establish a system of "free schools for the gratuitous instruction of all persons between five and twenty-one years of age," with state funds distributed on a per-student basis. The credit of the state or counties could never be loaned for any purpose without the consent of the people. No money could be paid out of the state treasury without an appropriation by law.

This new document was approved by the voters in the spring of 1868, and Arkansas was readmitted to the Union by Congress on June 22, 1868, overriding President Andrew Johnson's veto of the congressional approval.[31] Political factionalism among Democrats reinforced Republican rule. The corrupt legislature spent millions of dollars on fictitious railroads, levees, buildings that were never constructed, special commissions, and phantom projects. The state debt thus increased by 400 percent, with only a few public improvements to show for the increased expenditures.[32] The high taxes and hard times of this era spawned deep resentments and a depressed self-image.

Tax assessors were appointed by the governor and were given a percentage of the taxes levied as an incentive to raise assessment levels.

---

[29] Eugene Feistman, "Radical Disfranchisement in Arkansas, 1867–1868" *Arkansas Historical Quarterly*, 12, Nov. 2 (Summer 1953): 133.

[30] William Russ, "The Attempt to Create a Republican Party during Reconstmction," *Arkansas Historical Quarterly*, 1, no. 3 (September 1942): p. 212.

[31] Orval Driggs, "The Issues of the Powell Clayton Regime, 1868–1874," *Arkansas Historical Quarterly*, 8, no. 1 (Spring 1949): 1–5.

[32] Staples, Reconstruction, pp. 242–46.

The ex-Confederates, conservatives, and other Arkansas natives clamored for honest administration, a new constitution, and a new chance to gain control of their state government. Eventually, the Republicans began fighting among themselves, breaking into divisive factions and allowing the Democrats to take advantage of the political vacuum that was thus created.[33]

When Governor Powell Clayton was appointed to the U.S. Senate in 1871, a Radical Republican, Elisha Baxter, was elected governor over the opposition of moderate Republicans and Democrats, all of whom supported Joseph Brooks. After the Pulaski County Circuit Court ruled Baxter's election invalid, Brooks moved into the state capitol and appointed an adjutant general who seized the state armory and fortified the capitol grounds. After several weeks, the so-called Brooks-Baxter War created so much chaos and confusion that President Ulysses S. Grant declared Baxter the Governor.

THE 1874 CONSTITUTION TO RECOVER FROM RECONSTRUCTION

Shortly thereafter, the legislature set a date for the election of delegates to another constitutional convention. Amid allegations of voting fraud, the convention was authorized and delegates were selected.[34]

Arkansas had just passed through its most tempestuous period of history from 1861 to 1874: from nominal military rule, to three years of civil war, to four years of civil government loyal to the United States, to a military regime under federal generals, and finally political reconstruction, six years of Republican rule and Democratic upheaval.

The fifth Arkansas Constitutional Convention's proceedings, which lasted for most of the summer of 1874, were basically harmonious, with the Republicans outnumbered and the Democrats restrained. The central focus of the delegates was primarily in the areas most abused by the Radicals during congressional Reconstruction: taxation, elections, patronage, length of terms, public credit, anddebt.[35]

The president of the convention was Grandison D. Royston, a member of the state's first convention in 1836. J. F. White was the leader of the black delegates. A Washington County Granger had defeated the venerable David Walker, the president of the 1861 Convention, who had sought once again to be a delegate.

Sixty-nine of the 261 provisions dealt with financial matters, all negatively. Ridiculously low salaries for public officials, such as $4,000 for the governor, were written into the Constitution. Education was hamstrung by a two-mill

---

[33] Armitage Harper, *The Story of Arkansas* (Kansas City, Mo.: The Grolier Society, 1931), pp. 90–91.

[34] Thomas, *Arkansas and Its People*, p. 157.

[35] Staples, *Reconstruction*, p. 421.

state property tax limit and a five-mill local limit. The state and municipalities were prohibited from borrowing money. Maximum interest rates were set at 10 percent. Freedom of religion was affirmed, but atheists were disqualified from holding office. Property rights were granted to women.

Structurally, the new constitution was designed to keep the office of governor weak. Almost all offices were made elective, and the county unit was strongly emphasized in the document. The veto power was weak because it could be overridden by a simple majority of both houses and the governor's term fell from four to two years, rendering the office largely honorific. Politics in Arkansas thereafter took on a shapeless character, for in guarding against abusive deeds, the 1874 framers also prevented constructive developments. Constitutionally, the history of Arkansas from 1874 to the present has been the passage of amendment after amendment in a desperate attempt to catch up to modernization. That it would require amendments to create kindergartens, use voting machines, establish libraries and hospitals, or have an ongoing three-mill county road tax illustrates how repressive the document was.

Thus, the present Arkansas Constitution, its fifth, was approved on October 13, 1874, by a three-to-one margin and the Democrats swept the offices.[36] No Republican candidates were fielded on the state level.

This document incorporated more changes than any of the other constitutions in the state's history, and most of these revisions were highly rural, restrictive, and negative in nature.

The powers to tax and borrow were severely limited, the terms of elected officials were reduced from four years to two years, the number of county officials was increased from two to ten, and the legislative sessions were limited to sixty days every two years. In short, distrust of government was the theme, and detailed provisions abounded to prevent misunderstanding of the convention's intentions to preclude the misuse of any powers granted.[37]

Augustus H. Garland was elected governor. He had been an early opponent of secession, had been elected as a Confederate congressman and then a senator, and had served as a leader of the conservatives during Reconstruction. His primary mission as governor was to show the nation that the outcome of the Brooks-Baxter War had not harmed the essential economic, political and cultural order of the state. He supported economic policies to encourage development, as well as civil rights legislation for blacks.

However, Garland found the state house a wreck and did not even have enough money for firewood to heat his office. His departure to the U.S. Senate in 1877 to Powell Clayton's former seat was in part occasioned by the governor's small salary.

---

[36] Staples, *Reconstruction*, p. 421.

[37] Staples, *Reconstruction*, p. 421.

Garland was in many ways a typical Redeemer, a man elected as a Democrat who thought like a Whig, a "New Departure" Democrat. Garland was a Whig in background rather than a Democrat. An early opponent of secession, he first attracted statewide attention by his performance in the aborted attempt to avoid that action.

One major goal was to restore some fiscal integrity to state government. The Loughborough Bonds, amounting to $756,000, were issued to return the state to solvency. As of 1877, Arkansas carried a debt of $17, 752, 196 under a tedious web of bonds and debts, including $7 million in railroad bonds, more than $2 million in levee bonds, $1.7 million owed to the U.S. government, and a cash flow debt of $1 million. Pamphlets were written and heated words exchanged. Arkansas would lose national credibility if the debts were repudiated, but there was debate over that avenue.

In fact, between 1874 and 1884, the debt question was the leading single issue in Arkansas. Governor Garland supported repayment, while the agrarian wing under the influence, first of Grangerism and then of Greenbackism, came out for debt reduction or repudiation. It became the basis for the postwar success of western Arkansas's sometime Republican-turned Democrat William M. Fishback, who was also known as The Great Repudiator. He spoke loud and long on the subject of debt repudiation, telling the voters that the payment of Republican debts was a swindle. Many knew that he was a director of the Little Rock-Fort Smith Railroad and that voiding the railroad debts would relieve his company of one of its major liabilities.

The first step in debt repudiation was the work of the state Supreme Court. In a unanimous decision written by Associate Justice David Walker, the court held that the state law authorizing the people to vote for or against railroads had not been properly ratified. This being so, the election was a nullity and the bonds subsequently issued were not binding on the state, even in the hands of innocent parties. In another development, State Land Commissioner J. N. Smithee refused to honor levee bonds brought for payment. Again, the high court found defects in the law, and another repudiation resulted. Thus, by judicial interpretation, Arkansas erased $9 million dollars of obligations.

Since 1874, in necessary response to the detailed nature of the Arkansas Constitution, some 165 constitutional amendments have been voted on by the people, and 77 of these have been adopted, though because of contradictions, amendments of amendments, and court orders, only 69 are now in effect.[38] A listing of these proposals is included in the Table on pages 15 through 22.

Three constitutional conventions have been held since 1874 to revise the document, and all three proposed new constitutions have been rejected handily.

---

[38] James T. Atkinson, "The Adoption of the Constitution of 1874 and the Passing of the Reconstmction Regime," *Arkansas Historical Quarterly*, 5, no. 3 (Fall 1946): 292.

In 1887, the legislature passed a bill to submit the question of holding a convention to the voters, who, in turn, voted against it substantially.[39]

THE WORLD WAR I CONVENTION

In 1917–1918, the sixth Arkansas Constitutional Convention was called directly by the legislature, instead of the people, and drafted a proposed constitution which was rejected by the voters at a special election in December 1918.

This proposed new constitution provided for women's suffrage, statewide prohibition, limitation of office terms, and creation of the office of lieutenant governor; it left unchanged taxing and borrowing provisions.[40]

The proposed new constitution was submitted to the voters in a special election in December 1918 and was defeated, with participation at an all-time low. The weather was bad, the people were preoccupied by World War I, and there was a statewide flu epidemic. In many precincts, no vote was even reported.[41] Prohibition and female suffrage were controversial and aroused opposition, while too few other changes were made to engender active enthusiasm.

Early in the 1960s, a constitutional revision movement began under the leadership of then State Representative David Pryor of Camden and the late State Representative Virgil Butler of Batesville, who had served as campaign chairman for former Congressman Wilbur D. Mills's first race for Congress in 1938. The resulting momentum has lasted for thirty years. These so-called Young Turks attempted to pass legislation calling for a constitutional convention in 1961, 1963, and 1965, but met with opposition from Governor Orval E. Faubus, who was at the peak of his considerable power of his twelve-year tenure (1955–1967).

Faubus was succeeded by Governor Winthrop Rockefeller, the State's first Republican governor since Reconstruction and a strong advocate of constitutional revision.

THE ROCKEFELLER-YOUNG TURKS CONVENTION

In February 1967, the Arkansas General Assembly passed Act 121 of 1967, which established a thirty-member Arkansas Constitutional Revision Study Commission, appointed by the governor, speaker of the house, president pro tempore of the Senate, chief justice of the Supreme Court, and president of the Arkansas Bar Association. The commission's major conclusions were that a general revision of the 1874 Constitution was needed and that a constitutional

[39] Walter Nunn, "The Constitutional Convention of 1874," *Arkansas Historical Quarterly*, 28, no. 3 (Autumn 1968): 181.

[40] Robert A. Leflar, "Constitutional Revision in Arkansas," *Arkansas Law Review*, 24, no. 2 (Spring 1970): 155–56.

[41] Hemdon, Annals, p. 216.

convention was the best way to achieve it. Finally, it recommended that the General Assembly submit to the people the question of whether to call a constitutional convention.

The most powerful member of the Arkansas congressional delegation, the Honorable Wilbur D. Mills, endorsed the constitutional revision movement. As chairman of the House Ways and Means Committee, he was often referred to at that time as the second or third most powerful man in Washington, D.C.

Ted Boswell, a leading member of the study commission, ran for the Democratic nomination for governor with constitutional revision as the key issue in his campaign platform. He waged a reform-oriented race and only missed the runoff primary by. 1 percent of the vote.

The general election of 1968, at which the voters authorized a convention and selected delegates, was one that reflects the independent political thought of the Arkansas electorate. In addition to approving a convention, they supported Independent candidate George Wallace, the leading advocate of states' rights, for president; Democrat J. William Fulbright, the leading critic of the Vietnam War, for reelection to the U.S. Senate; and Republican Governor Winthrop Rockefeller, a leading moderate in the South and a member of the legendary New York Rockefellers, for reelection as governor.

The legislature had also created a three-member Constitutional Convention Advisory Commission to prepare for the holding of a convention that assisted with public education.

On January 6 and 7, 1969, the one hundred delegates to the seventh Arkansas Constitutional Convention held a two-day organizational meeting in the Chamber of the State House of Representatives in the state capitol and elected Distinguished Professor of Law Robert A. Leflar as president. From May 27 through August 21, the convention worked on a proposed constitution. All proposals were considered by committees before being debated and voted on by the entire convention.[42]

The initial tentative draft was distributed to the people immediately afterward, and the delegates spent that fall listening to their reactions and suggestions regarding the proposed document.

On January 12, 1970, the convention reconvened for a final thirty-day session to reconsider all the provisions previously adopted, deleting, adding, altering, and adopting them as they saw fit.[43]

A complete document was passed by the convention on February 10, 1970. It was composed of twelve articles instead of the nineteen articles of the 1874 Constitution, and contained only 13,573 words, about a fourth of the length of

---

[42] Arkansas Constitutional Revision Study Commission, Arkansas *Constitution*, p. 4.

[43] Arkansas Constitutional Convention, *The Proposed Arkansas Constitution of 1970* (Little Rock, Ark.: State of Arkansas), p. viii.

the 1874 Constitution.[44] Much of the reduction was due to the modernization of language, combination of sections, incorporation by reference, and deletion of contradictory and superfluous sections.

The delegates' presentation of the proposed document was accomplished positively:

> The Convention believes that certain provisions in the 1874 Constitution are good law but are not valid constitutional provisions; many of these may be reenacted as statutes by the General Assembly.[45]

The voters defeated the proposed Constitution soundly in the general election of 1970. Proponents, led by Governor Rockefeller, mounted a well-financed and expert campaign from the moment the document was presented by the convention, while the opponents, led primarily by property and judicial interests, started very late and spent little money. However, the vote was at a general, rather than a special, election, and the antitax, antichange campaign was very effective[46]

THE PRYOR-CLINTON CONVENTION

Then, newly inaugurated Governor David Pryor, long a constitutional revision advocate, led a push in the 1975 legislative session to call another convention. Consequently, an act was passed providing for thirty-five appointed delegates and prohibiting the convention from considering several controversial issues.

The Republican party filed a lawsuit challenging several of the procedures established for revising the Constitution. The Arkansas Supreme Court ruled shortly before the convention was to begin that the restriction on subject matter to be considered was an unconstitutional limitation on the people's right to change their constitution and their government.

Governor Pryor and the General Assembly, in turn, submitted the question of calling a convention to the voters in the 1976 general election. The question passed with a 56 percent majority, and with virtually no public discussion.

After meeting in its regular biennial session beginning in January 1977, the Arkansas General Assembly was called into an extraordinary session by an executive order of Governor Pryor in the summer of 1977 for the express purpose of drafting legislation to implement the calling of a convention. Consequently, Act 3 of the Special Session of 1977 called for the convening of a constitutional

---

44 Arkansas Constitutional Convention, *The Proposed Arkansas Constitution of 1970* (Little Rock, Ark.: State of Arkansas), p. ix.

45 Arkansas Constitutional Convention, *The Proposed Arkansas Constitution of 1970* (Little Rock, Ark.: State of Arkansas), p. X.

46 Arkansas Constitutional Convention, *The Proposed Arkansas Constitution of 1970* (Little Rock, Ark.: State of Arkansas), p. X.

convention from the second Monday in May 1979 until the third Monday in July 1979, with a second session to be held later.

Following a vote of the people in the 1978 general election to have the proposed constitution submitted at the 1980 general election and to choose convention delegates, the General Assembly passed Act 622 of 1979, amending Act 3 to allow the convention to come back into session from the third through fifth Mondays in June 1980 to reconsider earlier decisions and reactivate public attention.

These nonpartisan delegates met for an organizational meeting in December 1978, and, once again, they elected Distinguished Emeritus Professor of Law Robert A. Leflar as president of the eighth Arkansas Constitutional Convention; P. K. Holmes of Newport as vice president for the first congressional district; Cal Ledbetter, Jr., of Little Rock, for the second district; Steve Smith of Fayetteville for the third district; and Clint Huey of Warren for the fourth.

In the months that followed, prior to the convening of the first session of the convention, staff were hired and committee meetings held to draft initial proposals for the various sections of the proposed constitution.[47]

Between May 14 and July 16, 1979, the delegates met in the chamber of the House of Representatives in the state capitol. During that time, the convention worked on the proposed constitution. All proposals were considered by committees before being debated and voted on by the entire convention. By July 16, the convention had prepared a tentative draft of a proposed new constitution to take before the electorate over the next eleven months in an effort to obtain the people's reaction to the proposed document.[48]

On June 16, 1980, the convention reconvened for a final fifteen-day session. All provisions that had been adopted during the 1979 session were again placed before the delegates. Provisions were deleted, added, altered, or adopted as previously written. Each provision of the proposed constitution had to receive the approval of at least a majority (fifty-one votes) of the convention.[49]

According to Act 3, the convention had the option of submitting to the electorate either one document or separate or alternative parts. The convention chose to submit a single document, with only one issue, the method of choosing appellate court judges, being separated out to be voted on independently by the electorate.[50]

---

[47] Kay Collett and Walter Nunn, *Political Paradox* (New York: National Municipal League, 1973), p. 5.

[48] Arkansas Constitutional Convention, *Proposed Arkansas Constitution of 1980* (Little Rock, Ark.: State of Arkansas, 1980), p. ix.

[49] Arkansas Constitutional Convention, *Proposed Arkansas Constitution of 1980* (Little Rock, Ark.: State of Arkansas, 1980), p. ix.

[50] Arkansas Constitutional Convention, *Proposed Arkansas Constitution of 1980* (Little Rock, Ark.: State of Arkansas, 1980), p. ix.

The completed document was adopted by the convention on June 30, 1980. Ninety-eight of the one hundred delegates signed the document, and the two absent members signed it at a later date, thus providing unanimous approval for the proposed Constitution of 1980.[51]

On November 4, 1980, in the general election, Arkansas voters reflected a national negative mood, going against the reelections of President Jimmy Carter (after having given him his second highest majority in 1976) and of Governor Bill Clinton (the nation's youngest and most promising governor), as well as against the proposed new constitution.

Thus, the present Arkansas Constitution was written during a time when the nation lacked sophisticated modes of communication such as telephones, beepers, car phones, televisions, computers, facsimile machines, and copying equipment. Americans had developed no dependency on imported oil because the primary source of energy was wood; nuclear energy was a rather remote concept. In 1874, Arkansas had a distinctly rural agrarian economy. The people lived primarily on small, family-owned farms or were tenant farmers or sharecroppers. In 1900, only 8.5 percent of Arkansas's population lived within an incorporated town or city.[52] Today, however, more than 50 percent of the state population resides in incorporated areas.[53] With the increased mechanization and the influx of people from rural areas, Arkansas has undergone a great many changes:

> Little Rock, in 1880, had 13, 138 inhabitants, fairly good railroad connections, and was still a humming river port. It had 120 miles of streets, unpaved, and deep in mud or dust according to the weather; street cars drawn by mules and guided by 127 street gas lights.... There were only enough police to guard the business section, four blocks to an officer, leaving the suburbs at the mercy of burglars; cattle and hogs still roved at large throughout the city.[54]

In 1879, telephone service began in Little Rock with 10 subscribers. Electric street lights began shining in Little Rock in 1888.

Constitutionally, then, the history of Arkansas since 1874 to the present has been the passage of amendment after amendment and the calling of three constitutional conventions in numerous unsuccessful, and desperate, attempts to modernize its basic organic law.

Of the myriad of 169 amendments proposed during the 118 years since adoption, 78 pertained to taxes and finances, 18 to election procedures, 18 to salaries

---

[51] Arkansas Constitutional Convention, *Proposed Arkansas Constitution of 1980* (Little Rock, Ark.: State of Arkansas, 1980), p. ix.

[52] Arkansas Constitutional Convention, *Proposed Arkansas Constitution of 1980* (Little Rock, Ark.: State of Arkansas, 1980), p. ix.

[53] *Arkansas Almanac, 1954–1955* (Little Rock: Arkansas Almanac Company, 1957), p. 5.

[54] U. S. Department of Commerce, Bureau of Census, *1980 Census of Population, General Social and Economic Characteristics of Arkansas* (Washington, D.C.: U.S. Government Printing Office), p. 11.

for public officials, 14 to the organization and power of the executive branch, 13 to the organization and power of the judicial branch, 8 to education, and 3 to the organization and power of the legislative branch.

▪ PROPOSED AMENDMENTS TO THE ARKANSAS CONSTITUTION, 1874 TO 1992

Year	Subject Matter	Method by Which Proposed Action	Amendment Number	
1880	Holford Bonds	Legislature	Failed	
1884	Holford Bonds	Legislature	Adopted	1
1892	Poll Tax	Legislature	Adopted	
1894	Quorum courts to levy taxes for local improvements	Legislature	Failed	
1894	Governor to fill vacancies in township and county offices	Legislature	Invalidated	
1898	Regulation of transportation rates	Legislature	Adopted	2
1898	3-mill county road tax	Legislature	Adopted	3
1900	Sureties on official bonds	Legislature	Adopted	4
1902	Mileage and per diem for legislators	Legislature	Failed	
1904	Increase number of Supreme Court Justices	Legislature	Failed	
1904	Local bond issues by local vote	Legislature	Failed	
1906	7-mill local school tax	Legislature	Adopted	
1908	Poll tax	Legislature	Adopted	
1908	Local bond issues	Legislature	Adopted	
1910	Initiative and Referendum	Legislature	Adopted	
1910	Cotton mill tax exemption	Legislature	Failed	
1912	Education qualifications for voting	Legislature	Failed	
1912	Cotton mill tax exemption	Legislature	Failed	
1912	Mileage and per diem for legislators; 60-day session	Initiative	Adopted	
1912	Recall of elective officers	Initiative	Invalidated	
1912	Cities and towns to issue bonds	Initiative	Invalidated	
1912	Sixty-day session of legislature	Initiative	Adopted	5
1914	Cities and towns to issue bonds	Initiative	Invalidated	
1914	Legislative Salaries	Legislature	Failed	
1914	Create office of Lieutenant Governor	Legislature	Adopted	6
1916	3-mill county road and bonds tax	Legislature	Adopted	
1916	12-mill district school tax	Initiative	Adopted	
1916	Initiative and Referendum	Legislature	Failed	
1918	Municipal improvement bonds Initiative	Adopted		
1918	Increase number of Supreme Court justices	Legislature	Failed	
1918	State farm loans	Legislature	Failed	
1920	Initiative and Referendum	Initiative	Adopted	7
1920	Women's suffrage; poll tax	Legislature	Adopted	8

Year	Subject Matter	Method by Which Proposed Action	Amendment Number	
1922	Initiative and Referendum	Initiative	Failed	
1922	Increase school revenues	Initiative	Failed	
1922	Tax on personal property	Legislature	Failed	
1924	Legislative determination of salary and number of Supreme Court Justices	Legislature	Adopted	9
1924	City and county debt limitation	Legislature	Adopted	10
1924	Prohibition of local acts	Legislature	Invalidated	
1926	State mill tax and poll tax	Legislature	Adopted	11
1926	Cotton mill tax exemption	Legislature	Adopted	12
1926	Bond issue in cities	Initiative	Adopted	13
1926	Local acts prohibited	Initiative	Adopted	14
1928	Salaries of state officers	Legislature	Adopted	15
1928	Jury trial	Legislature	Adopted	16
1928	County construction and building tax	Legislature	Adopted	17
1928	Tax to aid industries	Initiative	Adopted	18
1930	Establishment of state schools	Legislature	Failed	
1930	Elective highway commission	Initiative	Failed	
1930	Prohibit tax increases	Initiative	Failed	
1930	Citizen's challenge of laws	Initiative	Failed	
1930	Special elections for referendum and vacancies	Initiative	Failed	
1930	Prohibit the reduction in judges' compensation	Initiative	Failed	
1930	Restriction on inheritance and death taxes	Initiative	Failed	
1930	Prohibit reassessment of property after tax paid	Initiative	Failed	
1932	Reorganization of state government	Legislature	Failed	
1932	1 percent sales tax	Legislature	Failed	
1932	Require popular vote for issuance of bridge bonds	Legislature	Failed	
1932	School fund to receive $6 per enumerated pupil	Initiative	Failed	
1932	Homestead exemptions	Initiative	Failed	
1934	Passage of laws	Legislature	Adopted	19
1934	State bonds	Legislature	Adopted	20
1934	4-year term for state and county officials	Initiative	Failed	
1936	Criminal prosecutions; prosecutors' salaries	Legislature	Adopted	21
1936	Homestead exemptions	Initiative	Adopted	22
1936	Board of Apportionment	Initiative	Adopted	23
1938	Chancery and probate matters	Legislature	Adopted	24
1938	Poll tax elimination	Legislature	Failed	
1938	County construction tax	Legislature	Adopted	25
1938	Workmen's compensation	Initiative	Adopted	26
1938	Highway bond refunding	Initiative	Failed	
1938	Consolidated textbook and education boards	Initiative	Failed	

Year	Subject Matter	Method by Which Proposed	Action	Amendment Number
1938	Tax exemption for new industries	Initiative	Adopted	27
1938	Regulation of practice of law	Initiative	Adopted	28
1938	Filling vacancies in office	Initiative	Adopted	29
1940	Repeal of double primary	Legislature	Failed	
1940	Pledging revenues for debt refunding	Legislature	Failed	
1940	Personal property exemption	Legislature	Failed	
1940	City libraries	Initiative	Adopted	30
1940	Police and firemen's pensions	Initiative	Adopted	31
1940	Game and Fish Commission	Initiative	Failed	
1940	Old age pension plan	Initiative	Failed	
1942	Junior college districts	Legislature	Failed	
1942	County or city hospitals	Legislature	Adopted	32
1942	Game and Fish Commission	Initiative	Failed	
1942	Boards and commissions governing state institutions	Initiative	Adopted	33
1944	County library tax	Initiative	Failed	
1944	Rights of labor	Initiative	Adopted	34
1944	Game and Fish Commission	Initiative	Adopted	35
1944	Poll tax exemption for members of armed forces	Initiative	Adopted	36
1944	4-year term for governor and lieutenant governor	Legislature	Failed	
1946	State officers' salaries	Legislature	Adopted	37
1946	County road tax	Initiative	Failed	
1946	County libraries	Legislature	Adopted	38
1948	Registration of voters	Legislature	Adopted	39
1948	Levy of school taxes	Initiative	Adopted	40
1948	Abolition of state property tax	Initiative	Failed	
1950	Public school finance	Initiative	Failed	
1950	4-year term for state and county officers	Initiative	Failed	
1952	Election of county clerks	Legislature	Adopted	41
1952	State Highway Commission	Legislature	Adopted	42
1952	Tax for industrial sites	Legislature	Failed	
1954	Property assessment equalization	Legislature	Failed	
1954	4-year term for governor	Legislature	Failed	
1954	Salaries of state, district, and county officers	Legislature	Failed	
1956	School tax limitation	Legislature	Failed	
1956	Municipal retirement	Legislature	Failed	
1956	Abolition of poll tax	Initiative	Failed	
1956	Salaries and expenses of judicial officers	Initiative	Adopted	43
1956	Interposition	Initiative	Adopted	44
1956	Legislative apportionment	Initiative	Adopted	45
1956	Prohibition of horse- and dog-race betting	Initiative	Failed	

Year	Subject Matter	Method by Which Proposed Action	Amendment Number	
1956	Horse racing and pari-mutuel wagering in Hot Springs	Initiative	Adopted	46
1956	Maximum interest rate	Initiative	Failed	
1958	State ad valorem tax prohibited	Legislature	Adopted	47
1958	Legislative salaries	Legislature	Adopted	48
1958	Industrial development bonds	Legislature	Adopted	49
1960	State and county officer salaries	Legislature	Failed	
1960	Municipal improvements	Legislature	Failed	
1960	Public schools	Legislature	Failed	
1962	Municipal improvements	Legislature	Failed	
1962	Public education	Legislature	Failed	
1962	Salaries of county officers	Legislature	Failed	
1962	Teacher retirement fund	Initiative	Failed	
1962	Voting machines	Initiative	Adopted	50
1964	Salaries of state executive officers; elimination of state land commissioner	Legislature	Failed	
1964	Hospital and industrial development districts	Legislature	Failed	
1964	City and county road tax	Legislature	Failed	
1964	Voter registration	Initiative	Adopted	51
1964	Garland County wagering	Initiative	Failed	
1964	County officers' salaries	Initiative	Failed	
1964	Community colleges	Initiative	Adopted	52
1966	None			
1968	Public kindergartens, adult education	Legislature	Adopted	53
1968	Legislature permitted to submit 8 amendments at once	Legislature	Failed	
1968	County government reorganization	Legislature	Failed	
1970	None			
1972	None			
1974	State printing contracts	Legislature	Adopted	54
1974	State salary commission	Legislature	Failed	
1974	County government reorganization	Legislature	Adopted	55
1974	Minimum interest rate	Initiative	Failed	
1976	Constitutional officers (salaries)	Legislature	Adopted	56
1976	Intangible personal property	Legislature	Adopted	57
1978	Court of Appeals	Legislature	Adopted	58
1980	Statewide property reappraisal and millage rollback	Legislature	Adopted	59
1980	Maximum rate of interest controlled by two-thirds of General Assembly	Initiative	Failed	
1980	Constitution of 1980 Convention	Failed		
1982	The 1982 Interest Rate Control Amendment	Legislature	Adopted	60

Year	Subject Matter	Method by Which Proposed Action	Amendment Number	
1982	Jurisdiction and venue of courts	Legislature	Failed	
1982	Three-mill county road tax	Legislature	Adopted	61
1984	Exempt household goods from ad valorem taxes	Legislature	Failed	
1984	Authorize local governments to issue capital improvements bonds	Legislature	Adopted	62
1984	Four-year terms for state constitutional officers	Initiative	Adopted	63
1984	The Unborn Child Amendment	Initiative	Failed	
1984	Garland County Lawful Wagering Amendment	Initiative	Failed	
1984	Game and Fish Commission sales	Initiative	Failed	
1986	Municipal courts	Legislature	Passed	64
1986	Limitation on abortion	Initiative	Failed	
1986	County officials—4 years	Initiative	Failed	
1986	Revenue bonds	Initiative	Passed	65
1988	Judicial discipline	Legislature	Passed	66
1988	Juveniles and bastardy	Legislature	Passed	67
1988	Prevent abortion funding	Initiative	Passed	68
1988	Repeal personal property tax	Initiative	Failed	
1990	Arkansas Compensation Commission	Legislature	Failed	
1990	Interest rate control	Initiative	Failed	
1990	To repeal amendment 44	Legislature	Adopted	69
1992	To raise salaries of state officials	Legislature	Adopted	70
1992	Exemption of personal property from taxation	Legislature	Adopted	71
1992	Library tax	Legislature	Adopted	72
1992	Term limits	Initiative	Adopted	73

	Adopted	Failed or Invalidated	Total
Submitted by the General Assembly	50	47	97
Submitted by Initiated Petition	31	41	72
Total Amendments Submitted	81	88	169

PART TWO

The Arkansas Constitution and Commentary

PREAMBLE

> We, the people of the State of Arkansas, grateful to Almighty God for the privilege of choosing our own form of government, for our civil and religious liberty, and desiring to perpetuate its blessings and secure the same to ourselves and posterity, do ordain and establish this Constitution.

This preamble is a restatement of the preamble to the Constitution of 1868. It contains a pointed reference to the people being grateful for achieving the opportunity to decide for themselves, rather than receive only the dictates of the federal government, and for resuming power over their own state and local affairs. Like many other state preambles, there is an invocation to God and a discourse on the desirability of liberty, but there is no reference to the purpose or importance of government.

The preambles to most state constitutions, like all of the Arkansas documents, reflect these two enduring characteristics of Americans: their belief in popular sovereignty and their faith in a Supreme Being.

Article I

Boundaries

We do declare and establish, ratify and confirm, the following as the permanent boundaries of the State of Arkansas, that is to say: beginning at the middle of the main channel of the Mississippi river, on a parallel of thirtysix degrees of north latitude, running thence west with said parallel of latitude to the middle of the main channel of the St. Francis River; thence up the main channel of said last named river to the parallel of thirty-six degrees, thirty minutes of north latitude; thence west with the southern boundary line of the State of Missouri to the southwest comer of said last named State; thence to be bounded on the west to the north bank of Red River, as by Act of Congress and treaties existing January 1, 1837, defining the western limits of the Territory of Arkansas and to be bounded across and south of Red river by the boundary line of the State of Texas as far as to the northwest comer of the State of Louisiana; thence easterly with the northern boundary of said last named State to the middle of the main channel of the Mississippi river; thence up the middle of the main channel of said last named river, including an island in said river known as "Belle Point Island," and all other land originally surveyed and included as a part of the Territory or State of Arkansas, to the thirty-sixth degree of north latitude, the place of beginning.

This boundary provision, which occupies a prominent position, reflects a territorial imperative and displays the traditional reaction to war. The boundary lines have remained relatively stable throughout state history. However, there has been litigation regarding the state line with Mississippi, Missouri, Tennessee, and Texas.

SEAT OF GOVERNMENT

> The seat of government of the State of Arkansas shall be and remain at Little Rock, where it is now established.

Little Rock is the most central geographic location. It is historically the most populous municipal corporation, and is the undisputed capital city. The capital was moved to Washington Post temporarily during the Civil War and was almost located in Georgetown in White County at one point.

Article II

Declaration of Rights

SECTION 1

All political power is inherent in the people, and government is instituted for their protection, security and benefit; and they have the right to alter, reform or abolish the same in such manner as they may think proper.

This section on source of power has been interpreted to mean that the position of delegate to the constitutional convention is not derived from the Constitution, but rather from the power inherent in the people (Harvey v. Ridge way, 1970).

SECTION 2

All men are created equally free and independent, and have certain inherent and inalienable rights, amongst which are those of enjoying and defending life and liberty; of acquiring, possessing, and protecting property and reputation; and of pursuing their own happiness. To secure these rights, governments are instituted among men, deriving just powers from the consent of the governed.

Changes in constitutional law must be authorized by a vote of the people, with constitutional delegates elected by the people and with a constitutional document ratified by the people (Pryor v. Lowe, 1975). The equal protection provision of this section requires equitable school financing (Dupree v. Alma School District No. 30, 1983). The right of a retailer to sell its own property at its low price is a right guaranteed by the Constitution as a valuable property right (Union Carbide and Carbon Corp. v. White River Distributors, Inc., 1955). Public hospitals are prohibited from acting arbitrarily and capriciously (Brandt v. St. Vincent Infirmary, 1985).

SECTION 3

The equality of all persons before the law is recognized, and shall ever remain inviolate; nor shall any citizen ever be deprived of any right, privilege or immunity, nor exempted from any burden or duty, on account of race, color or previous condition.

The state must establish a compelling interest for classifications in legislation (Boshears v. Arkansas Racing Commission, 1975). However, habitual criminal classification does not violate this section (Poe v. State, 1971). Fixing prices at which liquor can be sold is a valid exercise of police power (Gipson v. Morely, 1961). Denying aliens, who are incapable of becoming citizens and unprotected by treaty, the right to acquire property is not in conflict (Applegate v. Leem Jungluke, 1927). A prosecuting attorney may order a bank to produce copies of records of a depositor's account (First National Bank v. Roberts, 1967). The gender-neutral divorce statute is constitutional (Sweeney v. Sweeney, 1980).

SECTION 4

The right of the people peaceably to assemble to consult for the common good, and to petition, by address or remonstrance, the government, or any department thereof, shall never be abridged.

Private shopping centers may prohibit or regulate political, social, or religious expression or activity (38 *Arkansas Law Review* 4th 1219). "Terroristic threat" statutes are valid (45 ALR 4th 949). Local option elections can be required in an area before licenses permitting the sale of liquor can be granted (Havis v. Philpot, 1914). If disclosure of the membership list of the National Association of Colored People (NAACP) interferes with the right of association, local ordinances requiring it are unconstitutional (Bates v. City of Little Rock, 1960).

SECTION 5

The citizens of this state shall have the right to keep and bear arms for their common defense.

The right to bear arms here refers to arms used for purposes of war, and the legislature may prohibit the wearing of weapons not used in warfare or not contributing to the common defense (Fife v. State, 1876). The legislature may regulate the wearing of war arms, but may not prohibit it on a person's own premises or when people are acting in aid of a military officer (Wilson v. State, 1878). A statute making the wearing of concealed weapons a penal offense is constitutional (State v. Buzzard, 1842). Act prohibiting wearing or carrying any pistol unless it is uncovered and in the hand is constitutional (Haile v. State, 1882). Act making the sale of any pistol, except as used in the military, a misdemeanor is constitutional (Dabbs v. State, 1882). There has been no modernday litigation on this provision.

SECTION 6

The liberty of the press shall forever remain inviolate. The free communication of thought and opinions is one of the invaluable rights of man; and all persons may freely write and publish their sentiments on all subjects, being responsible for the abuse of such rights. In all criminal prosecutions for libel the truth may be given in evidence to the jury; and, if it shall appear to the jury that the matter charged as libelous is true, and was published with good motives and for justifiable ends, the party charged shall be acquitted.

Any restraint on the freedom of the press, even though narrow in scope and duration, is subject to the closest scrutiny and is upheld only upon a clear showing that an exercise of this right presents a clear and imminent threat to the fair administration of justice (Arkansas Gazette Co. v. Lofton, 1980). The printing of names of attorneys representing indigent peoples is permitted (Roberts v. Lowe, 1960).

SECTION 7

The right of trial by jury shall remain inviolate, and shall extend to all cases at law, without regard to the amount in controversy; but a jury may be waived by the parties in all cases in the manner prescribed by law.

This section was amended in 1928 by Amendment 16 to prescribe for jury trials in civil cases in order to make decisions by agreement of nine of the jurors, who will sign their names. Moreover, the new provisions made the section selfexecuting, requiring no enabling act by the legislature. The right to trial by jury extends only to the trial of issues of fact in civil and criminal causes (Jones v. Reed, 1979). A party is not entitled to trial by jury in contempt proceedings (Neel v. State, 1849). Legislature may dispense with a jury trial in contested elections (Govan v. Jackson, 1877). Trial by jury is not required in sanity hearings, either under common law or under this section (Scherz v. Peoples National Bank, 1949). A directed verdict, when the evidence is undisputed and unimpeached, does not deny the right to trial by jury (Darden v. State, 1906). The statutes may permit the court to fix punishment under certain circumstances (Froman v. State, 1960). A property owner's appeal from an assessment is not entitled to trial by jury (Missouri Pacific Railroad v. Conway County Bridge District, 1918).

After agreeing to a settlement, one cannot change one's mind and demand a trial by jury (Veasy v. Joshlin, 1974). A defendant must be given sufficient information to make a knowing and intelligent choice between a trial by jury or a decision by a judge (Williamson v. Lockhart, 1986).

SECTION 8

> No person shall be held to answer a criminal charge unless on the presentment or indictment of a grand jury, except in cases of impeachment or cases such as the General Assembly shall make cognizable by justices of the peace, and courts of similar jurisdiction; or cases arising in the army and navy of the United States; or in the militia when in actual service in time of war or public danger; and no person for the same offense, shall be twice put in jeopardy of life or liberty; but if, in any criminal prosecution, the jury be divided in opinion, the court before which the trial shall be had may, in its discretion, discharge the jury and commit or bail the accused for trial at the same or the next term of said court; nor shall any person be compelled, in any criminal cases to be a witness against himself; nor be deprived of life, liberty or property, without due process of law. All persons shall, before conviction, be bailable by sufficient sureties, except for capital offenses, when the proof is evident or the presumption great.

These provisions were extended by Section 1 of Amendment 21 in 1936 to provide also for prosecution by information filed by the prosecuting attorney, as well as by indictment by the grand jury. The offense of accessory before the fact to murder is a capital offense and is not bailable (State v. Williams, 1911). The court will agree to the denial of bail in a capital case (Pamell v. State, 1942). A determination on the application for bail will not be disturbed unless the trial court abused its discretion (Fikes v. State, 1952). A prior conviction for capital offense satisfies the "proof is evident" provision for depriving a defendant of the right to bail (Grigsby v. Mabry, 1983). It is a reversible error for a trial court to tell a defendant that if he or she takes the stand to testify as to his or her insanity, it will send him or her to a state mental hospital and not consider bail (Kozal v. State, 1978). First-degree rape is a bailable offense (Baumgardner v. Hall, 1974). If the same offense violates city ordinance and state law, the defendant cannot be tried in both local court and state court (Champion v. State, 1913). If the jury is discharged without consent of the defendant, double jeopardy may be invoked

(Jones v. State, 1959). If a defendant violates probation, despite having paid his or her fine, the court can revoke probation and impose a sentence (Diffee v. State, 1986). The Public Service Commission does not violate due process unless the rates it sets are confiscatory or the credit of the telephone company is impaired (Southwestern Bell v. Arkansas Public Service Commission, 1980). Delinquent tax sales without notice are not violations of due process (Benham v. Davis, 1938). A juvenile's first offense confession should be suppressed if counsel was not present, even if it was voluntary (Vault v. State, 1974).

SECTION 9

Excessive bail shall not be required, nor shall excessive fines be imposed; nor shall cruel or unusual punishment be inflicted; nor witnesses be unreasonably detained.

The right of bail after conviction, pending appeal, is up to judicial discretion (Lane v. State, 1950). Challenges to capital punishment have been held to be moot (Graham v. State, 1972). It is not up to the jury to decide how a defendant is to die (Swindler v. State, 1979). In the case of a defendant with three prior felony convictions who was convicted of four separate counts of aggravated robbery, a sentence of four consecutive life sentences was ruled to be neither an abuse of discretion nor cruel and unusual punishment (Duncan v. State, 1979).

SECTION 10

In all criminal prosecutions the accused shall enjoy the right to a speedy and public trial by an impartial jury of the county in which the crime shall have been committed; provided that the venue may be changed to any other county of the judicial district in which the indictment is found, upon the application of the accused, in such manner as now is, or may be, prescribed by law; and to be informed of the nature and cause of the accusation against him, and to have a copy thereof; to be confronted with the witnesses against him; to have compulsory process for obtaining witnesses in his favor, and to be heard by himself and his counsel.

Expedition of adjudication is urged (Maxwell v. State, 1950). The legislature may regulate the manner of securing the right to force payment of a fee for a copy of the indictment (Howard v. State, 1881). The right to counsel is guaranteed (Philyaw v. State, 1986). An accused has no constitutional right to have oral argument by counsel at the conclusion of an evidentiary hearing on a motion to suppress evidence (Brenneman v. State, 1978). Defendants have the right to know the accusations against them (State v. Cadle, 1858). An impartial jury is guaranteed (Bailey v. Henslee, 1961). Open trial may be asserted by the public, the press, and the accused (Taylor v. State, 1984). Prospective jurors who are opposed to the death penalty may be excused (Venable v. State, 1976). Fair and impartial proceedings are necessary for the benefit of litigants and to maintain the public's confidence in the judiciary (Oliver v. State, 1980).

SECTION 11

The privilege of the writ of habeas corpus shall not be suspended, except by the General Assembly in case of rebellion, insurrection or invasion, when the public safety may require it.

This section is almost identical to habeas corpus provisions included in all of the Arkansas constitutions throughout history, except for the Constitution of 1868, under which Arkansas state government was "reconstructed" by the federal government. Habeas corpus could issue wherever there is an unlawful restraint of personal liberty (Wright v. Johnson, 1844). The circuit Court has jurisdiction (Ex parte Dame, 1923; "Post-Conviction Relief in Arkansas," 24 *Arkansas Law Review* 57).

SECTION 12

No power of suspending or setting aside the law or laws of the State shall ever be exercised except by the General Assembly.

This provision resulted from adverse reactions to executive power exercised by the out-of-state Republican Reconstruction Administration under the 1868 Constitution. Moreover, the power of the governor to grant clemency is limited to individuals who are under sentence for a crime, penalty, or forfeiture, and does not extend to the granting of general amnesty, nor relief from civil penalties or forfeitures (Hutton v. McCleskey, 1918). The authority of the court in regulating the practice of law includes the preparation of rules determining the qualifications of one who desires to take the bar examination (In re Pitchford, 1979; L. J. Sailings, "Survey of Arkansas Law," 3 *UALR L.J.* 277).

SECTION 13

Every person is entitled to a certain remedy in the laws for all injuries or wrongs he may receive in his person, property or character; he ought to obtain justice freely, and without purchase, completely, and without denial, promptly, and without delay, conformably to the laws.

This section guarantees rights of individuals and does not restrict the power of the legislature to enact remedial laws (Peugh v. Oliger, 1961). Laws cannot deny citizens the right to free and untrammeled access to the courts (Bennett v. NAACP, 1963). Moreover, immunity to tort liability granted to subdivisions of the state is constitutional under this section (Thompson v. Sanford, 1984). A legitimate state purpose is served by the notice requirement for medical injuries (Simpson v. Fuller, 1984). When political rights are asserted under this section, there is no remedy (McFarlin v. Kelly, 1969). The Claims Commission does not have exclusive jurisdiction over tort claims against state employees or officials (Grimmett v. Digby, 1979). Recovery of damages for mental anguish in wrongful death actions does not violate this section (Peugh v. Oliger, 1961).

SECTION 14

Treason against the State shall only consist in levying and making war against the same, or in adhering to its enemies, giving them aid or comfort. No person shall be convicted of treason unless on the testimony of two witnesses to the same overt act, or on confession in open court.

This section is relatively new in Arkansas constitutional history in that only the current constitution and its immediate predecessor (in 1868) contained this provision, and it has never been litigated. However, limits on treason convictions or punishment are provided in thirty-six other state constitutions.

SECTION 15

The rights of the people of this State to be secure in their persons, houses, papers and effects against unreasonable searches and seizures shall not be violate, and no warrant shall issue except upon probable cause, supported, by oath or affirmation, and particularly describing the place to be searched and the person or thing to be seized.

This section is a limitation upon the power of government, but not upon the individual, and is not an authorization for the issuance of search warrants (Grimmett v. State, 1972). However, a public officer may enter a public place to make an arrest on probable cause that an unlawful act is being committed there because this provision extends only to private places (Gerard v. State, 1963). The state may compel corporations doing business with the state to produce books for investigation, whether kept in state or out (Hammond Packing Company v. State, 1908). A warrant is not required before administrative inspection of a regulated business, such as the distribution of pharmaceuticals (Hosto v. Brickell, 1979). Not all searches and seizures without a warrant are prohibited, but only those that are unreasonable (Mann v. City of Heber Springs, 1965). The state must produce a search warrant for evidence used at a trial (Russ v. Camden, 1974).

Time of day and validity of period must be indicated on an affidavit (Herrington v. State, 1985). The guarantee against search and seizure without a warrant may be waived (Williams v. State, 1964).

SECTION 16

No person shall be imprisoned for debt in any civil action, on mesne or final process, unless in cases of fraud.

Imprisonment for disobedience of an order directing payment of specific funds adjudged to be in the hands of the defendant is not imprisonment for debt (Meeks v. State, 1906; Harrison v. Harrison, 1965). Imprisonment for disobedience of an order to pay a sum into court without finding that the defendant had those funds is imprisonment for debt (Leonard v. State, 1926). Criminal provision for the failure of a contractor to satisfy a lien must make fraud a prerequisite of criminal offense (Pearis v. State, 1957). Imprisonment for disobeying an order to pay a sum into court, when the defendant does not have it, is imprisonment for debt (Leonard v. State, 1926; Godwin v. Godwin, 1980).

SECTION 17

No bill of attainder, ex post facto law, or law impairing the obligation of contracts shall ever be passed; and no conviction shall work corruption of blood and forfeiture of estate.

This is a succinct summary of five important rights for Arkansas citizens. In previous Arkansas constitutions, only ex post facto laws and laws impairing obligations of contracts were prohibited. All contracts are made, subject to the police power to change the contracts. The power to change utility rates does not impair the obligation of a contract (Camden v. Arkansas Power and Light Company, 1920). Ex post facto provisions pertain only to criminal proceedings (Taylor v. Governor, 1837). Statute impairing power to contract with an attorney is unconstitutional (Bennett v. NAACP, 1963). If the state contracts by law, the contracts cannot be impaired (Jones v. Cheney, 1973). Removal of an official from office does not impair contract (Hunter State Bank v. Mills, 1909).

SECTION 18

The General Assembly shall not grant to any citizen or class of citizens privileges or immunities which upon the same terms shall not equally belong to all citizens.

This equal protection clause does not prohibit legislation that recognizes degrees of evil, nor does it require that things that are different in fact or opinion be treated in law as though they were the same (J. W. Black Lumber Company V. Arkansas Department of Pollution Control and Ecology, 1986). The imposition of a progressive income tax does not deny equal protection (Stanley v. Gates, 1929). A corporation is not a citizen under this clause (Chicago, R. I. and P.R.R. v. State, 1908). An act requiring dentists to register with a board of examiners and be certified is constitutional (Gosnell v. State, 1889). A statute fixing prices, wages, and hours of barbers violates the privileges and immunities clause of the Constitution (Noble v. Davis, 1942). Additional pay for police and not other city employees is constitutional and reasonable (Piggott v. Woodard, 1977).

SECTION 19

Perpetuities and monopolies are contrary to the genius of a republic, and shall not be allowed; nor shall any hereditary emoluments, privileges or honors ever be granted or conferred in this State.

Monopolies in the field of common carriers are unconstitutional, for this antimonopoly provision is to be read and considered along with the police powers and public welfare powers. The reason is that if there is a clear showing of absence of the proper exercise of police and welfare powers, the statute is considered unconstitutional (North Little Rock Transportation Company v. City of North Little Rock, 1944). Liquor licenses meet the test (Ex parte Levy, 1884). The legislature may prohibit foreign insurance companies from doing business in the state if they are members of a rate-fixing combination anywhere in the world (Hartford Fire Insurance v. State, 1905).

SECTION 20

No distinction shall ever be made by law between resident aliens and citizens in regard to the possession, enjoyment or descent of property.

This provision has been interpreted to prohibit legislative acts denying to aliens who are ineapable of becoming citizens the right to acquire, possess, or transfer real estate (Applegate v. Lumjung Luke, 1927). Statutes fixing the prices of liquor are valid exercises of police power (Gipson v. Morley, 1950). Perpetuities are forbidden (Roemild v. Jones, 1957). Refusal to rezone property that is adjacent to property already zoned for business creates a monopoly and violates this clause (Blytheville v. Thompson, 1973).

SECTION 21

No person shall be taken or imprisoned or disseized of his estate, freehold, liberties or privileges; or outlawed; or in any manner destroyed or deprived of his life, liberty or property; except by the judgment of his peers or the law of the land; nor shall any person under any circumstances be exiled from the State.

One Arkansas statute, which has been held not to violate the banishment prohibition, allows the governor to grant pardons on condition that the convicted person leave the state (Ex parte Hawkins, 1895). Nor is the trial by the juvenile court of a minor a violation of his or her constitutional rights (Martin v. State, 1948). A statute fixing prices at which liquor could be sold was ruled a valid exercise of the police power and did not violate this clause (Gipson v. Morley, 1950). Repossession of collateral by a secured party does not violate the guaranteed rights (Teeter Motor Co. v. First National Bank, 1976). Due process requires the opportunity to be heard at a meaningful time and in a meaningful place before a person may be deprived of life, liberty, or property (Franklin v. State, 1979).

SECTION 22

The right of property is before and higher than any constitutional sanction; and private property shall not be taken, appropriated or damaged for public use, without just compensation therefor.

The right of eminent domain is inherent in the government but the legislature is bound to provide a fair compensation to the individual whose property is taken, and, until a just indemnity is afforded, the power cannot be legally exercised (Ex parte Martin, 1853). The words "just compensation" mean "full compensation" in accordance with appraised or market value (Arkansas Highway Commission v. Stupendi, 1953). However, property cannot be taken for private use through eminent domain (Ozark Coal Co. v. Pennsylvania Anthracite R. R., 1911). Moreover, outdoor advertising along highways can be regulated (City of Fayetteville v. S & H, Inc., 1977). Private property enjoys no constitutional privilege when it is knowingly used to traffic in illegal drugs (1982 Datsun 280ZX v. Bentley ex rel. North Little Rock Police Department, 1985). Just compensation means full compensation (Arkansas Highway Commission v. Stupendi, 1953). When purchased property is zoned for single families, the city's failure to rezone does not constitute taking of property for public use without just compensation (McMinn v. Little Rock, 1982).

SECTION 23

The State's ancient right of eminent domain and of taxation is herein fully and expressly conceded; and the General Assembly may delegate the taxing power with the necessary restriction, to the State's subordinate political and municipal corporations to the extent of providing for their existence, maintenance and well being, but no further.

Annexation of land for purposes only of taxation is prohibited (Saunders v. City of Little Rock, 1977). The legislature may classify corporations and corporate interests for purpose of taxation and may specify the mode of assessment, levy, and collection of taxes on corporate properties and interests (Arco Auto

Carriers, Inc. v. State ex rel. Bennett, 1960). A local improvement district is not a subordinate political agency to which tax privileges may be delegated (Whaley v. Northern Road Improvement District, 1922). The legislature has the power to make all property in the state subject to taxation, except for property that is specifically exempted by the Constitution (Arco Auto Carriers, Inc. v. State ex rel. Bennett, 1960).

SECTION 24

All men have a natural and indefeasible right to worship Almighty God according to the dictates of their own consciences; no man can, of right, be compelled to attend, erect or support any place of worship; or to maintain any ministry against his consent. No human authority can, in any case or manner whatsoever, control or interfere with the right of conscience; and no preference shall ever be given, by law, to any religious establishment, denomination or mode of worship above any other.

A provision for freedom of religion is found in all fifty state constitutions. The state may compel children to attend school or may appoint a guardian to have children vaccinated against small pox in order to permit them to attend even if the parents contend that vaccination is contrary to their religious beliefs (Cude v. State, 1964). The opening of a parochial school is a religious action and is subject to reasonable limitation (Abram v. City of Fayetteville, 1983). To claim protection under this section, a party's position must be rooted in religious belief (Gipson v. Brown, 1986).

SECTION 25

Religion, morality and knowledge being essential to good government, the General Assembly shall enact suitable laws to protect every religious denomination in the peaceable enjoyment of its own mode of public worship.

Only the 1868 Constitution previously contained this provision. For a general discussion, see 4 *Arkansas Law Review* 433. Also see Gipson v. Brown, 1986.

SECTION 26

No religious test shall ever be required of any person as a qualification to vote or hold office, nor shall any person be rendered incompetent to be a witness on account of his religious belief; but nothing herein shall be construed to dispense with oaths or affirmations.

This is also a relatively new provision in Arkansas constitutional history, coming several decades after the granting of statehood. Also see the reference to atheists in Article 19, Section 1.

SECTION 27

There shall be no slavery in this State, nor involuntary servitude, except as a punishment for crime. No standing army shall be kept in time of peace; the military shall at all times be in strict subordination to the civil powers; and no soldier shall be quartered in any house, or on any premises, without the consent of the owner, in time of peace; nor in time of war, except in a manner prescribed by law.

There has been no litigation of this clearly and strongly worded provision, which embodies the spirit of the Emancipation Proclamation and guarantees against abuses during any future civil wars. This provision can be said to protect persons against various forms of tyranny and against government discrimination. Its purpose is to keep the military in strict subordination to civil power. Similar sections are contained in forty state constitutions.

SECTION 28

All lands in this State are declared to be allodial; and feudal tenures of every description, with all their incidents, are prohibited.

This section was drafted in tandem with the immediately preceding section. For a general discussion, see Medieval Law in the Age of Space: Some Rules of Property in Arkansas, 22 *Arkansas Law Review* 248.

SECTION 29

This enumeration of rights shall not be construed to deny or disparage others retained by the people; and to guard against any encroachment on the rights herein retained, or any transgression of any of the higher powers herein delegated, we declare that everything in this article is excepted out of the general powers of the government, and shall forever remain inviolate; and that all laws contrary thereto, or to other provisions herein contained shall be void.

The legislature may proscribe any abortion by a person who is not a physician. A layperson thus charged with inducing an abortion has no standing in court to attack the constitutionality of such a legislative act (May v. State, 1973). A statute providing for a limited constitutional convention not ratified by the voters was unconstitutional. It allowed delegates to exercise power that is reserved to the people (Pryor v. Lowe, 1975). The state may grant or withhold the privilege of the authority to sell liquor and may impose any conditions (Wade v. Homer, 1914).

Article III

Franchise and Elections

SECTION 1

Every male citizen of the United States, or male person who has declared his intention of becoming a citizen of the same, of the age of twenty-one years, who has resided in the State twelve months, and in the county six months, and in the voting precinct or ward one month, next preceding any election, where he may propose to vote, shall be entitled to vote at all elections by the people. (See Amendments Nos. 8, 36, 39 and 51, Section 17.)

Superseded by Amendment 8.

SECTION 2

Elections shall be free and equal. No power, civil or military, shall ever interfere to prevent the free exercise of the right of suffrage; nor shall any law be enacted whereby the right to vote at any election shall be made to depend upon any previous registration of the elector's name; or whereby such right shall be impaired or forfeited; except for the commission of felony at common law; upon lawful conviction thereof.

The clause prohibiting the registration of voters has been superseded by Amendments 39 and 51. Election statutes are to be regarded as mandatory before, but not after, an election (Henderson v. Gladesh, 1939). The legislature has the power to make registration for voting in any election (Faubus v. Miles, 1964). If Board of Election commissioners has no authority to call an election, the court cannot issue a writ of mandamus to direct it to do so (Files v. Hill, 1980).

SECTION 3

All elections by the people shall be by ballot. Every ballot shall be numbered in the order in which it shall be received, and the number recorded by the election officers on the list of voters opposite the name of the elector who presents the ballot. The election officer shall be sworn or affirmed not to disclose how any elector shall have voted, unless required to do so as witness in a judicial proceeding, or a proceeding to contest an election.

Superseded by Amendment 50.

SECTION 4

Electors shall, in all cases (except treason, felony and breach of the peace), be privileged from arrest during their attendance at elections and going to and from the same.

These provisions set a high state priority on a voter's effort to cast a vote, which is in line with democratic principles.

SECTION 5

No idiot or insane person shall be entitled to the privileges of an elector.

This provision is the first in Arkansas constitutional history and has not been litigated, although it is often referred to in humor.

SECTION 6

Any persons who shall be convicted of fraud, bribery or other willful and corrupt violation of any election law of this State shall be adjudged guilty of a felony, and disqualified from holding any office of trust or profit in this State.

When this question arises, power is implied for the legislature to provide for a method of ascertaining and declaring the forfeiture of office (Speer v. Wood, 1917). For a general discussion, see "Official Misconduct under the Arkansas Criminal Code," 30 *Arkansas Law Review* 60; and Porter, "Removal of Discipline of Judges in Arkansas," 32 *Arkansas Law Review* 545.

SECTION 7

No soldier, sailor or marine in the military or naval service of the United States shall acquire a residence by reason of being stationed on duty in this State.

This provision reflects a concern for the historical precedence of Union soldiers staying on to hold office during the Reconstruction period and has been interpreted to mean that a soldier of the United States must meet residency requirements, apart from military service, for two months before filing a divorce suit in this state (Kennedy v. Kennedy, 1943; Mohr v. Mohr, 1944). A soldier may acquire residency by residing in state for three months with animus manendi (Mohr v. Mohr, 1944). A soldier residing in Arkansas for three months before a divorce suit is filed is considered a resident (Walther v. Walther, 1961).

SECTION 8

The general elections shall be held biennially, on the first Monday of September; but the General Assembly may by law fix a different time.

In 1916, the State legislature changed this election day to coincide with the federal election day.

SECTION 9

In trials of contested elections and in proceedings for the investigation of elections, no person shall be permitted to withhold his testimony on the ground that it may criminate himself or subject him to public infamy; but such testimony shall not be used against him in any judicial proceeding, except for perjury in giving such testimony.

This provision flies in the face of the Fifth Amendment to the U. S. Constitution and has not been litigated. It is new to the 1874 Constitution (not being contained in any of the four preceding constitutions), and is presumably of no force. For a general discussion, see "Theory of Testimonial Competency and Privilege," 4 *Arkansas Law Review* 377.

SECTION 10

No person shall be qualified to serve as an election officer who shall hold at the time of the election any office, appointment or employment in or under the government of the United States or of this State, or in any city or county or any municipal board, commission or trust in any city, save only the justices of the peace and aldermen, notaries public and persons in the militia service of the State. Nor shall any election officer be eligible to any civil office to be filled at an election at which he shall serve—save only to such subordinate municipal or local offices, below the grade of city or county officers, as shall be designated by general law.

This provision applies to all civil offices without respect to rank or grade until the legislature designates subordinate municipal or local offices as exempt (Faulkner v. Woodard, 1941). Incumbents can contest the eligibility of their successors to hold the office in cases where successors have acted as a judge of an election, and may continue in office until a successor is qualified (Faulkner v. Woodard). Election officials are recognized by the Constitution as constitutional officers (Henderson v. Gladish, 1939). There will be no exemptions unless made by the legislature in very specific terms (State ex rel. Robinson v. Jones, 1937).

SECTION 11

If the officers of any election shall unlawfully refuse or fail to receive, count or return the vote or ballot of any qualified elector, such vote or ballot shall nevertheless be counted upon the trial of any contest arising out of said election.

There was a great concern about election fraud at the time of the drafting of the Constitution. Under this provision, all legal votes cast at an election must be counted, whether returned or not, and whether or not any irregularities attended the election (Govan v. Jackson, 1877). If election is not held at the proper time, the court may not declare what would have been the voter's choice in case an election had been held (Chism v. Tucker, 1911). These provisions do not apply to party primaries, but the legislature may, by reference, make primaries subject to general election laws (Craig v. Sims, 1923).

SECTION 12

All elections by persons acting in representative capacity shall be viva voce.

This provision has not been litigated and has been applied primarily to the legislature and city boards of directors for the election of officers. It means they must use voice vote or live vote. The election of officers by the General Assembly is covered in Article V, Section 14.

Article IV

Departments

SECTION 1

The powers of the government of the State of Arkansas shall be divided into three distinct departments, each of them to be confined to a separate body of magistracy, to-wit: Those which are legislative to one, those which are executive to another, and those which are judicial to another.

This clear statement of the separation of powers has been a traditional provision of all of Arkansas's constitutions and is a matter-of-fact description. See "Legislative Delegation of Judicial Powers," 10 *Arkansas Law Review* 213; "Fusing the Division of Authority," 24 *Ark. Law Review*, 182; and J. D. Gingerich, "Mandamus of Unexecuted Executive Discretionary Powers," 33 *Arkansas Law Review* 765.

SECTION 2

No person or collection of persons, being of one of these departments, shall exercise any powers belonging to either of the others, except in the instance hereinafter expressly directed or permitted.

None of the three separate departments of government is subordinate to another. For example, the legislature cannot be coerced or controlled by the judiciary, and the legislature is not subject to judicial writ of mandamus (Wells v. Purcell, 1979). One can serve as a chief of police and a county sheriff at the same time, but not as state treasurer and justice of the peace (State v. Hutt, 1840; Peterson v. Culpepper, 1904; and State Bank v. Curran, 1849). The legislature has no right to delegate legislative power, but it may delegate the power to determine facts (McArthur v. Smallwood, 1955). Courts should not interfere with a constitutional convention as long as it is acting within its scope of framing a new constitution (Riviere v. Wells, 1980). The Amendment 60 provision for maximum interest rates at 5 percent above the federal discount rate did not violate the separation of powers (W. E. Tucker Oil Co. v. Portland Bank, 1985). The legislature may delegate the power or authority to determine the facts regarding the operation of a statute (Venhaus v. State ex rel. Lofton, 1985).

Article V

Legislative

SECTION 1

The Legislative power of this State shall be vested in a General Assembly, which shall consist of the Senate and House of Representatives.

This section has been partially superseded by Amendment 7, Section 1, which provides some legislative power to the people through the initiative and referendum process. This provision keeps the legislature from delegating its power to make laws, but allows it to make a law to delegate the power to determine some fact or state of things upon which its own action depends (Boyd v. Bryant, 1879). Municipalities may legislate only as authorized by the legislature (Leprarie v. City of Hot Springs, 1916). The legislature may enact a law imposing a condition on which it will be operative (Miller v. Witcher, 1923).

SECTION 2

The House of Representatives shall consist of members to be chosen every second year by the qualified electors of the several counties.

The legislature has the power to change the dates of biennial elections and of the beginning of terms of office (Hendricks v. Hodges, 1916).

SECTION 3

The Senate shall consist of members to be chosen every four years by the qualified electors of the several districts. At the first session of the Senate the senators shall divide themselves into two classes by lot, and the first class shall hold their places for two years only, after which all shall be elected for four years.

A suit by a voter seeking a declaratory judgment as to whether the Senate should be divided into two classes, as provided, was ruled defective because only the voters' senators were named as parties. Instead all must be named (Block v. Allen, 1967).

SECTION 4

No person shall be a senator or representative who, at the time of his election, is not a citizen of the United States, nor any one who has not been, for two years next preceding his election a resident of this State, and for one year next preceding his election a resident of the county or district whence he may be chosen. Senators shall be at least twenty-five years of age and representatives at least twenty-one years of age.

This residency requirement corresponds to residency requirements in many other state constitutions and has been held to meet the "reasonable basis" and the "compelling state interest" tests. Furthermore, one does not acquire residency by attending college in a district (Brewster v. Johnson, 1976). For a discussion of "The Constitutionality of Filing Fees for Political Candidates in Primary Elections," see 30 *Arkansas Law Review* 49, and "Survey of Arkansas Law," 1 *University of Arkansas at Little Rock Law Journal* 140.

SECTION 5

The General Assembly shall meet at the seat of government every two years on the first Tuesday after the second Monday in November until said time be altered by law.

This provision has been changed by legislative statute to the second Monday in January in odd-numbered years (in Section 10–2-101). For a general discussion, see "Survey of Arkansas Law: Public Law," 4 University of Arkansas at Little Rock Law Journal 243.

SECTION 6

The Governor shall issue writs of election to fill such vacancies as shall occur in either house of the General Assembly.

This provision further guarantees the system of checks and balances established by the separation of powers, a concept that was first expressed in the 1874 Constitution. This section was cited in Glover v. Henry, 1959.

SECTION 7

No judge of the supreme court, circuit or inferior courts of law or equity. Secretary of State, Attorney General for the State, Auditor, or Treasurer, recorder, clerk of any court of record, sheriff, coroner, member of Congress, nor any other person holding any lucrative office under the United States or this State (militia officers, justices of the peace, postmasters, officers of public schools and notaries excepted), shall be eligible to a seat in either house of the General Assembly.

Article IV provides the overall separation of powers, and this section provides additional specifics. In addition, this section was cited in State ex rel. Gray v. Hodges, 1913. After election, a legislator cannot acquire one of the listed positions (Williams v. Douglas, 1971).

SECTION 8

No person who now is or shall be hereafter a collector or holder of public money, nor any assistant or deputy of such holder or collector of public money, shall be eligible to a seat in either house of the General Assembly, nor to any office of trust or profit, until he shall have accounted for and paid over all sums for which he may have been liable.

This section originates from a specific incident under the 1868 Constitution during Reconstruction. It was adjudicated once shortly after its adoption to the effect that an official who was guilty of a violation of this section may be ousted (Swepston v. Barton, 1882). An identical provision from the 1836 Constitution was held to be not in violation of the U.S. Constitution (Taylor v. Governor, 1837).

SECTION 9

No person hereafter convicted of embezzlement of public monies, bribery, forgery or other infamous crime shall be eligible to the General Assembly or capable of holding any office of trust or profit in this State.

This restriction cannot be lifted by a gubernatorial or presidential pardon (Rideway v. Catlett, 1964). The legislature is the sole judge of its own members (Evans v. Wheatley, 1939). If a convicted person is replaced on the city council, the conviction is later reversed, and the person seeks to get an order for return to the position, facts are sufficient against demurrer (May v. Edwards, 1975).

SECTION 10

No Senator or Representative shall, during the term for which he shall have been elected, be appointed or elected to any civil office under this State.

A senator was elected as a constitutional convention delegate in 1968 and the Arkansas Supreme Court found him not in violation of this section because a delegate position was not considered a civil position under this article (Harvey v. Ridgeway, 1970). Furthermore, a state senator can run for Congress because it is a federal, and not a state, office. A member of the legislature cannot be appointed deputy prosecuting attorney (Martindale v. Honey, 1976). Legislators cannot serve on the State Board of Pardons and Paroles (Stames v. Sadler, 1963).

There is no conflict between this section and Article 5, **Section 7 (Williams v.** Douglas, 1971).

SECTION 11

Each house shall appoint its own officers and shall be sole judge of the qualifications, returns and elections of its own members. A majority of all the members elected to each house shall constitute a quorum to do business; but a smaller number may adjourn from day to day and compel the attendance of absent members in such manner and under such penalties as each house shall provide.

The chair of a party's state committee has no right to exclude the name of a candidate for state senator, even if convicted of a felony, as long as he or she complies with their rules (Irby v. Barrett, 1942). The courts do not have jurisdiction over election contests for legislative seats (State ex rel. Evans v. Wheatly, 1939; Pendergrass v. Sheid, 1967). When Senator Guy "Mutt" Jones, Sr., of Conway contested his expulsion from state senate, the trial court had jurisdiction to determine whether the Senate was lawfully in session (Reaves v. Jones, 1974).

SECTION 12

Each house shall have the power to determine the rules of its proceedings; and punish its members or other persons for contempt or disorderly behavior in its presence; enforce obedience to its process; to protect its members against violence or offers of bribe or private solicitations; and with the concurrence of two-thirds, expel a member, but not a second time for the same cause. A member expelled for corruption shall not thereafter be eligible to either house; and punishment for contempt or disorderly behavior shall not bar an indictment for the same offense. Each house shall keep a journal of its proceedings and from time to time publish the same, except such parts as require secrecy; and the yeas and nays on any question shall, at the desire of any five members, be entered on the journals.

The observance of rules adopted by the General Assembly for the conduct of its business is a matter entirely within its control and discretion and is not subject to review by the courts (Monroe v. Green, 1903). A house concurrent resolution providing both houses to recess and to reconvene is a matter of internal rule making and can be changed by the legislature at will (Reaves v. Jones, 1974). The failure to give notice to a senator, for proceedings at which he was expelled, did not violate due process (Reaves v. Jones). Double jeopardy does not apply to legislative judgment and action (Reaves v. Jones). Legislation requiring a financial impact statement of all state legislative mandates on counties and municipalities is constitutional (Howard County v. Rotenberry, 1985).

SECTION 13

The sessions of each house and of committees of the whole shall be open unless when the business is such as ought to be kept secret.

This relates to legislative committees as well as to the House and Senate as a whole. This section has not been litigated, but it has been discussed in John Watkins, "Access to Public Records under Arkansas Freedom of Information Act," 37 *Arkansas Law Review* 741, and John Watkins, "Open Meetings under the Arkansas Freedom of Information Act," 38 *Arkansas Law Review* 268.

SECTION 14

Whenever an officer, civil or military, shall be appointed by the joint or concurrent vote of both houses, or by the separate vote of either house of the General Assembly, the vote shall be taken viva voce and entered on the journals.

The voice vote requirement is contained in several places in this constitution in the Franchise and Elections article (3, Section 12), as well as the Legislative Department section, and refers to elections by persons acting as representatives.

SECTION 15

The members of the General Assembly shall in all cases except treason, felony, and breach, or surety of the peace, be privileged from arrest during their attendance at the sessions of their respective houses, and in going to and returning from the same; and for any speech or debate in either house they shall not be questioned in any other place.

The legislators have special license plates and are not subject to civil traffic violation citations during legislative sessions.

SECTION 16

The members of the General Assembly shall receive such per diem pay and mileage for their services as shall be fixed by law. No member of either house shall, during the term for which he has been elected, receive any increase of pay for his services under any law passed during such term. The term of all members of the General Assembly shall begin on the day of their election.

This section has been substantially superseded by Amendment 15, paragraph 3, and Amendment 48. Compensation of legislators is now governed by Amendment 56, Section 3, while the commencement of terms is governed by Article 8, Section 6, as amended (Berry v. Gordon, 1964). Commencement of terms is governed by Article 8, Section 6, as amended. Cited in Purcell v. Jones, 1967.

SECTION 17

The regular biennial session shall not exceed sixty days in duration, unless by a vote of two-thirds of the members elected to each house of said General Assembly. Provided that this section shall not apply to the first session of the General Assembly under this constitution, or when impeachments are pending.

This section has been restated and extended by five additional sections in Amendment 6. A regular session may exceed sixty days by a vote of two-thirds of members elected (State ex rel. Purcell v. Jones, 1967). There is no limit on such an extension (Wells v. Purcell, 1979). The Uniform Rules of Evidence of 1976 were not validly adopted because the legislature was not validly in session at the time of adoption and, therefore, they did not become law (Ricarte v. State, 1986). Later, the Arkansas Supreme Court adopted the Uniform Rules of Evidence.

SECTION 18

Each house, at the beginning of every regular session of the General Assembly, and whenever a vacancy may occur, shall elect from its members a presiding officer to be styled respectively, the President of the Senate and the Speaker of the House of Representatives; and whenever, at the close of any session, it may appear that the term of the member elected President of the Senate will expire before the next regular session, the Senate shall elect another president from those members whose terms of office continue over, who shall qualify and remain President of the Senate until his successor may be elected and qualified; and who, in the case of a vacancy in the office of Governor, shall perform the duties and exercise the powers of Governor, as elsewhere herein provided.

The newly elected president of the Senate assumes the duties of that office at noon on the day of adjournment (Powell v. Hays, 1907). This provision has been further defined by Amendment 6, Sections 1 and 5, and Amendment 37, Section 1. The lieutenant governor serves as president of the Senate. Section 19. The style of the laws of the State of Arkansas shall be; "Be it enacted by the General Assembly of the State of Arkansas." This enacting clause is customary in U.S. legislation and is essential to the validity of each act unless it is adopted by the people, instead of the legislature, in which case it should read: "Be it enacted by the People of the State of Arkansas," as provided by Amendment 7 (Ferrell v. Keel, 1912). The enacting clause is essential to the validity of an act (Vinsant v. Knox, 1871).

SECTION 20

The State of Arkansas shall never be made defendant in any of her courts.

The state has a state claims commission, appointed by the governor and funded by the legislature, which serves as a system for the redress of claims against the state. See Smolla, "Politics and Due Process Don't Mix: Should the State Claims Commission Be Abolished?" 1986 *Ark. Law Notes* 43. A state agency may become the subject of a suit by virtue of acting in "badfaith." The state may not be sued without its consent but this article clarifies that and expressly forbids all suits against the state (Pitcock v. State, 1909). Further, a suit against state officers is not a suit against the state. The state may become a suitor in its own courts (Arkansas Highway Commission v. Partain, 1937). Even when the state is not defendant, it is not certain that a suit can be filed (Ralls v. Mittlesteadt, 1980). A trial court can allow contract purchasers to intervene in eminent domain cases (Highway Commission v. Wilkinson, 1984). A suit against state officers is not a suit against the state (McConnell v. Arkansas Brick and Manufacturing Co., 1902). The state Highway Commission cannot be sued (Highway Commission V. Nelson Brothers, 1935).

SECTION 21

No laws shall be passed except by bill, and no bill shall be so altered or amended on its passage through either house as to change its original purpose.

The purpose of this section was to forbid amendments that are not germane to the subject as expressed by the title of the act (Loftin v. Watson, 1877). This does not prohibit the House from amending a Senate bill by striking it all after enacting clause and substituting a new bill, as long as the amendment does not change the original purpose (Reitzhammer v. Desha Road Improvement District, No. 2, 1919). The most recent judicial reference is Freeze v. Jones, 1976.

SECTION 22

Every bill shall be read at length on three different days in each house, unless the rules be suspended by two-thirds of the house, when the same may be read a second or third time on the same day; and no bill shall become a law unless on its final passage the vote be taken by yeas and nays, the names of the persons voting for and against the same be entered on the journal, and the majority of each house be recorded thereon as voting in its favor.

The requirements as to reading were to prevent hasty legislation by giving members time to do research and consult with their constituents. The first reading may be by title only and may be dispensed with upon a suspension of the rules. A bill may be read in both branches on the same day (Chicot County v. Davies, 1882). The Constitution of 1868 contained a provision similar to that found in this clause. It was held at that time that a bill did not become a law in cases where the House journal showed the number of votes given on its final passage in the affirmative and the names of those voting in the affirmative but had no entry of the names of those who voted in the negative (Smithee v. Garth, 1878). The same bill must be passed by both houses (Rogers v. State, 1904). Concurrent resolutions cannot be used to pass laws (Dickinson v. Johnson, 1915). The presumption of validity of the legislation signed by the governor and deposited with the secretary of state is not overcome by the fact that it was amended (Bradley Lumber Co. v. Cheney, 1956). A statute was ruled not valid because it passed only with vote of a senator who was unlawfully appointed by the governor (Smith v. Ridgeview Baptist Church, Inc., 1974).

SECTION 23

No law shall be revived, amended, or the provisions thereof extended or conferred by reference to its title only; but so much thereof as is revived, amended, extended or conferred shall be reenacted and published at length.

This section is an effort to make legislation more easily read and understood by average citizens, as well as by legal scholars. This section does not apply to municipal ordinances (Shepherd v. City of Little Rock, 1931). Repeals by implication are not within the meaning of this provision (City of Little Rock v. Quindley, 1896).

SECTION 24

The General Assembly shall not pass any local or special law changing the venue in criminal cases; changing the names of persons or adopting or legitimating children; grant divorces; vacating roads, streets or alleys.

This section may be superseded by Amendment 14, a much broader prohibition against local and special acts. The legislature can alter the procedure to change public roads (Tuggle v. Tribble, 1928; also cited in Laman v. Harrill, 1961).

SECTION 25

In all cases where a general law can be made applicable, no special law shall be enacted; nor shall the operation of any general law be suspended by the Legislature for the benefit of any particular individual, corporation or association; nor where the courts have jurisdiction to grant the powers or the privileges of the relief asked for.

This section may also be superseded by Amendment 14. It is left to the discretion of the legislature to determine the case in which the special law should be passed, as long as the legislature acts within its enumerated powers (Boyd v. Bryant, 1879). This section refers to cases in which the courts have jurisdiction independent of statute (School District v. West Hartford Special School District, 1912; also cited in Jackson v. Ozment, 1984).

SECTION 26

No local or special bill shall be passed, unless notice of the intention to apply therefor shall have been published in the locality where the matter or thing to be affected may be situated, which notice shall be at least thirty days prior to the introduction in the General Assembly of such bill, and in the manner to be provided by law. The evidence of such notice having been published shall be exhibited in the General Assembly before such act shall be passed.

The legislature is the sole judge of whether the requirement of notice has been satisfied (Davies v. Gaines, 1886). An act is void if not preceded by adequate notice (Booe v. Road Improvement District No. 4, 1919). This section may be superseded by Amendment 14.

SECTION 27

No extra compensation shall be made to any officer, agent, employee, or contractor after the service shall have been rendered or the contract made, nor shall any money be appropriated or paid on any claim, the subject matter of which shall not have been provided for by pre-existing laws; unless such compensation or claim be allowed by bill passed by twothirds of the members elected to each branch of the General Assembly.

This section prevents the legislature from making appropriations in the satisfaction of contracts that are not authorized by some law existing at the time the contract was made, unless upon a vote of two-thirds of the members of the legislature (Jobe v. Urquhart, 1912; Oliver v. Southern Trust Co., 1919).

SECTION 28

Neither house shall, without the consent of the other, adjourn for more than three days nor to any other place than that in which the two houses shall be sitting.

The houses of the legislature may not take this kind of strategic action against each other. They may block legislation, defeat bills, and use parliamentary rules against each other, but may not desert each other. There has been no litigation of this section.

SECTION 29

No money shall be drawn from the treasury except in pursuance of specific appropriations made by law, the purpose of which shall be distinctly stated in the bill, and the maximum amount which may be drawn shall be specified in dollars and cents; and no appropriations shall be for a longer period than two years.

All funds paid into the state treasury come within the meaning of this section (Dickinson v. Cliboum, 1916). A statute requiring that funds raised through bonds be used for a specific purpose was held to be a specific appropriation (Hudson v. Higgins, 1928). This section does not apply to moneys that are not in the treasury (Gipson v. Ingram, 1949). There is no restriction on the supreme power of the legislature regarding public revenues (McArthur v. Small wood, 1955). The Department of Correction was permitted to buy printing equipment as appropriate for maintenance and operations (Wells v. Heath, 1981).

SECTION 30

The general appropriation bill shall embrace nothing but appropriations for the ordinary expense of the executive, legislative and judicial departments of the State. All other appropriations shall be made by separate bills, each embracing only one subject.

The objective of this section was to prevent omnibus appropriation bills (Perkins v. DuVal, 1876). The inclusion of separate and unrelated appropriations in a single bill is prevented because that practice is widely believed to open the door to the past evils that were known as "logrolling" and "pork barrel" legislation (Cottrell v. Faubus, 1961). However, the subject of an appropriation is not destroyed by appropriating several sums for several specific objects if they are necessary or convenient for the accomplishment of one general design (State v. Sloan, 1899). The construction and maintenance of highways and roads do not have to be enumerated in separate appropriations (Hooker v. Parkin, 1962). The compensation of attorneys in collateral proceedings must be appropriated in separate items (Reed v. Jones, 1977). A judicial retirement bill was not able to transfer a county to a new judicial district (Clinton v. Taylor, 1984).

SECTION 31

No State tax shall be allowed, or appropriation of money made, except to raise means for the payment of the just debts of the State, for defraying the necessary expenses of government, to sustain common schools. to repel invasionand suppress insurrection, except by a majority of twothirds of both houses of the General Assembly.

The legislature has the right to determine what is a necessary expense of state government (State v. Moore, 1905). The state courts may make a determination as well (Belote v. Coffman, 1915). The maintenance of institutions of higher education is a necessary expense (Hudson v. Higgins, 1927). For further discussion, see "Property Tax Exemptions in Arkansas," 4 *Ark. Law Review* 433.

SECTION 32

No act of the General Assembly shall limit the amount to be recovered for injuries resulting in death, or for injuries to persons or property; and in case of death from such injuries the right of action shall survive and the General Assembly shall prescribe for whose benefit such action shall be prosecuted.

This section has been substantially amended and extended by Amendment 26. If damages awarded by a jury are excessive, the court may direct a revision (Little Rock and Fort Smith R.R. v. Barber, 1882).

SECTION 33

No obligation or liability of any railroad or other corporation held or owned by this State shall ever be exchanged, transferred, remitted, postponed or in any way diminished by the General Assembly; nor shall such liability or obligation be released except by payment thereof into the State Treasury.

Many railroad debts had been reduced or repudiated by the legislature in the post-Civil War period in Arkansas. No litigation has attended this section.

SECTION 34

No new bill shall be introduced in either house during the last three days of the session.

This does not apply in cases of special sessions of the legislature, when called by the governor via proclamation; these may last only three days (Spa Kennel Club v. Dunaway, 1966).

SECTION 35

Any person who shall, directly or indirectly, offer, give or promise any money or thing of value, testimonial, privilege or personal advantage to any executive or judicial officer or member of the General Assembly, and any such executive or judicial officer or member of the General Assembly who shall receive or consent to receive any such consideration, either directly or indirectly, to influence his action in the performance or non-performance of his public or official duty, shall be guilty of a felony and be punished accordingly.

This is Arkansas's definition of bribery and is also governed by the Arkansas Criminal Code of 1971 and the Code of Ethics Act of 1988. For a general discussion, see "Official Misconduct under the Arkansas Criminal Code," 30 *Arkansas Law Review* 160.

SECTION 36

Proceedings to expel a member for a criminal offense, whether successful or not, shall not bar an indictment and punishment, under the criminal laws, for the same offense.

This section has never been litigated and has been expanded by Amendment 19.

Article VI

Executive Department

SECTION 1

The executive department of this State shall consist of a Governor, Secretary of State, Treasurer of State, Auditor of State, and Attorney General, all of whom shall keep their offices in person at the seat of government, and hold their offices for the term of two years and until their successors are elected and qualified, and the General Assembly may provide by law for the establishment of the office of Commissioner of State Lands.

This section has been superseded with the addition of the Office of Lieutenant Governor. See Amendment 6, Sections 1, 4, 5, and 6, as well as Amendments 56 and 63. Executive officers are liable to damages if they execute a statute that violates the constitution (Little Rock and Fort Smith R.R. v. Worthen, 1885; also cited in State ex rel. Williams v. Karston, 1945).

SECTION 2

The supreme executive power of this State shall be vested in the chief magistrate, who shall be styled "the Governor of the State of Arkansas."

This section has been superseded by Amendment 6, Section 2. Cited in Curry v. State, 1983).

SECTION 3

The Governor, Secretary of State, Treasurer of State, Auditor of State, and Attorney General shall be elected by the qualified electors of the State at large at the time and places of voting for members of the General Assembly; the returns of each election therefor shall be sealed up separately and transmitted to the seat of Government by the returning officers, and directed to the Speaker of the House of Representatives, who shall during the first week of the session, open and publish the votes cast and given for each of the respective officers hereinbefore mentioned, in the presence of both houses of the General Assembly. The person having the highest number of votes for each of the respective offices shall be declared duly elected thereto; but if two or more shall be equal, and highest in votes for the same office, one of them shall be chosen by the joint vote of both houses of the General Assembly and a majority of all the members elected shall be necessary to a choice.

The lieutenant governor was added by Amendment 6, Section 3, and the state land commissioner was added by Amendment 37. These additions were reiterated by Amendment 56. This section does not require runoff primaries because it authorizes election by plurality votes (Rockefeller v. Matthews, 1970).

SECTION 4

Contested elections for Governor, Secretary of State, Treasurer of State, Auditor of State, and Attorney General shall be determined by the members of both houses of the General Assembly in joint session, who shall have exclusive jurisdiction in trying and determining the same, except as hereinafter provided in the case of special elections, and all such contests shall be tried and determined at the first session of the General Assembly after the election in which the same shall have arisen.

In 1874, at the time of the drafting of this constitution, the state's most infamous contested election occurred between two gubernatorial candidates and resulted in an armed skirmish known as the Brooks-Baxter War. A cannon reputedly fired in this battle is on display in Little Rock on the lawn of the Old State House, the former state capitol building (Baxter v. Brooks, 1874; also cited in Roger C. Mears, Jr. v. Hall, 1978).

SECTION 5

No person shall be elected to the office of Governor except a citizen of the United States who shall have attained the age of thirty years, and shall have been seven years a resident of this State.

The 1868 Constitution provided a minimum age of twenty-five years and five years of residency. The 1864 Constitution provides for thirty years of age and ten years of residency, as did the 1836 and 1861 constitutions. This provision would have made anyone residing in Arkansas for seven years, from 1867 to the present, eligible for governor. Cited in Glover v. Henry, 1959.

SECTION 6

The Governor shall be commander-in-chief of the military and naval forces of this State, except when they shall be called into the actual service of the United States.

This area of the law is also dealt with in Amendment 6, **Section 4.** Cited in Jones v. Clark, 1983.

SECTION 7

He may require information in writing from the officers of the executive department on any subject relating to the duties of their respective offices, and shall see that the laws are faithfully executed.

This is a traditional and typical provision of all Arkansas constitutions, and has not been litigated.

SECTION 8

He shall give to the General Assembly from time to time, and at the close of his official term to the next General Assembly, information by message concerning the condition and government of the State, and recommend for their consideration such measures as he may deem expedient.

Addresses to the legislature, reports, state of the state messages, inaugural addresses, and gubernatorial appearances before the Committee of the Whole are envisioned by this provision. Governor Bill Clinton has used this section more than any other Arkansas chief executive.

SECTION 9

A seal of the State shall be kept by the Governor, used by him officially, and called the "Great Seal of the State of Arkansas."

These seals are imprinted on legislation signed into law by the governor and are attached to proclamations, Arkansas Traveller Certificates, and other official documents of the governor's office. A legislator in the 1991 session proposed a change to "the Seal of the Great State of Arkansas," but it was not accepted for referral to the people.

SECTION 10

All grants and commissions shall be issued in the name and by the authority of the State of Arkansas, sealed by the Great Seal of the State, signed by the Governor, and attested by the Secretary of State.

This is an additional constitutional purpose for the official seal and is cited in Chism v. Martin, 1892.

SECTION 11

No member of Congress, or other person holding office under the authority of this State, or of the United States, shall exercise the office of Governor, except as herein provided.

This section was fashioned to protect Arkansas from influence from outside the state. It is a historic remnant from Reconstruction days and federal military district administration.

SECTION 12

In case of the death, conviction or impeachment, failure to qualify, resignation, absence from the State or other disability of the Governor, the powers, duties and emoluments of the office for the remainder of the term, or until the disability be removed, or a Governor elected and qualified, shall devolve upon and accrue, to the President of the Senate.

This section has probably been superseded by Amendment 6, Section 4.

SECTION 13

If, during the vacancy of the office of Governor, the President of the Senate shall be impeached, removed from office, refuse to qualify, resign, die, or be absent from the State, the speaker of the House of Representatives shall, in like manner, administer the government.

This provision, which was probably superseded by Amendment 6, Section 5, reflects an earlier era before modem transportation and advanced technology made it possible for a governor to stay in close communication while out of state. Cited in Futtrell v. Oldham, 1913. Now, the lieutenant governor becomes governor upon the latter's absence from the state.

SECTION 14

Whenever the office of Governor shall have become vacant by death, resignation, removal from office or otherwise, provided such vacancy shall not happen within twelve months next before the expiration of the term of office for which the late Governor shall have been elected, the President of the Senate or Speaker of the House of Representatives, as the case may be, exercising the powers of Governor for the time being, shall immediately call an election to be held to fill such vacancy, giving by proclamation sixty days previous notice thereof, which election shall be governed by the same rules prescribed for general elections of Governor as far as applicable; the returns shall be made to the Secretary of State, and the Acting Governor, Secretary of State and Attorney General shall constitute a board of canvassers, a majority of whom shall be decided as may be provided by law.

This section may have been superseded by Amendment 6, Sections 4 and 5. Cited in Futtrell v. Oldham, 1913.

SECTION 15

Every bill which shall have passed both houses of the General Assembly shall be presented to the Governor; if he approves it, he shall sign it; but if he shall not approve it, he shall return it, with his objections, to the house in which it originated, which house shall enter the objections at large upon their journal and proceed to reconsider. If, after such reconsideration, a majority of the whole number elected to that house shall agree to pass the bill, it shall be sent with the objections to the other house, by which likewise, it shall be reconsidered; and, if approved by a majority of the whole number elected to that house, it shall be a law; but in such cases the votes of both houses shall be determined by "yeas and nays," and the names of the members voting for or against the bill shall be entered on the journals. If any bill shall not be returned by the Governor within five days, Sunday excepted, after it shall have been presented to him, the same shall be a law in like manner as if he had signed it, unless the General Assembly, by their adjournment, prevented its return, in which case it shall become a law, unless he shall file the same, with his objections, in the office of the Secretary of State and give notice thereof by public proclamation within twenty days after such adjournment.

Bills need not be transmitted to the governor before adjournment of the assembly, but must be transmitted within twenty days of adjournment (Monroe v. Green, 1903). The governor cannot veto a resolution proposing a constitutional amendment (Mitchell v. Hopper, 1922). In the computation of time, the first day is not counted while the last day is (State ex rel. Hebert v. Hall, 1958). A bill becomes law without signature after five days, even if it becomes effective or operative later (Fletcher v. Bryant, 1968).

SECTION 16

Every order or resolution in which the concurrence of both houses of the General Assembly may be necessary, except on questions of adjournment, shall be presented to the Govemor, and before it shall take effect, be approved by him; or, being disapproved, shall be repassed by both houses, according to the rules and limitations prescribed in the case of a bill.

Concurrent resolutions have the force of law only within the limited sphere incident to the work or legislation which the legislature may complete before its final adjournment, but cannot be used in place of bills to enact laws (Dickinson v. Johnson, 1915). Vetoes are not allowed on resolutions, including those proposing a constitutional amendment (Mitchell v. Hopper, 1922).

SECTION 17

The Govemor shall have power to disapprove any item or items of any bill making appropriation of money, embracing distinct items, and the part or parts of the bill approved shall be the law, and the item or items of appropriation disapproved shall be void, unless repassed according to the rules and limitations prescribed by the passage of other bills over the executive veto.

The govemor has an "item veto" (Dickinson v. Page, 1915).

SECTION 18

In all criminal and penal cases, except in those of treason and impeachment, the Govemor shall have power to grant reprieves, commutation of sentence, and pardons after conviction; and to remit fines and forfeitures under such rules and regulations as shall be prescribed by law. In case of treason he shall have power, by and with the advice and consent of the Senate, to grant reprieves and pardons; and he may, in the recess of the Senate, respite the sentence until the adjournment of the next regular session of the General Assembly. He shall communicate to the General Assembly at every regular session each case of reprieve, commutation or pardon, with his reason therefor, stating the name and crime of the convict, the sentence, its date and the date of the commutation, pardon or reprieve.

The review of sentences, when not in excess of statutory limits and where there is no error, is not within the jurisdiction of the courts, as the exercise of clemency is given to the executive branch (Osborne v. State, 1963). The executive branch has the sole authority to grant clemency to deserving individuals (Smith v. State, 1977). Pardons may be granted by the governor even while a case is pending (Cole v. State, 1907). The governor may remit a forfeited bond (Tinkle v. State, 1959). A pardon does not discharge the convict from the costs of prosecution (Edwards v. State, 1851). Life imprisonment without parole was ruled not to violate this section (Tanner v. State, 1976).

SECTION 19

The Governor may, by proclamation, on extraordinary occasions, convene the General Assembly at the seat of government, or at a different place if that shall have become since their last adjournment dangerous from an enemy or contagious disease and he shall specify in his proclamation the purpose for which they are convened, and no other business than set forth therein shall be transacted until same shall have been disposed of, after which they may, by a vote of two-thirds of all members elected to both houses, entered upon their journals, remain in session not exceeding fifteen days.

The legislature may act freely within the Governor's official call upon all or any subjects specified, and every presumption will be in favor of the regularity of the action, but when the court determines that the act is not within the purposes specified, it is the court's duty to declare the act invalid (Jones v. State, 1922; Sims v. Weldon, 1924). There are only two types of legislative sessions: regular and special (State ex rel. Purcell v. Jones, 1967).

SECTION 20

In cases of disagreement between the two houses of the General Assembly, at a regular or special session with respect to the time of adjournment, the Governor may, if the facts be certified to him by the presiding officers of the two houses, adjourn them to a time not beyond the day of their next meeting; and, on account of danger from an enemy or disease, to such other place of safety as he may think proper.

This section is designed to promote the smoothest possible solution to any intralegislative disagreement and to allow the governor to settle differences and respond to emergencies. Cited in Wells v. Purcell, 1979.

SECTION 21

The Secretary of State shall keep a full and accurate record of all the official acts and proceedings of the Governor, and, when required, lay the same, with all papers, minutes and vouchers relating thereto, before either branch of the General Assembly. He shall also discharge the duties of Superintendent of Public Instruction, until otherwise provided by law.

Arkansas no longer has a superintendent of public instruction. The elementary and secondary education system is now administered by the State Board of Education, its general education director, and its vocational-technical education director. The secretary of state is specifically the custodian of all records pertaining to actions of the governor's office (Powell v. Hays, 1907).

SECTION 22

The Treasurer of State, Secretary of State, Auditor of State and Attorney General shall perform such duties as may be prescribed by law; they shall not hold any other office or commission, civil or military, in this State, or under any State, or the United States, or any other power, at one and the same time; and, in case of vacancy occurring in any of said offices, by death, resignation or otherwise, the Governor shall fill said office by appointment for the unexpired term.

This section, for example, prohibits officers of the U.S. Reserve from serving as constitutional officers in Arkansas (Jones v. Clark, 1983). The legislature has the right and power to prescribe the duties of the attorney general (Morley v. Berg, 1950). The legislature has right and power to prescribe duties of the attorney general (Parker v. Murry, 1953).

SECTION 23

When any office from any cause may become vacant, and no mode is provided by the Constitution and laws for filling such vacancy, the Govemor shall have the power to fill the same by granting a commission, which shall expire when the person elected to fill said office, at the next general election, shall be duly qualified.

Amendment 29 has particular relevance to this section, which relates only to elective offices (Cox v. State, 1904). This section does not apply to vacancies occurring in the office of mayor (Hogins v. Bullock, 1909). All commissions issued by the govemor expire no later than the next general election (Means v. Terral, 1920; cited in Glover v. Henry, 1959).

Article VII

Judicial Department

SECTION 1

The judicial power of the State shall be vested in one Supreme Court; in circuit courts, in county and probate courts, and injustices of the peace. The General Assembly may also vest such jurisdiction as may be deemed necessary in municipal corporation courts, courts of common pleas, where established, and when deemed expedient, may establish separate courts of chancery.

This provision is almost identical to the first sections in each of the previous Arkansas constitutions, except that it provides more flexibility to the legislature in creating local courts, such as municipal courts, county courts, juvenile courts (Ex parte King, 1919; Pulaski County Municipal Court v. Scott, 1981). States may require that matters be presented to the Public Service Commission and then to courts on appeal as long as a full and expeditious remedy is provided (McGehee v. MidSouth Gas Co., 1962). This section does not confer on the supreme court the exclusive authority to set rules of court procedure (Jackson v. Ozment, 1984). Law clerks do not have the power to decide cases (Brown v. State, 1986).

SECTION 2

The Supreme Court shall be composed of three judges, one of whom shall be styled chief justice, and elected as such; any two of whom shall constitute a quorum, and the concurrence of two judges shall, in every case, be necessary to a decision.

This section has probably been superseded by Amendment 9, Section 1, which increases the number of supreme court judges to five. It has not been litigated.

SECTION 3

When the population of the State shall amount to one million, the General Assembly, may, if deemed necessary, increase the number of judges of the Supreme Court to five; and, on such increase, a majority of judges shall be necessary to make a quoram or decision.

The legislature increased the number of judges to seven by Act 205 of 1925, Section 4.

SECTION 4

The Supreme Court, excepting cases otherwise provided by this Constitution, shall have appellate jurisdiction only, which shall be coextensive with the State, under such restrictions as may from time to time be prescribed by law. It shall have a general superintending control over all inferior courts of law and equity; and, in aid of its appellate and supervisory jurisdiction, it shall have power to issue writs of error and supersedes, certiorari, habeas corpus, prohibition, mandamus and quo warranto, and other remedial writs, and to hear and determine the same. Its judges shall be conservators of the peace throughout the State, and shall severally have power to issue any of the aforesaid writs.

Supreme court judges cannot issue warrants (Ex parte Levy, 1942). The jurisdiction of the court cannot be diminished or enlarged by the legislature, though its exercise may be regulated and restricted (Ex parte Anthony, 1844). The right of appeal must be exercised, however, under such restrictions as the legislature may impose (Smith v. State, 1886). This article was found not to be amended by Amendment 26 to allow direct appeal from the Workers' Compensation Commission (Ward School Bus Manufacturing, Inc. v. Fowler, 1977). Jurisdiction of the supreme court cannot be expanded by legislature (American Party v. Brandon, 1972). Notice is the foundation of due process and is required in the removal of a judge (Anderson v. State, 1979).

SECTION 5

In the exercise of original jurisdiction the Supreme Court shall have power to issue writs of quo warranto to the circuit judges and chancellors when created, and to officers of political corporations when the question involved is the legal existence of such corporation.

The original jurisdiction of the Supreme Court is conferred by this section (Ex parte Snoddy, 1905). The right to issue the writ of quo warranto includes information in the nature of the writ (State v. Leatherman, 1881). Writs of quo warranto are legal documents requiring a person to show by what authority he or she exercises a public office, franchise, or liberty.

SECTION 6

A judge of the Supreme Court shall be at least thirty years of age, of good moral character, and learned in the law; a citizen of the United States and two years a resident of the State, and who has been a practicing lawyer eight years, or whose service upon the bench of any court of record. when added to the time he may have practiced law, shall be equal to eight years. The judges of the Supreme Court shall be elected by the qualified electors of the State and shall hold their offices during the term of eight years from the date of their commissions; but at the first meeting of the court after the first election under this Constitution the judges shall by lot divide themselves into three classes, one of which shall hold his office for four, one for six and the other for eight years, after which each judge shall be elected for a full term of eight years. A record shall be made in the court of this classification.

All the previous constitutions provided for judges to be thirty years of age and to serve eight-year terms. However, the residency requirement and the reference to "good moral character" are new. Originally, in the state's first constitution in 1836, the judges were selected by the General Assembly. This section was cited in Jewett v. McConnell, 1914).

SECTION 7

The Supreme Court shall appoint its clerk and reporter, who shall hold their offices for six years, subject to removal for good cause.

Similar provisions are contained in each of the state's constitutions, beginning with the 1861 Charter. Initially, the term was for four years.

SECTION 8

The terms of the Supreme Court shall be held at the seat of government at the times that now are, or may be, provided by law.

This provision seeks to provide stability of the judicial system and is a new provision for Arkansas with this constitution.

SECTION 9

In case all or any of the judges of the Supreme Court shall be disqualified from presiding in any cause or causes, the court or the disqualified judge shall certify the same to the Governor, who shall immediately commission the requisite number of men learned in the law to sit in the trial and determination of such cases.

This section and process is used frequently and cited in Chism v. Martin, 1892 and Ferrell v. Keel, 1912. For reference, see Lawrence, "Precedential Value of the Opinions from an Equally Divided Court," 37 *Ark. Law Review* 418.

SECTION 10

The Supreme Court Judges shall at stated times receive a compensation for their services to be ascertained by law, which shall not be, after the adjournment of the next General Assembly, diminished during the time for which they shall have been elected. They shall not be allowed any fees or perquisites of office, nor hold any office of trust or profit under the State or the United States.

This provision (specifically the first sentence) is superseded in part by Amendment 9, Section 2, which was, in turn, superseded by Amendment 43.

SECTION 11

The circuit courts shall have jurisdiction in all civil and criminal cases, the exclusive jurisdiction of which may not be vested in some other court provided for by this constitution.

In cases where the circuit court has no legal jurisdiction specifically, its judgments have been held to be void (Drainage District v. Rolfe, 1913). Since the writ of mandamus is a common law writ and a remedy at law, the jurisdiction of such writ is vested in the circuit court, rather than in the chancery courts (Nethercutt v. Pulaski County Special School District, 1970). The circuit courts also have original jurisdiction over misdemeanors (State v. Devers, 1879). Chancery court has no jurisdiction to issue a writ of prohibition (Jeffery v. Jackson County Court, 1972). The writ of mandamus is vested in circuit courts (Nethercutt v. Pulaski County Special School District, 1970).

SECTION 12

The circuit courts shall hold their terms in each county at such times and places as are, or may be, prescribed by law.

The power of the legislature over terms, locations, and times is virtually unlimited, providing tremendous flexibility, which is unique to this otherwise restrictive constitution. If court is held at a time or place other than that provided by law, its proceedings are void (Ex parte James, 1871). Not every judicial act must be performed at a regular term of court (Central Coal and Coke Company v. Graham, 1917). For convenience, the legislature may require the circuit court to meet in several different places (Walker v. State, 1880). Statutes concerning the holding of special terms continue in force (Bell v. State, 1915).

SECTION 13

The State shall be divided into convenient circuits, each circuit to be made up of contiguous counties, for each of which circuits a judge shall be elected, who, during his continuance in office, shall reside in and be a conservator of the peace within the circuit for which he shall have been elected.

The right of a judge cannot be questioned collaterally (Keith v. State, 1887. The number of judges is not limited (State v. Martin, 1895). A district can contain only one county (Cockrell v. Dobbs, 1964).

SECTION 14

The circuit courts shall exercise a superintending control and appellate jurisdiction over county, probate, court of common pleas, and corporation courts and justices of the peace, and shall have power to issue, hear and determine all the necessary writs to carry into effect their general and specific powers, any of which writs may be issued under order of the judge of the appropriate court in vacation.

This section appears to be superseded by Section 35 of this same article, as amended, with respect to probate courts, by authorizing appeals directly to the Supreme Court. Matters of local concern pertaining to taxes, improvement, and disbursement for county purposes are under the jurisdiction of the county court (Ex parte Turner, 1883). The circuit court has the authority to issue orders staying judgment of county court pending appeal (Reese v. Steel, 1904). Certiorari cannot be used for the correction of errors in place of appeal, but where it appears from the record of the inferior court that it has no jurisdiction of the subject matter or person, its judgment may be quashed on certiorari by the circuit court (Baskins v. Wylds, 1882). The legislature may authorize court to be in session at all times (Miller v. Tatum, 1926). A county court's order on a local option liquor election is not subject to collateral attack in chancery court to enjoin the election (Biffle v. Priddy, 1936).

SECTION 15

Until the General Assembly shall deem it expedient to establish courts of chancery, the circuit courts shall have jurisdiction in matters of equity, subject to appeal to the Supreme court, in such manner as may be prescribed by law.

The legislature is without authority to give the chancery courts any jurisdiction other than that which chancery courts could exercise at the time of the adoption of the Constitution (Hester v. Bourland, 1906). Chancery courts have jurisdiction to render declaratory judgments in cases where the subject matter of the declaration is with equity jurisdiction (Jackson v. Smith, 1963). Equity jurisdiction is proper in action against issuance of securities based on allegations of fraud (Titan Oil and Gas v. Shipley, 1975). Chancery court has no jurisdiction to issue a write of prohibition (Jeffery v. Jackson County Court, 1972).

SECTION 16

A judge of the circuit court shall be a citizen of the United States, at least twenty-eight years of age, of good moral character, learned in the law, two years a resident of the State, and shall have practiced law six years, or whose service upon the bench of any court of record, when added to the time he may have practiced law, shall be equal to six years.

Special judges, appointed by the governor, do not have to have the same qualifications as regular judges (Maples v. Road Improvement District No. 2, 1919).

SECTION 17

The judges of the circuit courts shall be elected by the qualified electors of the several circuits, and shall hold their offices for the term of four years.

The legislature may not enlarge or abridge the constitutional term of office (Smith v. Askew, 1886). A statute could create a new division of a circuit court for a limited time (Wirges v. Roberts, 1966). The legislature does not have the power to enlarge the term of office of a circuit judge (Burns v. Britt, 1984).

SECTION 18

The judges of the circuit courts shall at stated times receive a compensation for their services, to be ascertained by law, which shall not, after the adjournment of the first session of the General Assembly, be diminished during the time for which they are elected. They shall not be allowed any fees or perquisites of office, nor hold any other office of trust or profit under this State or the United States.

Under this provision, the circuit courts are creatures of the state. An early act of the legislature making the salary of a circuit judge payable in part by the counties of the district was ruled invalid (Gotham v. Coffman, 1914). The mandate against holding other offices does not apply to special circuit judges (Maples v. Road Improvement District No. 2, 1919).

SECTION 19

The clerks of the circuit court shall be elected by the qualified electors of the several counties, for the term of two years, and shall be exofficio clerks of the county and probate courts and recorder; provided, that in any county having a population exceeding fifteen thousand inhabitants, as shown by the last federal census, there shall be elected a county clerk, in like manner as clerk of the circuit court, who shall be ex-officio clerk of the probate court of said county.

This provision was amended by Amendment 24, Section 3, which added the words "until otherwise provided, by the General Assembly." The provisions of this section limiting the election of a separate county clerk to those counties having a population exceeding 15,000 inhabitants were abolished by Amendment 41. The office of circuit clerk and recorder is a single office (Durden v. Sebastian Company, 1904). The Office of Clerk cannot be created for one county by statute (Huggins v. Wacaster, 1954).

SECTION 20

No judge or justice shall preside in the trial of any cause in the event of which he may be interested, or where either of the parties shall be connected with him by consanguinity or affinity, within such degree as may be prescribed by law; or in which he may have been of counsel or have presided in any inferior court.

Objections to a judge's qualifications must be made before judgment is rendered (Pettigrew v. Washington County, 1884). The interest that is disqualifying under this section is one in which liability, gain, or relief to the judge turns on the outcome of the suit (Foreman v. Marianna, 1884). Disqualification is discretionary with the judge, who will not be reversed unless there is some abuse (Woods v. State, 1983). Personal proprietary interest is disqualifying for a judge regarding the outcome of a case (Mears v. Hall, 1978). Disqualification is discretionary with the judge (Woods v. State, 1983). A prevailing party's attorney served as pallbearer for the judge's father after the trial and after the decision was made, but two days before it was communicated; this was ruled to bias the judge (Matthews v. Rodgers, 1983). A trial judge presiding at the previous trial of another person accused of the same crime is not disqualified (Welech v. State, 1984).

SECTION 21

Whenever the office of judge of the circuit court of any county is vacant at the commencement of a term of such court, or the judge of said court shall fail to attend, the regular practicing attorneys in attendance on said court may meet at 10 o'clock a.m. on the second day of the term and elect a judge to preside at such court, or until the regular judge shall appear; and if the judge of said court shall become sick or die or unable to continue to hold such court after its term shall have commended, or shall from any cause be disqualified from presiding at the trial of any cause then pending therein, then the regular practicing attorneys in attendance on said court may in like manner, on notice from the judge or clerk of said court, elect a judge to preside at such court or to try said causes, and the attorney so elected shall have the same power and authority shall cease at the close of the term at which the election shall be made. The proceedings shall be entered at large upon the record. The special judge shall be leamed in the law and a resident of the State.

The purpose of this section was to take care of emergency situations and to avoid a delay in trials. When a special judge, elected in the absence of the regular judge, is disqualified in a pirticular case, another special judge may be elected for that case (Little Rock and Fort Smith R.R. v. Barker, 1882). A motion suggesting a disqualification is not sufficient; rather, it must show a disqualification (Rowland v. State, 1948). A special judge can only hear cases pending at time of selection (State v. George, 1971). The statute cannot set a new system of selecting special judges (Wessell Brothers Foundry Drilling Co. v. Crossett Public School District, 1985).

SECTION 22

The judges of the circuit courts may temporarily exchange circuits or hold courts for each other under such regulations as may be prescribed by law.

It is not a reversible error for judges, under this section, to exchange circuits during the trial of a criminal case (York v. State, 1909). This language also applies to chancery courts in that chancellors may exchange with circuit judges as well as with other chancellors (McEachin v. Martin, 1937).

SECTION 23

Judges shall not charge juries with regard to matters of fact, but shall declare the law, and in jury trials shall reduce their charge or instructions to writing on the request of either party.

Juries in Arkansas are the sole judges of the evidence and witnesses (Texas and Pacific Railway v. Stephens, 1936). The main purpose of this section was to give counsel for either party an opportunity to make objections and exceptions in the judge's chambers, with no danger of the jury being influenced by rulings (Hicks v. State, 1956). The judge cannot advise the state's attorney to dismiss a prosecution for lack of evidence in the presence of the jury (State v. Wardlaw, 1884). If an instruction is applicable to the facts, it does not guarantee that it is proper (French v. State, 1974). Statute making the issue of a defendant's fitness to stand trial a question of law is constitutional (Rogers v. State, 1978). A judge's misstatement concerning whether the jury is the sole judge of issues is not a reversible error (Cobb v. State, 1979). Remarks of the court on the character of a witness violate this section (Williams v. State, 1927; West v. State, 1973).

SECTION 24

The qualified electors of each circuit shall elect a prosecuting attorney, who shall hold his office for the terms of two years, and he shall be a citizen of the United States, learned in the law, and a resident of the circuit for which he may be elected.

Prosecuting attorneys are constitutional officers acting in a quasi-judicial capacity (Griffin V. Rhoton, 1913). This section requires that each circuit have a prosecuting attorney (Riviere v. Hardegree, 1983). A circuit judge cannot appoint a special prosecutor unless the incumbent is being investigated for or charged with illegal activity (Venhaus v. Brown, 1985).

SECTION 25

The judges of the supreme, circuit, or chancery courts shall not, during their continuance in office, practice law or appear as counsel in any court, State or federal, within this State.

A judge may not appear as counsel under any situation (Wood v. Keith, 1895). For reference, see "Impeachment, Address and the Removal of Judges in Arkansas: An Historical Perspective," 32 *Ark. Law Review* 253.

SECTION 26

The General Assembly shall have power to regulate by law the punishment of contempt not committed in the presence or hearing of the courts, or in disobedience of process.

The power to punish for contempt is inherent in courts, allowing them to go beyond the powers given by statute (Carl Lee v. State, 1912). The chancery court cannot appoint a committee to investigate a law firm on contempt and code of professional ethics violations (Davis v. Merritt, 1972).

SECTION 27

The circuit court shall have jurisdiction upon information, presentment, or indictment to remove any county or township officer from office for incompetency, corruption, gross immorality, criminal conduct, mal-feasance, mis-feasance or non-feasance of office.

This section relates to the elective county and township officers created by this Constitution (Patton v. Vaughan, 1882). A public officer cannot be removed for acts committed prior to his present term of office (Rice v. State, 1942). The Constitution provides for declaring forfeitures of office and for removing officers, implying a prohibition against legislative interference (Speer v. Wood, 1917). Notice is the foundation of due process in the removal of a judge (Anderson v. State, 1979).

SECTION 28

The county courts shall have exclusive original jurisdiction in all matters relating to county taxes, roads, bridges, ferries, paupers, bastardy, vagrants, the apprenticeships of minors, the disbursement of money for county purposes, and in every other case that may be necessary to the internal improvement and local concerns of the respective counties. The county court shall be held by one judge, except in cases otherwise herein provided.

Many of these provisions are superseded by Amendment 55 and Act 742 of 1977, which provided for the complete reorganization of county government. For further reference, see "County Government Reorganization in Arkansas," 28 *Ark. Law Review* 226. Original jurisdiction for bastardy cases is in the county court (Puckett v. Puckett, 1986). Chancery court was found not to have jurisdiction in a divorce proceeding to determine the paternity of a child bom before marriage (Stain v. Stain, 1985). A county judge, when exercising administrative functions, is not entitled to judicial immunity (Clark v. Campbell, 1981). County property is under the jurisdiction of county court (Maroney v. Universal Leasing Co., 1978).

SECTION 29

The judge of the county court shall be elected by the qualified electors of the county for the term of two years. He shall be at least twentyfive years of age, a citizen of the United States, a man of upright character, of good business education and a resident of the State for two years before his election, and a resident of the county at the time of his election and during his continuance in office.

Efforts to amend this section to extend terms to four years have been unsuccessful. Very few county judges have only been twenty-five years of age when elected (one such was former Congressman Wilbur D. Mills, who was elected in White County in 1934, just after his twenty-fifth birthday). Qualifications, as fixed in this section, cannot be modified by the legislature (Mississippi County v. Green, 1940).

SECTION 30

The justices of the peace of each county shall sit with and assist the county judge in levying the county taxes and in making appropriations for the expenses of the county in the manner to be prescribed by law; and the county judge together with a majority of said justices, shall constitute a quorum for such purposes; and in the absence of the county judge, a majority of the justices of the peace may constitute the court, who shall elect one of their number to preside. The General Assembly shall regulate by law the manner of compelling the attendance of such quorum.

The General Assembly may impose duties on counties and require counties to pay therefor (Crawford County v. Van Buren, 1941). Quorum court cannot provide an open-ended appropriation to a county judge (Martin v. Bratton, 1954).

SECTION 31

The terms of the county court shall be held at the times that are now prescribed for holding the supervisors' courts, or as may hereafter be prescribed by law.

The importance of this process is greatly diminished by the constitutional reorganization of county government in the mid-1970s.

SECTION 32

The General Assembly may authorize the judge of the county court of any one or more counties to hold severally a quarterly court of common pleas in their respective counties, which shall be a court of record, with such jurisdiction in matters of contract and other civil matters not involving title to real estate as may be vested in such court.

Common pleas courts are no longer in existence, more for lack of use and need rather than by law. The governor fills judicial vacancies by the appointment of a special judge (Beauman v. Wells Fargo and Co. Express, 1905).

SECTION 33

Appeals from all judgments of county courts or courts of common pleas, when established, may be taken to the circuit court under such restrictions and regulations as may be prescribed by law.

This section provides authority for appeals from county court to circuit court, for fixing a time limit for appeals, and for establishing the absolute right to appeal without regard to merit (Hughes v. Jackson, 1948; Pettigrew v. Washington County, 1884). Additionally, the remedy is by mandamus to compel the county court to discharge a duty in the performance of which it has no discretion. The circuit court tries appeals from county court on a de novo basis (Pulaski County v. Horton, 1955).

SECTION 34

The judge of the county court shall be the judge of the court of probate and have such exclusive original jurisdiction in matters relative to the probate of wills, the estate of deceased persons, executors, administrators, guardians and persons of unsound mind and their estates as is now vested in the circuit court, or may be hereafter prescribed by law. The regular terms of the court or probate shall be held at the times that may hereafter be prescribed by law.

This section has been amended by Amendment 24, **Section 1.** The general rule is that the inherent jurisdiction of equity is not destroyed by the grant of jurisdiction in similar cases to another court (Shuman v. Phillips, 1890). Probate court had no authority to administer trust because exclusive jurisdiction resides with chancery court (Alexander v. Alexander, 1978). Probate court can appoint a guardian for an illegitimate child (Lee v. Grubbs, 1980). Probate court has only the power given in the Constitution (Carpenter v. Logan, 1984).

SECTION 35

Appeals may be taken from judgments and orders of the probate court to the circuit court under such regulations and restrictions as may be prescribed by law.

This section has been amended by Amendment 24, **Section 2.** An affidavit for appeal must be filed before the appeal is granted and acted on (Walker v. Noll, 1909). If objections are not made in trial court, they cannot be made before the supreme court (Umberger v. Westmoreland, 1951).

SECTION 36

Whenever a judge of the county or probate court may be disqualified from presiding in any cause or causes pending in his court he shall certify the facts to the Governor of the State, who shall thereupon commission a special judge to preside in such cause or causes during the time said disqualification may continue, or until such cause or causes may be finally disposed of.

Until the county judge certifies his or her disqualification, the governor has no authority to appoint a special county judge (Reed v. Bradford, 1919). If a judge of equity is disqualified from acting as probate judge, a special judge may be elected by counsel (Petty v. Clarke, 1974).

SECTION 37

The county judge shall receive such compensation for his service as presiding judge of the county court, as judge of the court of probate and judge of the court of common pleas, when established, as may be provided by law. In the absence of the circuit judge from the county, the county judge shall have power to issue orders for injunction and other provisional writs in their counties, returnable to the court having jurisdiction, provided that either party may have such order reviewed by any superior judge in vacation in such manner as shall be provided by law. The county judge shall have power, in the absence of the circuit judge from the county, to issue, hear and determine writs of habeas corpus under such regulations and restrictions as shall be provided by law.

The county judge may issue writs when the circuit judge is absent from the county and the case is pending in circuit court (Randolph v. Abbott, 1907).

SECTION 38

The qualified electors of each township shall elect the justices of the peace for the term of two years who shall be commissioned by the Governor, and their official oath shall be endorsed on the commission.

This provision has remained unchanged through the years, as well as from constitution to constitution, with justices of the peace being included among the elected officers soon after statehood.

SECTION 39

For every two hundred electors there shall be elected one justice of the peace, but every township, however small, shall have two justices of the peace.

This section has been amended by Amendment 55, under which counties are classified and have assigned a designated number of justices of the peace accordingly. The number of justices of the peace is based on population (Alford v. State, 1901). For further reference, see "County Government Reorganization in Arkansas," 28 *Ark. Law Review* 226.

SECTION 40

They shall have original jurisdiction in the following matters: First, exclusive of the circuit court in all matters of contract where the amount in controversy does not exceed the sum of one hundred dollars, excluding interest, and concurrent jurisdiction in matters of contract where the amount in controversy does not exceed the sum of three hundred dollars, exclusive of interest; second, concurrent jurisdiction in suits for the recovery of personal property where the value of the property does not exceed the sum of three hundred dollars, and in all matters of damage to personal property where the amount in controversy does not exceed the sum of one hundred dollars; third, such jurisdiction of misdemeanors as is now, or may be, prescribed by law; fourth, to sit as examining courts and commit, discharge or recognize offenders to the court having jurisdiction for further trial, and to bind persons to keep the peace or for good behavior; fifth, for the foregoing purposes they shall have power to issue all necessary process; sixth, they shall be conservators of the peace within their respective counties, provided a justice of the peace shall not have jurisdiction where a lien on land or title or possession thereto is involved.

The jurisdiction of a court is determined by the amount sought to be recovered and not merely by the amount that is actually recovered (St. Louis Southwestern Railway v. O'Neal, 1924). Municipal courts cannot be given greater jurisdiction than the justices of the peace (Peel v. Kelley, 1980). Jurisdictional questions should be determined in the court in which they first arise (Cabot v. Morgan, 1958).

SECTION 41

A justice of the peace shall be a qualified elector and a resident of the township for which he is elected.

A party nominee who is a resident of the district at the time of nomination is still qualified after moving temporarily into another residence (Booth v. Smith, 1977).

SECTION 42

Appeals may be taken from the final judgment of the justices of the peace to the circuit courts under such regulations as now are, or may be, provided by law.

When the proper affidavit is filed, an appeal is a matter of right regardless of the amount involved (Townsend v. Timmons, 1884; Chicago R.I. and P. Ry. v. Langley, 1906). The legislature may set deadlines (Wadkins v. Merchants Bank, 1910).

SECTION 43

Corporation courts for towns and cities may be invested with jurisdiction concurrent with justices of the peace in civil and criminal matters, and the General Assembly may invest such of them as it may deem expedient with jurisdiction of any criminal offenses not punishable by death or imprisonment in the penitentiary, with or without indictment, as may be provided by law, and until the General Assembly shall otherwise provide, they shall have the jurisdiction now provided by law.

Since the passage of Amendment 55, justices of the peace have only legislative, not judicial, powers. A suit regarding a contract may be located in either the county it was to be performed or the county in which the defendant resides (Peel v. Kelley, 1980). The jurisdiction of the municipal court over misdemeanors is exclusive (Lee v. Watts, 1968).

SECTION 44

The Pulaski Chancery Court shall continue in existence until abolished by law, or the business pending at the adoption of this Constitution shall be disposed of, or the pending business be transferred to other courts. The judge and clerk of said court shall hold office for the terms of two years, and shall be elected by the qualified voters of the State. All suits and proceedings which relate to sixteenth section lands or to money due for said lands, shall be transferred to the respective counties where such lands are located in such manner as shall be provided by the General Assembly at the next session.

This section, while recognizing the existence of the Pulaski County Chancery Court, does not create a new class of constitutional courts or deprive the General Assembly of express powers (Weber v. Pryor, 1976).

SECTION 45

The separate criminal courts established in this State are hereby abolished, and all the jurisdiction exercised by said criminal courts is vested in the circuit courts of the respective counties; and all causes now pending therein are hereby transferred to said circuit courts respectively. It shall be the duty of the clerks of said criminal courts to transfer all the records, books and papers pertaining to said criminal courts to the circuit courts of their respective counties.

This provision was an effort to streamline the state judicial system and diminish the number of courts.

SECTION 46

The qualified electors of each county shall elect one sheriff, who shall be ex-officio collector of taxes, unless otherwise provided by law; one assessor, one coroner, one treasurer, who shall be ex-officio treasurer of the common school fund of the county, and one county surveyor, for the term of two years, with such duties as are now or may be prescribed by law. Provided, that no percentum shall ever be paid to assessors upon the valuation or assessment of property by them.

Amendment 55 partially supersedes this section and gives power to the voters of a county to change or merge these offices. The legislature may extend the duties of the sheriff (Cain v. Woodruff County, 1909). County boards of equalization are constitutional (Pulaski County Board of Equalization, 1887). The Collector's Office is under control of the legislature (Newton v. Edwards, 1941).

SECTION 47

The qualified electors of each township shall elect a constable for the term of two years, who shall be furnished by the presiding judge of the county court with a certificate of election, on which his official oath shall be endorsed.

This section establishes the office of constable as an executive officer (State V. Hutt, 1840). Terms may be set by the legislature (Hutcheson v. Pitts, 1926).

SECTION 48

All officers provided for in this article, except constable, shall be commissioned by the Governor.

This provision elevates the other county offices over the office of constable.

SECTION 49

All writs and other judicial process shall run in the name of the State of Arkansas, bear test and be signed by the clerks of the respective courts from which they issue. Indictments shall conclude: "Against the peace and dignity of the State of Arkansas."

To be valid, each count of an indictment must conclude: "against the peace and dignity of the state" (Williams v. State, 1886). A defendant may object to the manner of service of a summons (Storey v. Brewer, 1960; Rogers v. State, 1986).

SECTION 50

All vacancies occurring in any office provided for in this article shall be filled by special election, save that in the case of vacancies occurring in county and township offices six months, and in other offices nine months, before the next general election; such vacancies shall be filled by appointment by the Governor.

This section may be superseded by the Constitutional Amendment 29, Section 1, as it relates to judicial officers other than municipal court officers (Johnson County V. Holman, 1983). The governor may fill a vacancy on a temporary basis until the next election (Cobb v. Hammock, 1907). Where someone who is elected to office dies before qualifying, there is no vacancy (Rice v. Palmer, 1906).

SECTION 51

That in all cases of allowances made for or against counties, cities or towns, an appeal shall lie to the circuit court of the county, at the instance of the party aggrieved, or on the intervention of any citizen or resident or taxpayer of such county, city or town, on the same terms and conditions on which appeals may be granted to the circuit court in other cases; and the matter pertaining to any such allowances shall be tried in the circuit court de novo. In case an appeal be taken by any citizen he shall give a bond, payable to the proper county, conditioned to prosecute the appeal and save the county from costs on account of the same being taken.

An order of the county court prohibiting the sale of liquors was not an allowance against the county (Holmes v. Morgan, 1889). A resident, citizen, or taxpayer has the right to appeal from an order of allowance against the county, whether he or she intervened before or after the allowance was ordered (Van Hook v. McNeil Monument Company, 1911). County court is acting in a judicial capacity when it passes on claims (Arkansas Association of County Judges v. Green, 1960). Cases against the sheriff can be heard in chancery court (Crittenden County v. Williford, 1984).

SECTION 52

That in all cases of contest for any county, township or municipal office, an appeal shall lie at the instance of the party aggrieved, from any inferior board, council or tribunal to the circuit court in other cases, and on such appeals the case shall be tried de novo.

This section gives the circuit court the original jurisdiction in election contest cases. The board of education may be designated by the legislature to hear election contests regarding school elections (Stafford v. Cook, 1923).

Article VIII

Apportionment

SECTION 1

[This article is a lengthy five-column section describing each legislative district and is superseded completely by Amendment XXIII.]

Article IX

Exemptions

SECTION 1

The personal property of any resident of this State who is not married or the head of a family, in specific articles to be selected by such resident, not exceeding in value the sum of two hundred dollars in addition to his or her wearing apparel, shall be exempt from seizure on attachment, or sale on execution, or other process from any court issued for the collection of any debt by contract; provided, that no property shall be exempt from execution for debts contracted for the purchase money therefor while in the hands of the vendee.

Exemption laws are not a part of a contract and pertain only to a remedy (Person v. Williams-Echols Dry Goods Co., 1914). A person who is domiciled in Arkansas but is temporarily absent may claim exemptions (Birdson v. Tuttle, 1889). A judgment debtor is not entitled to exemption in cases where the suit is based on collusion and negligence (Hill v. Bush, 1936). This section exempts a debtor's bank account from garnishment if it is entirely owned by the debtor (Rawleigh Co. v. Castleberry, 1941). The personal property exemption does not apply to a liability created by statute (Watson v. State Department of Finance and Administration, 1984).

SECTION 2

The personal property of any resident of this State who is married or the head of a family, in specific articles to be selected by such resident, not exceeding in value the sum of five hundred dollars in addition to his or her wearing apparel, and that of his or her family, shall be exempt from seizure on attachment, or sale on execution, or other process from any court on debt by contract.

Exemptions may be claimed by either or both spouses (Memphis and L.R. R.R. V. Adams, 1885). The legislature may prescribe the method of selecting the property that is claimed as exempt from execution (Andrews v. Briggs, 1942). A homestead may be claimed as exempt, even when not referenced in the foreclosure (In re Powers, 1962). A debtor may amend the schedule of exemptions to show his or her actual assets (Williams v. Swann, 1952).

SECTION 3

The homestead of any resident of this State, who is married or the head of a family, shall not be subject to the lien of any judgment, or decree of any court, or to sale under execution or other process thereon, except such as may be rendered for the purchase money or for specific liens, laborers' or mechanics' liens for improving the same, or for taxes, or against executors, administrators, guardians, receivers, attorneys for monies collected by them and other trustees of an express trust for monies due from them in their fiduciary capacity.

Arkansas law permits the acquisition and retention of a homestead, regardless of the rights of creditors. However, the homestead exemption does not extend to dead people as an estate interest (Sulcer v. Northwestern National Insurance Co., 1978). A lien can be enforced even if unrecorded if it is valid (Cloverleaf Development v. Provence, 1981). Acquisition of a homestead is permitted, regardless of the rights of creditors (Stanley v. Snyder, 1884). A creditor of an ex-husband cannot secure a homestead acquired by the ex-wife, even if the homestead exemption is not claimed (Campbell v. Geheb, 1975). Insurance proceeds from a homestead are exempt for a time (Exchange Bank and Trust v. Matthews, 1969).

SECTION 4

The homestead outside any city, town or village, owned and occupied as a residence, shall consist of not exceeding one hundred and sixty acres of land, with the improvements thereon, to be selected by the owner, provided the same shall not exceed in value the sum of twenty-five hundred dollars, and in no event shall the homestead be reduced to less than eighty acres, without regard to value.

All provisions for homesteads are to be construed liberally toward the debtor and strictly toward the creditor in Arkansas (Bank of Sun Prairie v. Hovig, 1963). Homestead exemptions in particular are liberally construed in favor of the person asserting the exemption (Scott County Bank v. McCraw, 1985). A twenty-acre piece of land in a municipal incorporation used exclusively for agricultural purposes and also as the defendant's home qualified for the homestead exemption (Farmers Coop v. Stevens, 1976).

SECTION 5

The homestead in any city, town or village, owned and occupied as a residence, shall consist of not exceeding one acre of land with improvements thereon, to be selected by the owner, provided the same shall not exceed in value the sum of two thousand five hundred dollars, and in no event shall such homestead be reduced to less than one quarter of an acre of land, without regard to value.

Arbitrary selection of a homestead is not allowed (Sparks v. Day, 1896). In an urban setting, owners are entitled to select a quarter of an acre as a homestead (Rowe v. Gose, 1966).

SECTION 6

If the owner of a homestead dies, leaving a widow, but no children, the said widow has no separate homestead in her own right, the same shall be exempt and the rents and profits thereof shall vest in her during her natural life, provided that if the owner leaves children, one or more, said child or children, shall share with said widow and be entitled to half the rents and profits till each of them arrives at twenty-one years of age—each child's right to cease at twenty-one years of age—and the shares to go to younger children, and then all go to the widow, and provided that said widow or children may reside on the homestead or not; and in case of death of the widow all of said homestead shall be vested in the minor children of the testator or intestate.

This section has been held to violate the equal protection clause of the U.S. Constitution in that it discriminates between widows and widowers (Stokes v. Stokes, 1981). After a married male cotenant of a property dies, the other cotenants may seek partition after his death, even if the property is claimed by his widow as homestead (Allen v. Smith, 1984). The homestead exemption does not run in favor of a dead person, and is neither an estate nor a vested interest (Sulcer V. Northwestern National Insurance Co., 1978).

SECTION 7

The real and personal property of any femme couverte in this State acquired either before or after marriage, whether by gift, grant, inheritance, devise or otherwise, shall

> so long as she may choose, be and remain her separate estate and property and may be devised, bequeathed or conveyed by her the same as if she was a femme sole, and the same shall not be subject to the debts of her husband.

A married woman may convey property without her husband joining in and without private examination and acknowledgment of the deed (Roberts v. Wilcoxin, 1880). An equal division of property is correct, even when the wife earns more than the husband (Stuart v. Stuart, 1983).

SECTION 8

> The General Assembly shall provide for the mode of scheduling the separate personal property of married women.

This section is self-explanatory and traditional. "Scheduling" in this context means "dividing" in case of divorce. The legislature has set forth the method of scheduling property.

SECTION 9

> The exemptions contained in the Constitution of 1868 shall apply to all debts contracted since the adoption thereof and prior to the adoption of this Constitution.

This section was adopted to provide continuity and clarity, and it revives the Homestead Exemption Act of 1852.

SECTION 10

> The homestead provided for in this article shall inure to the benefit of the minor children, under the exemptions herein provided, after the decease of the parents.

Abandonment by a widow and mother of the interest she acquired in a homestead in no manner affects the rights of minor children (Smith v. Scott, 1909). A minor's homestead cannot be sold, even by order of the court (Hart v. Wimberly, 1927). The homestead right does not cease until minor children reach twenty-one years of age (Hargett v. Hill, Fontaine and Co., 1911). The sale of a minor's homestead is void (Bank of Mulberry v. Frazhier, 1928). For further reference, see Brantley and Effland, "Inheritance, the Share of Surviving Spouse, and Wills: Arkansas Law and the Uniform Probate Code Compared," 3 *UALR Law Journal* 361.

Article X

Agriculture, Mining and Manufacture

SECTION 1

The General Assembly shall pass such laws as will foster and aid the agriculture, mining and manufacturing interests of the State, and may create a bureau to be known as the Mining, Manufacturing and Agricultural Bureau.

A Bureau of Mines, Manufactures and Agriculture was created by Act 30 of 1889 and abolished by Act 153 of 1933.

SECTION 2

The General Assembly, when deemed expedient, may create the office of State Geologist, to be appointed by the Governor, by and with the advice and consent of the Senate, who shall hold his office for such time and perform such duties and receive such compensation as may be prescribed by law. Provided, that he shall be at all times subject to removal by the Governor for incompetency or gross neglect of duty.

This method of appointment has always been used, and the duties of the state geologist have adhered to this description.

SECTION 3

The General Assembly may, by general law, exempt from taxation for the term of seven years from the ratification of this Constitution the capital invested in any or all kinds of mining and manufacturing business in this State, under such regulations and restrictions as may be prescribed by law.

Such exemptions were never adopted during this period of seven specified years.

Article XI

Militia

SECTION 1

The militia shall consist of all able-bodied male persons, residents of the State, between the ages of eighteen and forty-five years, except such as may be exempted by the laws of the United States or this State, and shall be organized, officered, armed and equipped and trained in such manner as may be provided by law.

The Arkansas National Guard is a part of the executive branch of state government (and the governor is the commander-in-chief). An appropriation for the National Guard is considered an appropriation to meet the necessary expenses of government (State v. Moore, 1905). The governor has the discretionary authority to create a detached officers' list for the National Guard (Baker v. Harris, 1929).

SECTION 2

Volunteer companies of infantry, cavalry or artillery may be formed in such manner and with such restrictions as may be provided by law.

This section is designed to provide the necessary flexibility for emergency situations (Adams v. Hale, 1948).

SECTION 3

The volunteer and militia forces shall in all cases (except treason, felony and breach of the peace) be privileged from arrest during their attendance at muster and the election of officers, and in going to and returning from the same.

This section is intended to ensure the independence of the military from unnecessary obstacles, a privilege also provided to state legislators, while in session.

SECTION 4

The Governor shall, when the General Assembly is not in session, have power to call out the volunteers or militia, or both, to execute the laws, repel invasion, repress insurrection and preserve the public peace in such manner as may be authorized by law.

This section follows the national principle of civilian supremacy over the military (Belote v. Coffman, 1915).

Article XII

Municipal and Private Corporations

SECTION 1

All existing charters or grants of special or exclusive privileges under which a bona fide organization shall not have taken place and business been commenced in good faith at the time of the adoption of this Constitution shall thereafter have no validity.

This section clears the law books of the hodgepodge of acts pertaining to municipalities which were adopted throughout the nineteenth century.

SECTION 2

The General Assembly shall pass no special act conferring corporate powers, except for charitable, educational, penal or reformatory purposes, where the corporations created are to be and remain under the patronage and control of the State.

Special acts must contain population classifications and legal justifications or they will be struck under this section (City of Little Rock v. Parish, 1880). The general laws under which a municipal corporation is formed constitute its charter (Lumber Co. v. Biddle, 1908). Reserve powers of the state are subject to some limitations (Fort Smith Light and Traction Company v. Board of Imps, 1925).

SECTION 3

The General Assembly shall provide, by general laws, for the organization of cities (which may be classified) and incorporated towns, and restrict their power of taxation, assessment, borrowing money and contracting debts, so as to prevent the abuse of such power.

The grant of power to the legislature to provide for the organization of cities and to restrict their powers does not confer any powers on the cities (Hendricks v. Block, 1906); also see Amendments 30 and 31. Cities may hire finance directors (Besharse v. Blytheville, 1973).

SECTION 4

No municipal corporation shall be authorized to pass any laws contrary to the general laws of the State; nor levy any tax on real or personal property to a greater extent, in one year, than five mills on the dollar of the assessed value of the same provided, that, to pay indebtedness existing at the time of the adoption of this Constitution, an additional tax of not more than five mills on the dollar may be levied.

Amendment 10 adds to this section. A municipal corporation has only those powers expressly conferred by the legislature and those necessarily or fairly implied (Bennett v. Hope, 1942). A city may levy a charge for service because it is not a tax (Holman v. Dierks, 1950). A city council has the exclusive power to levy a tax in order to pay a bond issue (Rhodes v. Stuttgart, 1936).

SECTION 5

No county, city, town or other municipal corporation shall become a stockholder in any company, association or corporation, or obtain an appropriate money for, or loan its credit to, any corporation, association, institution or individual.

A city council is prohibited from appropriating money to a railroad to induce the building of the railroad line (Luxora v. Jonesboro L.C. & F.R.R., 1907). A county may appropriate funds to an improvement district to aid in street improvements (Shofner v. Dowell, 1925). The Urban Development Law is constitutional (Rowe v. Housing Authority, 1952). A waterworks revenue pledge for the payment of bonds must be used for the payment of bonds (Little Rock v. Community Chest, 1942).

SECTION 6

Corporations may be formed under the general laws, which laws may, from time to time, be altered or repealed. The General Assembly shall have the power to alter, revoke or annul any charter of incorporation now existing and revokable at the adoption of this Constitution, or any that may hereafter be created, whenever, in their opinion, it may be injurious to the citizens of the State, in such manner, however, that no injustice shall be done to the corporators.

Corporations possess only powers that are conferred by their charter, and these powers may be modified by the legislature (Ozan Lumber Co. v. Biddie, 1908). Changes must be reasonable, made in good faith, and consistent with the scope and object of the act of incorporation (Arkansas Stave Company v. State, 1910). Charters are constitutional unless their effect is to confiscate the stock or property of a corporation (Bank of Blytheville v. State, 1921). The state can evaluate stock with no par value for the purpose of taxation. (State v. Margay Oil Corp., 1925). State may not surrender police power (Phillips Petroleum v. Jenkins, 1936).

SECTION 7

Except as herein provided, the State shall never become a stockholder in, or subscribe to, or be interested in, the stock of any corporation or association.

Acts authorizing cities and towns to purchase memberships in local industrial development corporations are unconstitutional under this provision (Halbert v. Helena-West Helena Industrial Development Corp., 1956).

SECTION 8

No private corporation shall issue stock or bonds, except for money or property actually received or labor done, and all fictitious increase of stock or indebtedness shall be void; nor shall the stock or bonded indebtedness of any private corporation be increased except in pursuance of general laws, nor until the consent of the persons holding the larger amount in value of stock shall be obtained at a meeting held after notice given for a period of not less than sixty days, in pursuance of law.

This section reflects a strong desire to inject an ethical standard for business operations that had not previously been the rule. For example, assets of an insolvent bank cannot be sold to a new bank if stock is to be purchased by checks against the insolvent bank (Krumpen v. Taylor, 1931). A note given for stock in a private corporation is void, except in the hands of an innocent purchaser (Bank of Manila v. Wallace, 1928; Roy v. Recker, 1963). Unless prohibited, a corporation may issue its stock in payment for services (Town and Country v. Godwin, 1961).

SECTION 9

No property, nor right-of-way, shall be appropriated to the use of any corporation until full compensation therefor shall be first made to the owner, in money, or first secured to him by a deposit of money, which compensation, irrespective of any benefit from any improvement proposed by such corporation, shall be ascertained by a jury of twelve men, in a court of competent jurisdiction, as shall be prescribed by law.

This section does not suggest that the right of eminent domain is limited to corporations (Young v. Energy Transportation Systems, 1983). A public utility's right to condemn private property is governed by this section (AP&L v. Pottach, 1986). This provision does not apply to municipal corporations (Paragould v. Milner, 1914). In a case in which a gas company condemned the easement for a pipeline, the owner was permitted to use the surface provided he or she did not ask for severance damages (Arkansas Louisiana Gas Co. v. Burkley, 1967). A private corporation as condemnor is liable for fair market value and damages (Arkla v. James, 1985).

SECTION 10

No act of the General Assembly shall be passed authorizing the issue of bills, notes or other paper which may circulate as money.

This section rules out regional legal tender, such as Confederate dollars, recognizing the U.S. Treasury and U.S. Government Mint as sole sources of legal tender.

SECTION 11

Foreign corporations may be authorized to do business in this State under such limitations and restrictions as may be prescribed by law. Provided, that no such corporation shall do any business in this State except while it maintains therein one or more known places of business and an authorized agent or agents in the same upon whom process may be served; and, as to contracts made or business done in this State, they shall be subject to the same regulations, limitations and liabilities as like corporations of this State, and shall exercise no other or greater powers, privileges or franchise than may be exercised by like corporations of this State, nor shall they have power to condemn or appropriate private property.

The power to designate by statute the officer on whom service may be made in suits against foreign corporations relates only to business transactions within the state, and not beyond the state (Protas v. Modem Investment Corporation, 1939). A foreign corporation is subject to the same regulations as a domestic corporation (Phillips Petroleum Corp. v. Jenkins, 1936; Arkansas Louisiana Electric Coop v. Arkansas Public Service Commission, 1946). The state has the authority to regulate the manner in which foreign corporations do business in

Arkansas (Missouri Pacific Railroad v. W. S. Fox and Sons, 1971). This section does not apply to the computation of franchise taxes (Franklin Electric Co. v. Heath, 1977).

SECTION 12

Except as herein otherwise provided, the State shall never assume or pay the debt or liability of any county, town, or city, or other corporation whatsoever, or any part thereof, unless such debt or liability shall have been created to repel invasion, suppress insurrection or to provide for the public welfare and defense. Nor shall the indebtedness of any corporation to the State ever be released or in any manner discharged save by payment into the public treasury.

The practice of the state being required to cover the debts of local governments was prohibited by this act. However, this does not apply to school districts (Ruff v. Womack, 1927). A matured tax claim is an indebtedness within the meaning of this section (Federal Express v. Skelton, 1979). If a student from a closed school attends a private school, any resulting liability will be payable to the school, and not by it (Fitzhugh v. Ford, 1959). The constitutional prohibition against the state assumption of debt does not apply to school districts (Ruff v. Womack, 1927).

Article XIII

Counties, County Seats and County Lines

SECTION 1

No county now established shall be reduced to an area of less than six hundred square miles nor less than five thousand inhabitants; nor shall any new county be established with less than six hundred square miles and five thousand inhabitants. Provided, that this section shall not apply to the Counties of Lafayette, Pope and Johnson, nor be so construed as to prevent the General Assembly from changing the line between the Counties of Pope and Johnson.

A county is a political subdivision of the state which, for the more convenient administration of justice and for some purposes of local self-government, is invested with a few functions of corporate existence (Pulaski v. Reeve, 1883). A county derives all its power from the legislature (Eagle v. Beard, 1878; see also Wells v. White, 1981).

SECTION 2

No part of the county shall be taken off to form a new county or part thereof without the consent of a majority of the voters in such part proposed to be taken off.

The power to change county lines is inherent in the legislature, except to extend constitutional borders (Reynolds v. Holland, 1879). The legislature may change the boundaries with the consent of the inhabitants, except in cases where a part is to be taken off to form a new county (Reynolds v. Holland).

SECTION 3

No county seat shall be established or changed without the consent of a majority of the qualified voters of the county to be affected by such change, nor until the place at which it is proposed to establish or change such county seat shall be fully designated. Provided, that in formation of new counties the county seat may be located temporarily by provision of law.

This provision refers to the removal of the county seat from one city to another and not to a removal from one site to another in the same town (Graham v. Nix, 1912). The county court has exclusive original jurisdiction regarding the changing of a county seat (Russell v. Jacoway, 1878). A majority of those voting at an election is sufficient to change a county seat (Vance v. Johnson, 1965; see also Rockefeller v. Matthews, 1970).

SECTION 4

In the formation of new counties no line thereof shall run within ten miles of the county seat of the county proposed to be divided, except the county seat of Lafayette County.

This right to form new county lines gives the legislature the right to change district lines, as by annexation (Smalley v. Fort Smith, 1965).

SECTION 5

Sebastian County may have two districts and two county seats, at which county, probate and circuit courts shall be held, as may be provided by law, each district paying its own expenses.

The county court of the Fort Smith district and the county court of the Greenwood district each have exclusive jurisdiction, as if they were in separate counties (Scaramuzza v. McLeod, 1944). Sebastian County is one unit regarding the county board of education and the county school supervisor (Reeves v. Been, 1950). A jury may be drawn from only one district in a county (Morgan v. State, 1981).

Article XIV

Education

SECTION 1

Intelligence and virtue being the safeguards of liberty and bulwark of a free and good government, the State shall ever maintain a general, suitable and efficient system of free schools, whereby all persons in the State between the ages of six and twenty-one years may receive gratuitous instruction.

This section has been superseded by Amendment 53.

SECTION 2

No money or property belonging to the public school fund, or to this State for the benefit of schools or universities, shall ever be used for any other than the respective purposes to which it belongs.

Any use of school funds raised from taxation that results in benefits to school funds or school property would be constitutional; for example, the payment of assessments for local improvements that are beneficial to school property (Rainwater V. Haynes, 1968). The reading of the Bible and recitation of the Lord's Prayer over the school intercom, as well as the distribution of Gideon Bibles, even if with the knowledge of the school board and superintendent, is unconstitutional (Goodwin v. Cross County School District No. 7, 1973).

SECTION 3

The General Assembly shall provide by general laws for the support of common schools by taxes, which shall never exceed in any one year two mills on the dollar on the taxable property of the state, and by annual per capita tax of one dollar, to be assessed on every male inhabitant of this State over the age of twenty-one years. Provided, the General Assembly may by general law authorize school districts to levy by a vote of the qualified electors of such district a tax not to exceed five mills on the dollar in any one year for school purposes. Provided, further, that no such tax shall be appropriated to any other purpose nor to any other district than that for which it was levied.

This section has been superseded by Amendments 11 and 40. For further reference, see "Educational Financing and Equal Protection," 26 *Arkansas Law Review* 69.

SECTION 4

The supervision of public schools and the execution of the laws regulating the same shall be vested in and confided to such officers as may be provided for by the General Assembly.

This section authorizes the creation of a state board of education to run the day-to-day administration of the public schools. The section has not been litigated but was cited in Reeves v. Been, 1950.

Article XV

Impeachment and Address

SECTION 1

The Governor and all State officers, judges of the supreme and circuit courts, chancellors and prosecuting attorneys shall be liable to impeachment for high crimes and misdemeanors and gross misconduct in office, but the judgment shall go no further than removal from office and disqualification to hold any office of honor, trust or profit under this State. An impeachment, whether successful or not, shall be no bar to an indictment.

These provisions provide a complete plan for the suspension and removal of state officers (Speer v. Wood, 1917). For further reference, see "Official Misconduct Under the Arkansas Criminal Code," 30 *Arkansas Law Review* 160, and "Removal and Discipline of Judges in Arkansas," 32 *Arkansas Law Review* 545.

SECTION 2

The House of Representatives shall have sole power of impeachment. All impeachments shall be tried by the Senate. When sitting for that purpose, the senators shall be upon oath or affirmation; no person shall be convicted without the concurrence of two-thirds of the members thereof. The Chief Justice shall preside unless he is impeached or otherwise disqualified, when the Senate shall select a presiding officer.

The state's impeachment process parallels the process contained in the national Constitution for the national process. For further reference, see Scott Stafford, "Separation of Powers and Arkansas Administrative Agencies: Distinguishing Judicial Power and Legislative Power," 7 *UALR Law Journal* 279.

SECTION 3

The Governor, upon the joint address of two-thirds of the members elected to each house of the General Assembly, for good cause, may remove the Auditor, Treasurer, Secretary of State, Attorney General, Judges of the Supreme and Circuit Courts, Chancellors and Prosecuting Attorneys.

The address process is an alternative to the trial-like process of the impeachment procedure. For further reference, see "Impeachment, Address and the Removal of Judges in Arkansas: An Historical Perspective," 32 *Arkansas Law Review* 253.

Article XVI

Finance and Taxation

SECTION 1

Neither the State nor any city, county, town or other municipality in this State shall ever loan its credit for any purpose whatever; nor shall any county, city, town or municipality ever issue any interest-bearing evidences of indebtedness, except such bonds as may be authorized by law to provide for and secure the payment of the present existing indebtedness, and the State shall never issue any interest-bearing treasury warrants or scrip.

Localities have the power constitutionally to donate money for a public purpose designated by the legislature (Kerr v. East Central Arkansas Housing Authority, 1945). Municipal improvement districts may levy assessments based on consent of two-thirds in value of property holders (Ray v. Mountain Home, 1958). Banks purchasing interest-bearing notes were found to have no infirmities if not given notice of a contract violating this section (Goodwin v. State, 1962). The Arkansas Development Finance Corporation Act is constitutional (Andres v. First Arkansas Development Finance Corporation, 1959). State highway refunding bonds do not violate this section because these use credit and do not lend it (Beaumont v. Faubus, 1965). Student loan authority bonds do not constitute an obligation of the state because they are repaid from income derived from loan notes and investments, with interest payments made by the federal government (Turner v. Woodruff, 1985). A city may lease a hospital to be run by a nonprofit corporation (Arkansas Uniform and Linen v. Institutional Service Corporation, 1985).

SECTION 2

The General Assembly shall, from time to time, provide for the payment of all just and legal debts of the State.

The legislature has created a state claims commission to hear these claims. For further reference, see "Politics and Due Process Don't Mix: Should the State Claims Commission Be Abolished?" 1986 *Arkansas Law Notes* 43.

SECTION 3

The making of profit out of public monies or using the same for any purpose not authorized by law, by any officer of the State or member or officer of the General Assembly, shall be punishable as may be provided by law; but part of such punishment shall be disqualification to hold office in this State for a period of five years.

This was an early and elementary ethical standard for public service. Under this section, the chancery court has jurisdiction to prevent illegal exactions, even in cases of state legislators who illegally hold a state civil office during their terms (Stames v. Sadler, 1963).

SECTION 4

The General Assembly shall fix the salaries and fees of all officers in the State, and no greater salary or fee than that fixed by law shall be paid to any officer, employee or other person, or at any rate other than par value; and the number and salaries of the clerks and employees of different departments of the State shall be fixed by law.

The goal of this section was some uniformity and continuity throughout the state. This power is lodged solely in the legislature (Legislative Research Bureau v. Mackrell, 1947). Agencies cannot use cash funds that are not appropriated by the legislature to enhance salaries beyond the level set by that body (Gipson v. Ingram, 1949). A statute fixing salaries of tax collectors in sixteen counties, where this function is separate from the sheriff's office is not local, since it has a general application (Inman v. Kelley, 1958). The state hospital board cannot establish positions that are different from those set by legislature (Gipson v. Crawfis, 1956).

SECTION 5

All property subject to taxation shall be taxed according to its value, that value to be ascertained in such manner as the General Assembly shall direct, making the same equal and uniform throughout the State. No one species of property from which a tax may be collected shall be taxed higher than another species of property of equal value, provided the General Assembly shall have power from time to time to tax hawkers, peddlers, ferries, exhibitions and privileges in such manner as may be deemed proper. Provided, further, that the following property shall be exempt from taxation: Public property used exclusively for public purposes; churches used as such; cemeteries used exclusively as such; school buildings and apparatus; libraries and grounds used exclusively for school purposes, and buildings and grounds and materials used exclusively for public charity.

When a private corporation leases public land, it is not exempted from ad valorem taxation (B.D.T., Inc. v. Moore, 1976). An excise tax on real estate transfers is not a property tax (Borchert v. Scott, 1970). This section was repealed by Amendment 59; see also Amendments 22, 27, and 12; "Recovery of Tax Paid on Exempt Property," 25 *Arkansas Law Review* 4th 186; and "Property Tax Exemptions in Arkansas," 4 *Arkansas Law Review* 433.

SECTION 6

All laws exempting property from taxation other than as provided in this Constitution shall be void.

This section limits legislature on passing exemptions. (Brodie v. Fitzgerald, 1893). It was superseded by Amendments 12, 22, and 27.

SECTION 7

The power to tax corporations and corporate property shall not be surrendered or suspended by any contract or grant to which the State may be a party.

The power to tax corporations was established long before progressive individual income taxes were declared constitutional. Arkansas experienced much controversy on this point concerning railroads during the nineteenth century.

SECTION 8

The General Assembly shall not have power to levy State taxes for any one year to exceed in aggregate one per cent of the assessed valuation of the property of the State for that year.

This section refers exclusively to property tax and does not prevent the selection of other objects of taxation and fixing of the rate. See Amendment 47.

SECTION 9

No county shall levy a tax to exceed one-half of one per cent for all purposes, but may levy an additional one-half of one per cent to pay indebtedness existing at the time of the ratification of this Constitution.

This section creates a limitation on the taxation power of the counties, except in exceptional cases arising under prior contracts. Neither the legislature, the state courts, nor the federal courts can force a county to make a valid levy in excess of this limitation (Cope v. Collins, 1881). A levy over limit is void, as is sale for failure to pay taxes (Sherrill v. Faulkner, 1940; see also Bell v. Crawford County, 1985).

SECTION 10

The taxes of counties, towns, and cities shall only be payable in lawful currency of the United States, or the orders or warrants of said counties, towns and cities respectively.

This section simply defines funds to which one may pay taxes that are levied for county purposes (Powell v. Durden, 1895). County warrants are receivable for county taxes (St. Louis National Bank v. Marion County, 1903).

SECTION 11

No tax shall be levied except in pursuance of law, and every law imposing a tax shall state distinctly the object of the same; and no monies arising from a tax levied for one purpose shall be used for any other purpose.

This section establishes the distinction between general and special revenues and the possibility of earmarking revenues and setting up trust funds for specific purposes. A referendum is required to enact a tax (Ragan v. Venhaus, 1986). An ordinance requiring interest on school funds to be deposited in a county general fund is unconstitutional (Mears v. Little Rock School District, 1980). A sheriff's expenses cannot be paid from moneys raised for school purposes (Special School District v. Sebastian County, 1982).

SECTION 12

No money shall be paid out of the treasury until the same shall have been appropriated by law, and then only in accordance with said appropriation.

There is no restriction on the power of the legislature to deal with public revenues prior to the time that such revenues are placed in the state treasury

(McArthur v. Smallwood, 1955). An appropriation is absolutely required before any funds may be drawn from the state treasury (Dickinson v. Clibourn, 1916). This section does not apply to state revenue department building funds (Holmes v. Cheney, 1962).

SECTION 13

Any citizen of any county, city or town may institute suit in behalf of himself and all others interested, to protect the inhabitants thereof against the enforcement of any illegal exactions whatever.

See Amendment 59, Sections 14, 15, and 16, for related provisions for the protection of taxpayers' rights. A taxpayer also may maintain a suit to prevent a misapplication of public funds and secure an injunction against such unlawful expenditures (Taylor, Cleveland and Company v. Pine Bluff, 1879). This section does not limit the rights of citizens (Samples v. Grady, 1944). A citizen may sue on conflict of interest of a city utility commission (Price v. Edmonds, 1959). A taxpayer need show only that the exaction is illegal to obtain relief (Mackey v. McDonald, 1974). An illegal exaction suit may proceed even when there are other adequate remedies (Jackson v. Munson, 1986). Amendments proposed during an extended session of the legislature could be subject to a suit seeking an injunction (Wells v. Riviere, 1980). Public officials and employees are not authorized attorneys' fees from public funds (Hall v. Thompson, 1984). Expense allowances for county officials are unconstitutional (Tedford v. Mears, 1975). Illegal fees fixed by a court can be recovered with a taxpayer's suit (Parker v. Laws, 1970).

Article XVII

Railroads, Canals and Turnpikes

SECTION 1

All railroads, canals and turnpikes shall be public highways, and all railroads and canal companies shall be common carriers. Any association or corporation organized for the purpose shall have the right to construct and operate a railroad between any points within this State and to connect at the State line, with railroads of other States. Every railroad company shall have the right with its road to intersect, connect with or cross any other road, and shall receive and transport each the other's passengers, tonnage and cars, loaded or empty, without delay or discrimination.

A de facto corporation can exercise the right of eminent domain, and a railroad resisting the condemnation of a crossing, for example, must do so in a court of equity (Cairo T. and S.R.R. v. Arkansas Short Line, 1926). One railroad may intersect with another (St. Louis, I.M. and S.Ry. v. Fort Smith & Van Buren Ry., 1912). It is Arkansas policy to regulate transportation agencies (Southeast Arkansas Freight Lines v. Arkansas Corp. Comm., 1942). See also 13 *American Jurisprudence* 2d, Carriers, Section 25.

SECTION 2

Every railroad, canal or turnpike corporation operated or partly operated in this State shall maintain one office therein, where transfers of its stock shall be made and where its books shall be kept for inspection by any stockholder or creditor of such corporation, in which shall be recorded the amount of capital stock subscribed or paid in, and the amounts owned by them respectively, the transfers of said stock and the names and places of residence of the officers.

This provision was included to prevent absentee management and diminished service caused by distance. This is an early example of consumer protection.

SECTION 3

All individuals, associations and corporations shall have equal rights to have persons and property transported over railroads, canals and turnpikes, and no undue or unreasonable discrimination shall be made in charges for, or in facilities for transportation of freight or passengers, within the State, or coming from or going to any other State. Persons and property transported over any railroad shall be delivered at any station at charges not exceeding the charges of transportation of persons and property of the same class in the same direction to any more distant station; but excursion and commutation tickets may be issued at special rates.

A railroad corporation cannot prevent picketing on grounds that they are prevented from supplying service when railroad employees refuse to cross the picket line and enter a struck plant (Missouri Pacific R.R. v. United Brick and Clay Workers Union, 1951).

SECTION 4

No railroad, canal or other corporation, or the lessees, purchasers or managers of any railroad, canal or corporation, shall consolidate the stock, property or franchise of, such corporation with, or lease or purchase the work or franchise of, or in any way control any other railroad or canal corporation owning or having under its control a parallel or competing line, nor shall any officer of such railroad or canal corporation act as an officer of any other railroad or canal corporation owning or having control of a parallel or competing line; and the question whether railroads or canals are parallel or competing lines, shall, when demanded by the party complainant, be decided by a jury as in other civil issues.

This section prevents what had been a problem during the Civil War and the subsequent Reconstruction period, namely, monopolistic moves and other deals to diminish the competition and control the market preparatory to raising prices.

SECTION 5

No president, director, officer, agent or employee of any railroad or canal company shall be interested diredcy or indirectly in the furnishing of materials or supplies to such company or in the business of transportation as a common carrier of freight or

> passengers over the works owned, leased, controlled or worked by such company; nor in any arrangement which shall afford more advantageous terms or greater facilities than are offered or accorded to the public. And all contracts and arrangements in violation of this section shall be void.

This is a code of ethics for railroad management, which is considered a public servant because of the public investments in railroad establishment, development, and operation.

SECTION 6

> No discrimination in charges or facilities for transportation shall be made between transportation companies and individuals or in favor or either by abatement, drawback or otherwise, and no railroad or canal comArticle pany or any lessee, manager or employee thereof shall make any preference in furnishing cars or motive power.

A railroad may make reasonable regulations for the reception of commodities to be carried (Choctaw, O. and G. Ry. v. State, 1904). The legislature may enforce prompt delivery, upon payment of freight charges, by making a railroad liable for damages equal to freight charges for each day withheld (Little Rock and F.S. Ry. v. Hanniford, 1887).

SECTION 7

> The General Assembly shall prevent by law the granting of free passes by any railroad or transportation company to any officer of this State, legislative, executive or judicial.

The legislature has subsequently permitted free transportation for certain officers.

SECTION 8

> The General Assembly shall not remit the forfeiture of the charter of any corporation now existing, or alter or amend the same or pass any general or special law for the benefit of such corporation, except on condition that such corporation shall thereafter hold its charter subject to the provisions of this Constitution.

This mechanism prevents special legislation bestowing inequitable and unethical concessions that are based on politics.

SECTION 9

> The exercise of the right of eminent domain shall never be abridged or so construed as to prevent the General Assembly from taking the property and franchise of

incorporated companies and subjecting them to public use the same as the property of individuals.

The legislature may provide the procedure for the condemnation of private property for public use within constitutional bounds (Helena v. Arkansas Utilities Company, 1945).

SECTION 10

The General Assembly shall pass laws to correct abuses and prevent unjust discrimination and excessive charges by railroad, canal and turnpike companies for transporting freight and passengers, and shall provide for enforcing such laws by adequate penalties and forfeitures.

This section is extended by Amendment 2 in a way that allows the legislature to create offices and commissions and to vest them with powers to regulate charges or to abolish them. For example, it could pass an act abolishing the railroad commission and transferring its powers and duties to Arkansas Corporation Commission (Helena Water Co. v. Helena, 1919). State policy is to regulate transportation agencies (Southeast Arkansas Freight Lines v. Arkansas Corporation Commission, 1942). For further reference, see "The Growth of Utility Regulation in Arkansas: A Functional Survey," 21 Arkansas Law Review 539.

SECTION 11

The rolling stock and all other movable property belonging to any railroad company or corporation in this State shall be considered personal property of individuals, and the General Assembly shall pass no law exempting any such property from execution and sale.

This section sets up the manner in which railroad property is to be treated by the law and for taxation purposes.

SECTION 12

All railroads which are now or may be hereafter built and operated, either in whole or in part, in this State, shall be responsible for all damages to persons and property, under such regulations, as may be prescribed by the General Assembly.

A person seeking a claim under this section would have to show negligence, even if he or she were an employee or a passenger of the railroad (Kansas City, F.S. and M.R.R. v. Becker, 1899). A railroad was found liable for injuries to a passenger who was injured through the road's negligence, even though the passenger was riding on a free pass stipulating that the passenger assumed all risks (St. Louis, I.M.&S. Railway v. Pitcock, 1907). A plaintiff must show negligence in claims against a bus company or any other person, except against a railroad company (Wade v. Brocato, 1936).

SECTION 13

The directors of every railroad corporation shall annually make a report under oath to the Auditor of Public Accounts of all their acts and doings, which report shall include such matters relating to railroads as may be prescribed by law, and the General Assembly shall pass laws enforcing, by suitable penalties, the provisions of this section.

A required report to the public was intended to increase the integrity of the operation.

Article XVIII

Judicial Circuits

This is a very lengthy article in which judicial districts for all circuit and chancery courts are spelled out specifically and geographically, naming each district and its counties. The judicial apportionment stood, until changed by the legislature. For further reference, see "The Arkansas Judiciary at the Crossroads," 17 *Arkansas Law Review* 259.

Article XIX

Miscellaneous Provisions

SECTION 1

No person who denies the being of a God shall hold any office in the civil departments of this State nor be competent to testify as a witness in any court.

One who believes in a supreme being but not God is competent to testify (Mueller v. Coffman, 1918). Writing a pamphlet is proof of belief in God (Farrell v. State, 1914). Atheists have unsuccessfully challenged this section as unconstitutional; however, the section is presumably no longer valid following the supreme court's decision in *Torasco* (Flora v. White, 1982). See "Theory of Testimonial Competency and Privilege," 4 *Arkansas Law Review* 377.

SECTION 2

No person who may hereafter fight a duel, assist in the same as second, or send, accept, or knowingly carry a challenge therefor shall hold any office in the State for a period of ten years, and may be otherwise punished as the law may prescribe.

This antiquated constitutional provision is one of the most frequently cited by those advocating comprehensive revision using a constitutional convention as a mechanism for modernization.

SECTION 3

No person shall be elected to or appointed to fill a vacancy in any office who does not possess the qualifications of an elector.

A special judge must be a qualified elector but not necessarily a registered voter (White v. Reagan, 1869). A city marshall who was not a resident of the city was found unqualified for the office (Thomas v. Sitton, 1948). In a case in which an alderman moved out of state and voted there, he was found ineligible to serve as alderman and was not a qualified elector, even though he claimed to be an Arkansas resident. (Charisse v. Eldred, 1972).

SECTION 4

All civil officers for the State at large shall reside within the State, and all district, county and township officers within their respective district, counties and townships, and shall keep their offices at such places therein as are now or may hereafter be required by law.

In determining the residency of a candidate, his or her conduct and actions are considered, both of which must be in conformity with the stated residency intent (Brick v. Simonetti, 1983). A justice of the peace nominee who was a qualified elector and a resident of his district at the time of nomination was held to be a qualified candidate even though he had temporarily moved outside his district (Booth v. Smith, 1977).

SECTION 5

All officers shall continue in office after the expiration of their official terms until their successors are elected and qualified.

This provision means that, in the event that a person who was elected to office fails to qualify, the office is not, in fact, considered vacant, but rather is to be filled by the incumbent until a qualified successor is elected (Justice v. Campbell, 1967). Special elections for sheriff are unconstitutional (McCraw v. Pate, 1973).

SECTION 6

No person shall hold or perform the duties of more than one officer in the same department of the government at the same time, except as expressly directed or permitted by this Constitution.

This section applies only to state officers, and not to local officials. A police chief, for example, can also serve as a deputy sheriff (Peterson v. Culpepper, 1906).

Additionally, one may hold a state judicial office and a municipal judicial office (State ex rel. Murphy v. Townsend, 1904). The right of certain officers to hold executive or judicial office is spelled out in Article 19, Section 26.

SECTION 7

Absence on business of the State, or of the United States, or on a visit, or on necessary private business, shall not cause a forfeiture of residence once obtained.

Military employees and public officials, for example, do not change their domicile, although they may actually live out of state for years (Central Manufacturer's Mutual Insurance Co. v. Friedman, 1948). Similarly, former Congressman Wilbur D. Mills lived in the Washington, D.C., area from 1939 to 1991 but was always considered a resident of Arkansas for all purposes.

SECTION 8

It shall be the duty of the General Assembly to regulate by law in what cases and what deductions from the salaries of public officers shall be made for neglect of duty in their official capacity.

This section has never been used, cited, or litigated.

SECTION 9

The General Assembly shall have no power to create any permanent State office not expressly provided for by this Constitution.

Creating the post of superintendent for a school for the blind is not a violation (Lucas v. Futtrell, 1907). A county superintendent of schools is not a state officer (Board of Education v. Ashdown School District, 1923). The Employment Security Division is an administrative agency that was created under police power, and its creation is not a violation (Hickenbottom v. McCain, 1944). An office created by the General Assembly is subject to the legislative will and may be abolished at any time; in this sense, it is temporary.

SECTION 10

Returns for all elections for officers who are to be commissioned by the Governor, and for members of the General Assembly, except as otherwise provided by this Constitution, shall be made to the Secretary of State.

A large part of the responsibilities of the secretary of state pertains to elections. The Election Services Division of the office is one of the largest in terms of employees.

SECTION 11

The Governor, Secretary of State, Auditor, Treasurer, Attorney General, judges of the Supreme Court, judges of the circuit court. Commissioner of State Lands and prosecuting attorneys shall each receive a salary, to be established by law, which shall not be increased or diminished during their respective terms, nor shall any of them, except the prosecuting attorneys, after the adoption of this Constitution, receive to his own use any fees, costs, perquisites of office or other compensation; and all fees that may hereafter be payable by law for any services performed by any officer mentioned in this section, except prosecuting attorneys, shall be paid in advance into the State Treasury. Provided, that the salaries of the respective officers herein mentioned shall never exceed per annum. For Governor the sum of $4,000; for the Secretary of State, the sum of $2,500; for Treasurer, the sum of $3,000; for Auditor, the sum of $3,000; for Attorney General, the sum of $2,500; for Commissioner of State Lands, the sum of $2,500; for judges of the Supreme Court, each the sum of $4,000; for judges of the circuit courts and chancellors, each the sum of $3,000; for prosecuting attorneys, the sum of $400.

This section has been superseded by Amendments 21, Section 2; 43, Section 1; and 56, Section 2. Prosecuting attorneys are constitutional state officers acting in a quasi-judicial capacity (Smith v. Page, 1936). Salaries of circuit court judges are paid from state revenue only (Cotham v. Coffman, 1914).

SECTION 12

An accurate and detailed statement of the receipts and expenditures of the public money, the several amounts paid, to whom and on what account, shall, from time to time, be published as may be prescribed by law.

This section requires the publication of detailed statements of receipts and expenses of the public money (Jeffery v. Trevathan, 1949; Clark v. Hampbleton, 1962).

SECTION 13

All contracts for a greater rate of interest than ten per centum per annum shall be void, as to principal and interest, and the General Assembly shall prohibit the same by law, but when no rate of interest is agreed upon the rate shall be six per centum per annum.

This section, which is now superseded by Amendment 60, was one of the most popular and highly litigated provisions of the 1874 constitution through the years, until it was blamed for an economic crisis in the 1970s in Arkansas due to the difficulty of businesses in securing capital. It was the severest usury provision ever enacted since the penalty for usurious interest rates was the forfeiture of both interest and principal.

SECTION 14

No lottery shall be authorized by this State, nor shall the sale of lottery tickets be allowed.

Most of the litigation over this section has centered around the definition of a lottery, which is determined by the element of chance involved in an activity. Pari-mutuel betting on horse races at Oaklawn Park in Hot Springs is not unconstitutional because even though the element of chance is present, it is not controlling, as the condition, speed, and endurance of the horse, as well as the skill and management of the rider, enter in (Longstreth v. Cook, 1949). This section forbids the legalization of lotteries and the sale of lottery tickets (Scott v. Dunaway, 1958). The punishment for lottery prosecutions is limited to a fine (State v. Bass, 1955). A lottery is defined as the distribution of prizes of chance among persons who have paid or agreed to pay a valuable consideration for an opportunity to obtain a prize (Shuffield v. Raney, 1956). No statute can legalize pari-mutuel betting (Longstreth v. Cook, 1949).

SECTION 15

All stationery, printing, paper, fuel, for the use of the General Assembly and other departments of government, shall be furnished, and the printing, binding and distributing of the laws, journals, department reports and all other printing and binding, and the repairing and furnishing the halls and rooms used for the meeting of the General Assembly and its committees shall be performed under contract to be given to the lowest responsible bidder, below such maximum price and under such regulations as shall be prescribed by law. No member or officers of any department of the government shall in any way be interested in such contracts, and all such contracts shall be subject to the approval of the Govemor, Auditor and Treasurer.

This section has been repealed by Amendment 54, Section 2.

SECTION 16

All contracts for erecting or repairing public buildings or bridges in any county, or for materials therefor, or for providing for the care and keeping of paupers where there are no alms houses, shall be given to the lowest responsible bidder under such regulations as may be provided by law.

A contract entered into by a county judge while on vacation, and not ratified by the county court, is void (Ross Drainage District v. Clark County, 1922). The competitive bid process is a constitutional requirement, no matter what extenuating circumstances may be asserted.

SECTION 17

The laws of this State, civil and criminal, shall be revised, digested, arranged, published and promulgated at such times and in such manner as the General Assembly may direct.

The Statute Revision Commission codifies all laws. The Secretary of State's Office publishes a volume of acts after every legislative session.

SECTION 18

The General Assembly, by suitable enactments, shall require such appliances and means to be provided and used as may be necessary to secure as far as possible the lives, health and safety of persons employed in mining and persons traveling upon railroads and by the other public conveyances, and shall provide for enforcing such enactments by adequate pains and penalties.

This state police power has always been a cornerstone of public safety and protection.

SECTION 19

It shall be the duty of the General Assembly to provide by law for the support of institutions for the education of the deaf and dumb and of the blind, and also for the treatment of the insane.

The legislature has a mandated duty to provide separate and special system of instruction for blind and deaf students, including state schools for the deaf and for the blind in Little Rock (Lucas v. Futtrall, 1907). Permanent school fund money may not be spent on the school for the blind (Walls v. State Board of Education, 1938).

SECTION 20

Senators and Representatives and all judicial and executive State and County officers, and all other officers, both civil and military, before entering on the duties of their respective offices, shall take and subscribe to the following oath or affirmation: "I, ___________, do solemnly swear (or affirm) that I will support the Constitution of the United States, and the Constitution of the State of Arkansas, and that I will faithfully discharge the duties of the office of ___________, upon which I am now about to enter."

It was found that the failure of an assessor to append the proper oath to his return is not grounds for an injunction (Equalization Board v. Landowners, 1889). Road commissioners are not required to take this oath (Nail v. Kelley, 1915). The oath of office taken by commissioners of the levee and drainage district was found to be in substantial compliance with this section (O'Kane v. McClean Bottom Levee and Drainage District #3, 1947).

SECTION 21

The sureties upon the official bonds of all State officers shall be residents of, and have sufficient property within the State not exempt from sale under execution, attachment or other process of any court, to make good their bonds; and the sureties upon the official bonds of all county officers shall reside within the counties where such officers reside, and shall have sufficient property therein, not exempt from such sale, to make good their bonds.

The legislature is authorized to prescribe the kind and character of bonds that all state and county officers should make and file (Gower v. Looney, 1939). This section has been superseded by Amendment 4.

SECTION 22

Either branch of the General Assembly at a regular session thereof may propose amendments to this Constitution, and, if the same be agreed to by a majority of all the members elected to each house, such proposed amendments shall be entered on the journals with the yeas and nays, and published in at least one newspaper in each county, where a newspaper is published, for six months immediately preceding the next general election for Senators and Representatives, at which time the same shall be submitted to the electors of the State for approval or rejection; and if a majority of the electors voting at such election adopt such amendments the same shall become a part of this Constitution; but no more than three amendments shall be proposed or submitted at the same time. They shall be so submitted as to enable the electors to vote on each amendment separately.

This section must be read in conjunction with Amendment 7, perhaps the most discussed and utilized constitutional provision, which enhances and extends the power of the people to govern themselves as an outgrowth of the

Progressive Era. The governor's approval is not necessary for the legislature's proposed amendments (Coulter v. Dodge, 1939).

SECTION 23

No officer of this State, nor of any county, city or town, shall receive, directly or indirectly, for salary, fees and perquisites, more than five thousand dollars net profit per annum in par funds, and any and all sums in excess of this amount shall be paid into the State, county, city or town treasury, as shall hereafter be directed by appropriate legislation.

This section was modified partially by Amendments 37, 48, and 63, and then repealed completely by Amendment 56.

SECTION 24

The General Assembly shall provide by law the mode of contesting elections in cases not specifically provided for in this Constitution.

The legislature has conferred original jurisdiction on the circuit court for county and municipal election contests, including school consolidation votes (Sumpter v. Duffle, 1906). The circuit court has exclusive jurisdiction over election contests (Purdy v. Glover, 1939). The circuit court has jurisdiction to hear election contests for the consolidation of school districts (Adams v. Dixie School District #7, 1978).

SECTION 25

The present seal of the State shall be and remain the Seal of the State of Arkansas until otherwise provided by law, and shall be kept and used as provided in this Constitution.

The same seal has been used by Arkansas since its inception including the motto, "Regnat Populus" (the people rule).

SECTION 26

Militia officers, officers of the public schools and notaries may be elected to fill any executive or judicial office.

There is no incompatibility among these offices, unless the military position is one appointed by the president and thus is not under the control of the state (Jones v. Clark, 1983). Only qualified electors are qualified to hold the office of notary public (Gray v. Hodges, 1913). See also Jeffrey, Nelson, Nunnally, and Robertson, "Constitutional Law Survey," 7 *UALR Law Journal* 179.

SECTION 27

Nothing in this Constitution shall be so construed as to prohibit the General Assembly from authorizing assessments on real property for local improvements in the towns and cities, under such regulations as may be prescribed by law, to be based upon the consent of a majority in value of the property holders owning property adjoining the locality to be affected; but such assessments shall be ad valorem and uniform.

An assessment for local improvements must be approved by a majority of the property owners (Rector v. Board of Improvement, 1887). The provision that a majority in value of property owners must consent to a local improvement is mandatory (Craig v. Waterworks Improvement District, 1907). In forming a drainage district to control flood waters, rural property owners could include part of a city in the district even if consent of the property owners in the city is not obtained (Curlin v. Harding Drain Improvement District, 1952). If the assessment is higher than the benefit, it amounts to the taking of private property without just compensation (Kirst v. Street Improvement District #120, 1908). If property is included in a district, it will be interpreted as being affected by improvements (Little Rock v. Katzenstein, 1889; McAllister v. Forrest City Improvement District #11, 1981).

Schedule

SECTION 1

All laws now in force which are not in conflict or inconsistent with this Constitution shall continue in force until amended or repealed by the General Assembly, and all laws exempting property from sale on execution or by decree of a court which were in force at the time of the adoption of the Constitution of 1868 shall remain in force with regard to contracts made before that time. Until otherwise provided by law, no distinction shall exist between sealed and unsealed instruments concerning contracts between individuals executed since the adoption of the Constitution of 1868; provided, that the statutes of limitation with regard to sealed and unsealed instruments in force at the time continue to apply to all instruments afterward executed until altered or repealed.

This section was designed to provide a smooth legal transition from the old to the new constitution.

SECTION 2

In civil actions no witness shall be excluded because he is a party to the suit or interested in the issue to be tried. Provided, that in actions by or against executor, administrators or guardians in which judgment may be rendered for or against them, neither party shall be allowed to testify against the other as to any transaction with or statements of the testors, intestate or ward, unless called to testify thereto by the opposite party. Provided further, that this section may be amended or repealed by the General Assembly.

This section was repealed by legislation via Act 1143 of 1975, which was passed in an invalid legislative session and then repassed in 1987.

SECTION 3

An election shall be held at the several election precincts of every county of the State on Tuesday the 13th day of October, 1874, for Governor, Secretary of State, Auditor, Treasurer, Attorney General, Commissioner of State Lands for two years, unless the office is sooner abolished by the General Assembly, chancellor and clerk of the separate chancery court of Pulaski County, Chief Justice and two Associate Justices of the Supreme Court, a circuit judge and prosecuting attorney for each judicial circuit provided for in this Constitution, Senators and Representatives to the General Assembly, all county and township officers provided for in this Constitution; and also for the submission of this Constitution to the qualified electors of the State for its adoption or rejection.

This section was operative only for the first election under the new Constitution.

SECTION 4

The qualification of voters at the election to be held as provided in this schedule shall be the same as is now prescribed by law.

This section establishes the qualification of voters in an effort to prevent contests or questions being raised.

SECTION 5

The State Board of Supervisors hereinafter mentioned shall give notice of said election immediately after the adoption of this Constitution by this convention by proclamation in at least two newspapers published at Little Rock, and such other newspapers as they may select. And each county board of supervisors shall give public notice in their respective counties of said election immediately after their appointment.

This section also governs the first election and the mechanisms designed to conduct it.

SECTION 6

The Governor shall also issue a proclamation enjoining upon all peace officers the duty of preserving good order on the day of said election and preventing any disturbance of the same.

This section governs the governor's role, emphasizing the role of the state government rather than the federal government in elections.

SECTION 7

Augustus H. Garland, Gordon H. Peay and Dudley E. Jones are hereby constituted a State Board of Supervisors of said election, who shall take an oath faithfully and impartially to discharge the duties of their office, a majority of whom shall be a quorum, and who shall perform the duties herein assigned them. Should a vacancy occur in said board by refusal to serve, death, removal, resignation or otherwise, or if any member should become incapacitated from performing said duties, the remaining members of the board shall fill the vacancy by appointment. But, if all the places on said board become vacant at the same time, the said vacancies shall be filled by the president of this convention.

This section exemplifies the legislative nature of some of the 1874 convention's activities and provisions.

SECTION 8

Said State Board shall at once proceed to appoint a board of election supervisors for each county of this State, consisting of three men of known intelligence and uprightness of character, who shall take the same oath as above provided for the State Board. A majority of each board shall constitute a quorum and shall perform the duties herein assigned to them; and vacancies occurring in the county board shall be filled by the State Board.

The state government establishes the county system for conducting state elections.

SECTION 9

The State Board shall provide the form of poll books, and each county board shall furnish the judges of each election precinct with three copies of the poll books in the form prescribed and with ballot boxes at the expense of the county.

This system was followed closely until voter registration was adopted in 1964.

SECTION 10

The State Board of Supervisors shall cause to be furnished in pamphlet form a sufficient number of copies of this Constitution to supply each county supervisor and judge of election with a copy, and shall forward the same to the county election boards for distribution.

This system of public education is used as a basic plan for constitutional amendments or proposed constitutions.

SECTION 11

The boards of county election supervisors shall at once proceed to appoint three judges of election for each election precinct in their respective counties, and the judges shall appoint three election clerks for their respective precincts, all of whom shall be good, competent men, and take an oath as prescribed above. Should the judges of any election precinct fail to attend at the time and place provided by law, or decline to act, the assembled electors shall choose competent persons in the manner provided by law to act in their places, who shall be sworn as above.

This provision had limited application, as it is just for the first election.

SECTION 12

Said election shall be conducted, in accordance with existing laws, except as herein provided. As the electors present themselves at the polls to vote, the judges of the election shall pass upon their qualifications and the clerks of the election shall register their names on the poll-books if qualified; and such registration by said clerks shall be a sufficient registration in conformity with the Constitution of this State, and then their votes shall be taken.

Same-day registration was initially permitted. Increased requirements and complications accumulated over time.

SECTION 13

Each elector shall have written or printed on his ticket "For Constitution" or "Against Constitution," and also the officers and names of the candidates for the office for whom he desires to vote.

This type of ballot question has been included in each ballot on a proposed constitution since the adoption of this constitution: in 1918, 1970, and 1980.

SECTION 14

The judges shall deposit the tickets in the ballot-box; but no elector shall vote outside of the township or ward in which he resides. The names of the electors shall be numbered and the corresponding numbers shall be placed on the ballots by the judges when deposited.

This system is still used and raises the question of tracing votes, a method fashioned in response to the perceived need to check to see if votes were counted as cast.

SECTION 15

All dram shops and drinking houses in this State shall be closed during the day of said election and the succeeding night, and any person selling or giving away intoxicating liquors during said day or night shall be punished by fine not less than two hundred dollars for each and every offense, or imprisoned not less than six months, or both.

Liquor stores are closed on Election Day in Arkansas until polls are closed, and restaurants are prohibited from serving alcoholic beverages until the polls close.

SECTION 16

The polls shall be open at eight o'clock in the forenoon and shall be kept open until sunset. After the polls are closed the ballots shall be counted by the judges at the place of voting as soon as the polls are closed, unless prevented by violence or accident, and the results by them certified on the poll books and the ballots sealed up. They shall be returned to the county board of election supervisors, who shall proceed to cast up the votes and ascertain and state the number of votes cast for the Constitution and the number cast against the Constitution, and also the number of votes cast for each candidate voted for any office, and shall forthwith forward to the State Board of Supervisors, duly certified by them, one copy of the statement or abstract of the votes so made out by them, retain one copy in their possession and file one copy in the office of the county clerk, where they shall also deposit for safekeeping the ballots, sealed up, and one copy of the poll books retaining possession of the other copies.

Election results are published at the precinct, county, and state levels.

SECTION 17

The State Board of Supervisors shall at once proceed, on receiving such returns from the county board, to ascertain therefrom and state the whole number of votes given for the Constitution and the whole number of votes given against it, and if a majority of all votes cast be in favor of the Constitution, they shall at once make public that fact by publication in two or more of the leading newspapers published in the City of Little Rock, and this Constitution, from that date, shall be in force; and they shall also make out and file in the office of the Secretary of State an abstract of all the votes cast for the Constitution and all the votes cast against it, and also an abstract of all votes cast for every candidate voted for at the election, and file the same in the office of the Secretary of State, showing the candidates elected. They shall also make out and certify and lay before each house of the General Assembly a list of the members elected to that house, and shall also make out, certify and deliver to the Speaker of the House of Representatives an abstract of all votes cast at the election for any and all persons for the office of Governor, Secretary of State, Treasurer of State, Auditor of State, Attorney General and Commissioner of State Lands, and the said Speaker shall cast up the votes and announce the names of the person elected to these offices; The Governor, Secretary of State, Treasurer of State, Auditor of State, Attorney General and Commissioner of State Lands, chosen at said election shall qualify and enter upon the discharge of the duties of their respective offices within fifteen days after the announcement of their election as aforesaid.

This section governs the reporting of election results, most of which is handled by the Secretary of State's Office in conjunction with the County Clerk.

SECTION 18

All officers shown to be elected by the abstract of said election filed by the State Board of Supervisors in the office of the Secretary of State, required by this Constitution to be commissioned, shall be commissioned by the Governor.

This section establishes a process whereby the governor attaches a state seal to an election certificate. This is known as a commission.

SECTION 19

At said election the qualified voters for each county and senatorial district, as defined in Article Eight of this Constitution, shall elect respectively Representatives and Senators according to the number and apportionment contained in said article. The Board of Election supervisors of each county shall furnish certificates of election to the person or persons elected to the House of Representatives as soon as practicable after the result of the election has been ascertained and such board of election supervisors in each county shall make a correct return of the election for senator and senators to the board of supervisors of the county first named in the senatorial apportionment, and said board shall furnish certificates of election to the person or persons elected as Senator or Senators in said senatorial districts as soon as practicable.

This section apportions the legislature and establishes the election process for legislators.

SECTION 20

All officers elected under this Constitution, except the Governor, Secretary of State, Auditor of State, Attorney General, and Commissioner of State Lands, shall enter upon the duties of their several offices when they shall have been declared duly elected by said State Board of Supervisors and shall have been duly qualified. All such officers shall qualify and enter upon the duties of their office within fifteen days after they have been duly notified of their election.

The terms of office begin on the date on which the election results are officially declared, and the person elected cannot postpone the date of the beginning of the term through a delay in taking office (Jewett v. McConnell, 1914).

SECTION 21

Upon the qualification of the officers elected at said election the present incumbents of the offices for which the election is held shall vacate the same and turn over to the officers thus elected and qualified all books, papers, records, monies and documents belonging or pertaining to said offices by them respectively held.

This section was added so that there would be no legal standing for Reconstruction officials to retain their positions.

SECTION 22

The first session of the General Assembly under this Constitution shall commence on the first Tuesday after the Second Monday in November, 1874.

The first legislative session was needed immediately in order to implement the new Constitution. Since then, legislative sessions have begun on the second Monday in January.

SECTION 23

The County courts provided for in this Constitution shall be regarded in law as a continuation of the boards of supervisors now existing by law, and the circuit courts shall be regarded in law as continuations of the criminal courts wherever the same may have existed in their respective counties, and the probate courts shall be regarded as continuations of the circuit courts for the business within the jurisdiction of such probate courts, and the papers and records pertaining to said courts and jurisdictions shall be transferred accordingly and no suit or prosecution of any kind shall abate because of any change made in this Constitution.

The county courts were continuations of the former boards of supervisors and were given exclusive original jurisdiction in all matters that are necessary to the internal improvement and local concerns of their respective counties.

SECTION 24

All officers now in office whose offices are not abolished by this convention shall continue in office and discharge the duties imposed on them by law until their successors are elected and qualified under this Constitution. The office of Commissioner of State Lands shall be continued, provided that the General Assembly at its next session may abolish or continue the same in such manner as may be prescribed by law.

This section prevents vacancies from occurring in the case that there are offices for which there are no candidates.

SECTION 25

Any election officer appointed under the provisions of this schedule who shall fraudulently and corruptly permit any person to vote illegally, or refuse the vote of any qualified elector, cast up or make a false return of said election, shall be deemed guilty of a felony, and on conviction thereof shall be imprisoned in the penitentiary not less than five years nor more than ten years. And any person who shall vote when not a qualified elector, or vote more than once, or bribe any one to vote contrary to his wishes, or intimidate or prevent any elector by threats, menace or promises from voting, shall be guilty of a felony, and upon conviction thereof, shall be imprisoned in the penitentiary not less than one nor more than five years.

Fraud was expected and discussed rather raatter-of-factly at this convention.

SECTION 26

All officers elected at the election provided for in this schedule shall hold their office for the respective periods provided for in the foregoing Constitution, and until their successors are elected and qualified. The first general elections after the ratification of this Constitution shall be held on the first Monday in September, A.D. 1876. Nothing in this Constitution and the schedule thereto shall be so construed as to prevent the election of Congressmen at the time as now prescribed by law.

Initially, state elections were held at different times than federal elections.

SECTION 27

The sum of five thousand dollars is hereby appropriated out of any money in the treasury not otherwise appropriated to defray the expenses of the election provided for in this schedule, and the Auditor of State shall draw his warrant on the Treasurer for such expenses not exceeding said amount on the certificate of the State Board of Supervisors of Election.

The total cost of a statewide election in 1874 was $5,000; now it is $1 million and is primarily paid for by candidates' filing fees, political parties, and counties.

SECTION 28

For the period of two years from the adoption of this Constitution, and until otherwise provided by law, the respective officers herein enumerated shall receive for their services the following salaries per annum:

For Governor, the sum of $3,500; for Secretary of State, the sum of $2,000; for Commission of State Lands, the sum of $2,000; for judges of the Supreme Court, each the sum of $3,500; for judges of the circuit and chancery courts, each, the sum of $2,500; for prosecuting attorney, each, the sum of $400; for members of the General Assembly, the sum of $6.00 per day and twenty cents per mile for each mile traveled in going to and returning from the seat of government over the most direct and practicable route.

The transitional salaries were limited to existing levels and thus were fixed.

Amendments to the Constitution of 1874

AMENDMENT 1: "HOLFORD" BONDS (ARTICLE 20)

The General Assembly shall have no power to levy any tax, or make any appropriation, to pay either the principal or interest, or any part thereof, of any of the following bonds of the State, or the claims, or pretended claims, upon which they may be based, to-wit: Bonds issued under an act of the General Assembly of the State of Arkansas, entitled "An Act to provide for the funding of the public debt of the State," approved April 6th, A.D. 1869, and numbered from four hundred and ninety-one to eighteen hundred and sixty, inclusive, being the "funding bonds," delivered to F. W. Caper, and sometimes called "Holford Bonds;" or bonds known as railroad aid bonds, issued under an act of the General Assembly of the State of Arkansas, entitled "A n Act to aid in the construction of railroads," approved July 21, A.D. 1868; or bonds called "levee bonds," being bonds issued under an act of the General Assembly of the State of Arkansas, entitled "A n Act providing for the building and repairing of the public levees of the State, and for other purposes," approved March 16, A.D. 1869; and the supplemental act thereto, approved April 12, 1869; and the Act entitled "A n Act to amend an act entitled an act providing for the building and repairing of the public levees of this State," approved March 23, A.D. 1871; and any law providing for any such tax or appropriation, shall be null and void.

The state thus formally reneged on this bond issue, which was owned mostly by the British. This historic amendment caused lively and embarrassed discussion during each of the three succeeding constitutional conventions. It was added to the Constitution after the legislature proposed it in January 1883 and put it on the ballot. The popular vote in 1884 favored the amendment: 119,806 for and 15,492 against.

AMENDMENT 2: REGULATION OF TRANSPORTATION RATES

The General Assembly shall pass laws to correct abuses and prevent unjust discrimination and excessive charges by railroads, canals and turnpike companies for transporting freight and passengers, and shall provide for enforcing such laws by adequate penalties and forfeitures, and shall provide for the creation of such offices and commissions and vest in them such authority as shall be necessary to carry into effect the powers hereby conferred.

This amendment, along with Amendment 1, reflects the importance of railroads during the early history and initial development of Arkansas and emphasizes public concern for the related financial transactions.

AMENDMENT 3: THREE-MILL COUNTY ROAD TAX

The county courts of the State in their respective counties, together with a majority of the justices of the peace of such county, in addition to the amount of county tax allowed to be levied, shall have the power to levy not exceeding three mills on the dollar on all taxable property of their respective counties, which shall be known as the County Road Tax, and when collected shall be used in the respective counties for the purpose of making and repairing public roads and bridges of the respective counties, and for no other purpose, and shall be collected in United States currency or county warrants legally drawn on such road tax fund, if a majority of the qualified electors of such county shall have voted public road tax at the general election for State and county officers preceding such levy at each election.

This amendment was repealed by Amendment 61, Section 2, which provided that the road tax would be a continuous levy. This was a needed provision in view of the fact that some counties forgot to include it on the ballot in some years while some counties defeated the tax from time to time.

AMENDMENT 4: SURETIES ON OFFICIAL BONDS BY BONDING COMPANIES

SECTION 1

The sureties upon the official bonds of all State officers shall be residents of, and have sufficient property within the State, not exempt from sale under execution, attachment or other process of any court, to make good their bonds and the sureties upon the official bonds of all county officers shall reside within the counties where such officers reside, and shall have sufficient property therein, not exempt from such sale, to make good their bonds. Provided, however, that any surety, bonding or guaranty company. organized for the purpose of doing a surety or bonding business, and authorized to do business in this State, may become surety on the bonds of all State, county and municipal officers under such regulations as may be prescribed by law.

This provision amended Article 19, Section 21, and was proposed by the General Assembly in 1899 and passed by the people in 1900 by almost a threeto-one margin. The legislature is authorized to prescribe the kind and character of bonds that all state and county officers should make and file (Gower v. Looney, 1939).

AMENDMENT 5: SIXTY-DAY SESSION OF THE LEGISLATURE

Each member of the General Assembly shall receive six dollars per day for his services during the first sixty days of any regular session of the General Assembly, and if any regular session be extended, such member shall serve without further per diem. Each member of the General Assembly shall also receive ten cents per mile for each mile traveled going to and returning from the seat of government, over the most direct and practicable route. When convened in extraordinary session by the Governor, they shall each receive three dollars per day for their services during the first fifteen days, and if such extraordinary session shall extend beyond fifteen days, they shall receive no further per diem. They shall be entitled to the same mileage for any extraordinary session as herein provided for regular sessions. The terms of all members of the General Assembly shall begin on the day of their election, and they shall receive no compensation, perquisite or allowance whatever except as herein provided.

This provision amends Article 5, Section 16, and reflects public thought that protection was needed from extravagant government. Compensation of the General Assembly is now governed by Amendment 56, Section 3.

AMENDMENT 6: GOVERNOR AND LIEUTENANT GOVERNOR

Executive Department

SECTION 1

The Executive Department of this State shall consist of a Governor, Lieutenant Governor, Secretary of State, Treasurer of State, Auditor of State, and Attorney General all of whom shall keep their office in person at the seat of government and hold their offices for the term of two years and until their successors are elected and qualified. And the General Assembly may provide by law for the establishment of the office of Commissioner of State Lands.

This provision was probably superseded by Amendment 37, Section 1, which, in turn, was repealed by Amendment 56, Section 5, and replaced by Section 1 of Amendment 56. The latter was then superseded by Amendment 63, Section 1.

SECTION 2

The executive power shall be vested in a Governor, who shall hold office for two years; a Lieutenant Governor shall be chosen at the same time and for the same term. The Governor and Lieutenant Govemor elected next preceding the time when this section shall take effect shall hold office until and including the second Monday in September, and their successors shall be chosen at the general election in that year.

This section on executive power has been superseded by Amendment 63 concerning terms of office. See also Article 6, Section 2, regarding the power of the govemor.

SECTION 3

The Govemor and Lieutenant Govemor shall be elected at the time and places of choosing members of the Assembly. The persons respectively having the highest number of votes for Govemor and Lieutenant Govemor shall be elected, but in case two or more shall have an equal and the highest number of votes for Govemor, or for Lieutenant Govemor, the two houses of the Legislature, at the next annual session shall forthwith, by joint ballot, choose one of the said persons so having an equal and the highest number of votes for Govemor or Lieutenant Govemor.

This section on election of the govemor and the lieutenant govemor is very similar to Article 6, Section 3.

SECTION 4

In case of the impeachment of the Govemor or his removal from office, death, inability to discharge the powers and duties of the said office, resignation or absence from the State, the powers and duties of the office shall devolve upon the Lieutenant Govemor for the residue of the term, or until the disability shall cease. But when the Govemor shall, with the consent of the Legislature, be out of the State, in time of war, at the head of the military force thereof, he shall continue commander-in-chief of all the military forces of the State.

This section, delineating when the lieutenant govemor will act as govemor, supersedes Article 6, Sections 12 and 14.

SECTION 5

The Lieutenant Govemor shall possess the same qualifications of eligibility for the office as the Govemor. He shall be President of the Senate, but shall have only a casting vote there in case of a tie vote. If during a vacancy of the office of Govemor, the Lieutenant Govemor shall be impeached, displaced, resign, die or become incapable of performing the duties of his office or be absent from the State, the President of the Senate shall act as Governor until the vacancy be filled or the disability shall cease; and if the President of the Senate for any of the above causes shall become incapable of performing the duties pertaining to the office of Governor, the Speaker of the Assembly shall act as Governor until the vacancy be filled or the disability shall cease.

This provision, establishing the qualifications and duties of lieutenant governor and the success to the governorship, supersedes Article 6, Sections 13 and 14. In this provision, absence from the state means simply being out of state, even for a very short period of time. There is no restriction on the power and authority that transfers to the lieutenant governor upon absence from the state by the governor.

SECTION 6

The Lieutenant Governor shall receive for his services an annual salary of two thousand dollars and shall not receive or be entitled to any other compensation, fee or perquisite, for any duty or service he may be required to perform by the Constitution or by law.

This section, establishing the salary of the lieutenant governor, was superseded by Amendment 56, Section 2.

AMENDMENT 7: INITIATIVE AND REFERENDUM

The legislative power of the people of this State shall be vested in a General Assembly, which shall consist of the Senate and House of Representatives, but the people reserve to themselves the power to propose legislative measures, laws and amendments to the Constitution, and to enact or reject the same at the polls independent of the General Assembly; and also reserve the power, at their own option, to approve or reject at the polls any entire act or any item of an appropriation bill.

The supreme court will make a more detailed examination of the proposed ballot title than it does of the popular name. The question does not concern the wisdom of a proposed amendment, but rather whether the conditions for referral to the people have been met. It is the function of the court to see that the ballot title (and popular name) are: (1) intelligible, (2) honest, and (3) impartial (Ferstle v. McCuen, 1988). The title of the act may be used as the ballot title if it fairly alleges the general purpose of the act (Coleman v. Sherrill, 1934). The ballot title must be free from any misleading tendency, whether by amplification, omission, or fallacy; it must not be tinged with partisan coloring. It is difficult to prepare a perfect ballot title; it is sufficient if it informs the voters with such clarity that they can case their ballot with a fair understanding of the issue presented (Ferstle v. McCuen, 1988). The ballot title need not recite all the details of the proposal; however, if the information would give the elector "s e rious ground for reflection," it is not a mere detail, and it must be disclosed. The ballot title must accurately reflect the general purposes and fundamental provisions of the proposed initiative, so that electors do not vote for a proposal based on its description in the ballot title when, in fact, the vote is for a position that they might oppose (Gaines v. McCuen, 1988).

Under Article 19, Section 22, the standard of review applied to ballot titles is: whether the ballot title is a "manifest fraud upon the public." This is a different, and less demanding, standard than the standard that is applicable to initiatives under this amendment and Becker v. McCuen, 1990. There is no language in this amendment pertaining to ballot titles for legislative proposals of constitutional amendments (Chaney v. Bryant, 1976; Becker v. Riviere, 1982).

In determining the sufficiency of a ballot title, the Supreme Court will determine that it reserves to the people the right to adopt, reject, approve, or disapprove legislation (Gaines v. McCuen, 1988).

The popular name is designed to make it easy for voters to discuss the proposal prior to the election by giving them a label with which to identify it. The supreme court has declared popular names invalid because they were misleading or used biased language. However, because so little is required of a popular name, the court has never held a proposed measure invalid solely because of an incomplete description of the act by the popular name (Gaines v. McCuen).

This amendment does not govern constitutional amendments proposed by the General Assembly (Becker v. McCuen, 1990).

> **Initiative**—The first power reserved by the people is in the initiative. Eight per cent of the legal voters may propose any law and ten per cent may propose a Constitutional Amendment by initiative petition, and every such petition shall include the full text of the measure so proposed. Initiative petitions for State-wide measures shall be filed with the Secretary of State not less than four months before the election at which they are to be voted upon; provided, that at least thirty days before the aforementioned filing, the proposed measure shall have been published once, at the expense of the petitioners, in some paper of general circulation.

This provision is a clear statement of the philosophy of the Progressive Era, which was initiated by Robert LaFollette in Wisconsin in the early part of the twentieth century. Under this amendment, the people of the county cannot enact a law contrary to a general law that operates uniformly throughout the state (Tindall v. Searan, 1936; Allen v. Langston, 1949).

The enacting clause provided in the amendment refers only to bills initiated by the people and does not repeal Article 5, Section 19, which provides the style for legislative bills (Jackson v. State, 1912; Ferrell v. Keel, 1912).

A petition proposing an initiated act for a county was ruled invalid because it did not contain an enacting clause (Hailey v. Carter, 1952).

Cases construing acts that contained an unconstitutional delegation of legislative power include: Crowley v. Thombrough, 1956; Cheney v. St. Louis, 1965; and Czech v. Baer, 1984.

Amendments proposed by the legislature are entirely different from those initiated under this amendment and are governed by an entirely different procedure. This amendment does not apply to amendments submitted by the legislature (Berry v. Hall, 1960).

Referendum—The second power reserved by the people is the referendum and any number not less than six per cent of the legal voters may, by petition, order the referendum against any general act, or any item of an appropriation bill, or measure passed by the General Assembly, but the filing of a referendum petition against one or more items, sections or parts of any such act or measure shall not delay the remainder from becoming operative. Such petition shall be filed with the Secretary of State not later than ninety days after the final adjournment of the session at which such act was passed, except when a recess or adjournment shall be taken temporarily for a longer period than ninety days, in which case such petition shall be filed not later than ninety days after such recess or temporary adjournment. Any measure referred to the people by referendum petition shall remain in abeyance until such vote is taken. The total number of votes cast for the office of Governor in the last preceding general election shall be the basis upon which the number of signature of legal voters upon statewide initiative and referendum petitions shall be computed.

Upon all initiative or referendum petitions provided for in any of the sections of this article, it shall be necessary to file, from at least fifteen counties of the State, petitions bearing the signature of not less than onehalf of the designated percentage of the electors of such county.

The right of referendum, under this provision, is granted to the people on legislation of every type, whether it affects all or some of the citizens.

Emergency—If it shall be necessary for the preservation of the public peace, health and safety that a measure shall become effective without delay, such necessity shall be stated in one section, and if upon a yea and nay vote twothirds of all the members elected to each house, or two-thirds of all the members elected to city or town councils, shall vote upon a separate roll call in favor of the measure going to immediate operation, such emergency measure shall become effective without delay. It shall be necessary, however, to state the fact which constitutes such emergency. Provided, however, that an emergency shall not be declared on any franchise or special privilege or act creating any vested right or interest or alienating any property of the State. If a referendum is filed against any emergency measure, such measure shall be a law until it is voted upon by the people, and if it is then rejected by a majority of the electors voting thereon, it shall be thereby repealed. The provisions of this subsection shall apply to city or town councils.

The amendment is self-executing and, although it is within the legislative discretion to determine that an emergency exists, that fact must be stated, as otherwise the proposed act is subject to the operation of this amendment. Moreover, ninety days are given from the final adjournment in which to demand or order the referendum thereon. Consequently, an act cannot take effect until ninety days after such adjournment (Arkansas Tax Commission v. Moore, 1912).

If a legislative act contains a valid emergency clause, it is effective from and after its passage, and remains in force and effect until an adverse vote has been registered by the people (Hanson v. Hodges, 1913; Railey v. Magnolia, 1939; Fulkerson v. Refunding Bd., 1940).

Prior to the adoption of this amendment, the emergency clause was attached to almost all laws enacted, and, to prevent this practice, a requirement that the facts constituting the emergency be stated was inserted in the Constitution (Gentry v. Harrison, 1937).

The courts will not disturb a finding by the General Assembly that a particular fact comprises an emergency if the fact is recited and if fair-minded and intelligent people might reasonably differ as to the sufficiency and truth of the recited fact as a basis for declaring an emergency (State v. Ziegenbein, 1984).

The emergency clause may not be attached if an act creates a vested right or interest, no matter how great the emergency (Fulkerson v. Refunding Board, 1940).

Municipalities and Counties—The initiative and referendum powers of the people are hereby further reserved to the legal voters of each municipality and county as to all local, special and municipal legislation of every character in and for their respective municipalities and counties, but no local legislation shall be enacted contrary to the Constitution or any general law of the State, and any general law shall have the effect of repealing any local legislation which is in conflict therewith.

Municipalities may provide for the exercise of the initiative and referendum as to their local legislation.

General laws shall be enacted providing for the exercise of the initiative and referendum as to counties. Fifteen per cent of the legal voters of any municipality or county may order the referendum, or invoke the initiative upon any local measures. In municipalities the number of signatures required upon any petition shall be computed upon the total vote cast for the office of mayor at the last preceding general election; in counties, upon the office of Circuit Clerk. In municipalities and counties the time for filing an initiative petition shall not be fixed at less than sixty days nor more than ninety days before the election at which it is to be voted upon; for a referendum petition at not less than thirty days nor more than ninety days after the passage of such measure by a municipal council; nor less than ninety days when filed against a local or special measure passed by the General Assembly.

Every extension, enlargement, grant or conveyance of a franchise or any rights, property, easement, lease, or occupation of or in any road, street, alley or any part thereof in real property or interest in real property owned by municipalities, exceeding in value three hundred dollars, whether the same be by statute, ordinance, resolution, or otherwise, shall be subject to emergency legislation.

This amendment has no application to the local option petitions, which are governed by statute (McFerrin v. Knight, 1979). This amendment does not apply to an election to change the form of a city government (Dingle v. City of Eureka Springs, 1967). The effectiveness of an emergency ordinance not providing for fine, penalty, or forfeiture should not be suspended until publication, provided it is published within a reasonable time (Kemp v. Simmons, 1968).

While the setting of the date for referendum on a municipal ordinance is a matter of legislative discretion, in cases where the election was set at more than twenty-one months in the future, it was an attempt to thwart the purpose of this amendment, as such election must be held within a reasonable time (Lewis v. Conlee, 1975). Publication of initiative measures affecting local or county government is governed by the general law concerning legal notices (Johnson v. Munger, 1976). The matter of calling a special election, if not exercised by the electors, rests on the discretion of the county judge and the quorum court, either of which may determine the necessity (Quattlebaum v. Davis, 1979).

Under this amendment, the people of the county cannot enact a law contrary to a general law that operates uniformly throughout the state (Allen v. Langston, 1949). The mayor is not an elected member of the city council but only an exofficio member by virtue of his or her executive position, and, therefore, his or her vote cannot be used in amending or repealing any part of an initiated act (Thompson v. Younts, 1984). An act fixing the salaries of county officers can be initiated and adopted by county electors (Tindall v. Searan, 1936). Chancery courts have the jurisdiction to review the action of a county or city clerk in determining the sufficiency of petitions for elections (Rich v. Walker, 1964).

The adoption of this provision was intended to reserve to the people the right to pass all local laws affecting the counties (Tindall v. Searen, 1936). After sponsors of an initiative or referendum have been notified by the city clerk that a petition is insufficient, they have ten days within which to correct or amend it, and any appeal from the decision of the clerk shall be taken to chancery court (Bradley v. Galloway, 1983). The right of referendum is granted to the people on legislation of every character, whether the legislation affects all or part of the citizens of the municipality affected (Carpenter v. Paragould, 1939). Only legislative action of the city council, as distinguished from administrative action, is subject to referendum, inasmuch as this amendment was not intended to frustrate administrative action that is essential to the efficient administration of a city's affairs. The test resorted to in determining whether the proposition is one that makes new law or executes a law was already in existence (City of North Little Rock v. Gorman, 1978).

General Provisions

Definition—The word "measure" as used herein includes any bill, law, resolution, ordinance, charter, constitutional amendment or legislative proposal or enactment of any character.

This provision establishes the broadest possible application.

No Veto—The veto power of the Governor or Mayor shall not extend to measures initiated by or referred to the people.

This provision establishes the priority of initiated statutes over regular legislative statutes.

Amendment and Repeal—No measure approved by a vote of the people shall be amended or repealed by the General Assembly or by any City Council, except upon a yea and nay vote on roll call of two-thirds of all the members elected to each house of the General Assembly, or of the City Council, as the case may be.

Any initiated act can be amended or repealed by a two-thirds vote of both houses of the General Assembly, a city council, or a county quorum court (Townsend v. Helena, 1968).

Election—All measures initiated by the people, whether for the State, county, city or town, shall be submitted only at the regular elections, either State, congressional or municipal, but referendum petitions may be referred to the people at special elections to be called by the proper official, and such special elections shall be called when fifteen per cent of the legal voters shall petition for such special election, and if the referendum is invoked as to any measure passed by a city or town council, such city or town council may offer a special election.

This provision gives higher priority to the protest referendum over the proposed initiative, thus providing more timely relief to an unpopular act.

Majority—Any measure submitted to the people as herein provided shall take effect and become a law when approved by a majority of the votes cast upon such measure, and not otherwise, and shall not be required to receive a majority of the electors voting at such elections. Such measures shall be operative on and after the 30th day after the election at which it is approved, unless otherwise specified in the act.

This section shall not be construed to deprive any member of the General Assembly of the right to introduce any measure, but no measure shall be submitted to the people by the General Assembly, except a proposed constitutional amendment or amendments as provided for in this Constitution.

This provision provides an effective date for an amendment to become law and states that such an amendment becomes law when approved by a majority of the votes cast.

Canvass and Declaration of Results—The results of the vote upon any State measure shall be canvassed and declared by the State Board of Election Commissioners (or legal substitute therefor); upon a municipal or county measure, by the County Election Commissioners (or legal substitute therefor).

The same procedure is used for this as for other election results.

Conflicting Measures—If conflicting measures initiated or referred to the people shall be approved by a majority of the votes severally cast for and against the same at the same election, the one receiving the highest number of affirmative votes shall become law.

This provision has never been used, but it is designed to prevent any possible confusion in case of the conflict of laws that are initiated in any election.

The Petition

Title—At the time of filing the petitions, the exact title to be used on the ballot shall by the petitioner be submitted with the petition, and on statewide measures, shall be submitted to the State Board of Election Commissioners, who shall certify such title to the Secretary of State, to be placed upon the ballot; on county and municipal measures such title shall be submitted to the County Election Board and shall by said board be placed upon the ballot in such county or municipal election.

The ballot title, if submitted with the petitions to the appropriate authority, may be used if it fairly alleges the general purpose of the act. This does not apply to legislative proposals of constitutional amendments.

Limitation—No limitation shall be placed upon the number of constitutional amendments, laws or other measures which may be proposed and submitted to the people by either initiative or referendum petition as provided in this section. No petition shall be held invalid if it shall contain a greater number of signatures than required herein.

This contrasts to the limit of three amendments that can be submitted by the General Assembly at each regular, biennial legislative session.

Verification—Only legal voters shall be counted upon petitions. Petitions may be circulated and presented in parts, but each part of any petition shall have attached thereto the affidavit of the person circulating the same, that all signatures thereon were made in the presence of the affiant, and that to the best of the affiant's knowledge and belief each signature is genuine, and that the person signing is a legal voter, and no other affidavit or verification shall be required to establish the genuineness of such signatures.

The verification process that has developed over the years includes county clerks providing the secretary of state with lists of registered voters.

Sufficiency—The sufficiency of all State-wide petitions shall be decided in the first instance by the Secretary of State, subject to review by the Supreme Court of the State, which shall have original and exclusive jurisdiction over all such causes. The sufficiency of all local petitions shall be decided in the first instance by the county clerk or the city clerk, as the case may be, subject to review by the Chancery Court.

The secretary of state usually hires college students as counters every summer prior to general elections for this purpose. They count and verify signatures to determine whether a sufficient number of valid signatures of qualified voters has been secured in order to certify a proposed constitutional amendment or statutory act for inclusion on the ballot.

After sponsors of an initiative or referendum have been notified by the city clerk that the petition is insufficient, they have ten days within which to correct or amend the petition. Any appeal from the decision of the clerk shall be taken to chancery court (Bradley v. Galloway, 1983).

When an initiated petition consists of several parts, all the parts constitute one petition and must be considered together (Czech v. Baer, 1984). The statute providing that the minimum number of signatures required on a referendum petition should be computed on the basis of the highest vote cast for a city director at the preceding general election is not a violation of the amendment (Czech v. Munson, 1984).

Court Decisions—If the sufficiency of any petition is challenged such cause shall be a preference cause and shall be tried at once, but the failure of the courts to decide prior to the election as to the sufficiency of any such petition shall not prevent the question from being placed upon the ballot at the election named in such petition, nor militate against the validity of such measure, if it shall have been approved by a vote of the people.

The state supreme court cannot enjoin the secretary of state from acting on the sufficiency of signatures on petitions because until the secretary of state certifies the signatures, the supreme court has nothing to review (Rambo v. Hall, 1938).

The amendment did not vest any original jurisdiction in the supreme court in proceedings relating to anything except initiated legislation with a statewide effect or a reference to acts of the General Assembly (American Party v. Brandon, 1972). The supreme court was found to have no authority to decide an original action questioning the ballot title of an initiated act until the petitions are submitted to the secretary of state, who was to declare them sufficient or insufficient (Scott v. McCuen, 1986).

> **Amendment of Petition**—If the Secretary of State, county clerk or city clerk, as the case may be, shall decide any petition to be insufficient, he shall without delay notify the sponsors of such petition, and permit at least thirty days from the date of such notification, in the instance of a State-wide petition, or ten days in the instance of a municipal or county petition, for correction or amendment. In the event of legal proceedings to prevent giving legal effect to any petition upon any grounds, the burden of proof shall be upon the person or persons attacking the validity of the petition.

The secretary of state cannot grant additional time, beyond thirty days from notification, for the correction or amendment of petitions (Wait v. Hall, 1938).

> **Unwarranted Restrictions Prohibited**—No law shall be passed to prohibit any person or persons from giving or receiving compensation for circulating petition, not in any manner interfering with the freedom of the people in procuring petitions; but laws shall be enacted prohibiting and penalizing perjury, forgery and all other felonies or other fraudulent practices in the securing of signatures or filing of petitions.

Circulators are often compensated by sponsoring organizations and interest groups on the basis of the number of signatures obtained.

> **Publication**—All measures submitted to a vote of the people by petition under the provisions of this section shall be published as is now, or hereafter may be provided by law.

This publication requirement is similar to that for other enactments by the legislature, quorum courts, and city councils.

> **Enacting Clause**—The style of all the bills initiated and submitted under the provisions of this section shall be, "Be It Enacted by the People of the State of Arkansas" (municipality, or county as the case may be). In submitting measures to the people, the Secretary of State and all other officials shall be guided by the general election laws or municipal laws, as the case may be, until additional legislation is provided therefor.

The enacting clause provided in the amendment refers only to statutes initiated by the people and does not repeal Article 5, Section 19, which provides the style for legislative bills (Jackson v. State, 1912). If a proposed act does not include a proper enacting clause, the petitions will be declared invalid (Hailey v. Carter, 1952).

> **Self-Executing**—The section shall be self-executing, and all its provisions shall be treated as mandatory, but laws may be enacted to facilitate its operation. No legislation shall be enacted to restrict, hamper or impair the exercise of the rights herein reserved to the people.

This amendment does not require implementing legislation.

AMENDMENT 8: EQUAL SUFFRAGE

Every citizen of the United States of the age of twenty-one years, who has resided in the State twelve months, in the county six months, and in the precinct, town or ward one month, next preceding any election at which they may propose to vote, except such persons as may have committed some felony be deprived of the right to vote by law passed by the General Assembly and who shall exhibit a poll tax receipt or other evidence that they have paid their poll tax at the time of collecting taxes next preceding such election, shall be allowed to vote at any election in the State of Arkansas; provided, that persons who make satisfactory proof they have attained the age of twenty-one years since the time of assessing taxes next preceding said election and possess the other necessary qualifications, shall be permitted to vote; and, provided further, that the said tax receipt shall be so marked by dated stamp or written endorsement by judges of election to whom it may be first presented as to prevent the holder thereof from voting more than once at any election. It is declared to be the purpose of this amendment to deny the right of suffrage to aliens and it is declared to be the purpose of this amendment to confer suffrage equally upon both men and women, without regard to sex. Provided, that women shall not be compelled to serve on juries.

This amends Article 3, Section 1. It was proposed in the 1919 legislative session and voted on at the general election of 1920. It was declared to be in force by the attorney general (Brickhouse v. Hill, 1925; Combs v. Gray, 1926). The poll tax requirement of this amendment was repealed by Amendment 51, Section 17.

AMENDMENT 9: STATE SUPREME COURT

This amendment was proposed by the General Assembly at the 1923 session (*see Acts 1923*, p. 796) and approved at the general election of October 7, 1924. It was declared adopted in Brickhouse v. Hill, 1925.

SECTION 1

The Supreme Court shall be composed of five judges, one of whom shall be styled Chief Justice and elected as such, any three of whom shall constitute a quorum, and the concurrence of at least three judges shall in every case be necessary to a decision. Provided, if it should hereafter become necessary to increase the number of judges of the Supreme Court, the Legislature may provide for two additional judges and may also provide for the court sitting in divisions under such regulations as may be prescribed by law; provided, further, that should the court sit in divisions, in all cases where the construction of the Constitution is involved, the cause shall be heard by the court in banc, and in all cases when a judge of a division dissents from the opinion therein, at the request of the Chief Justice, or such dissenting justice, the cause shall be transferred to the court in banc for its decision.

This provision, enlarging the state supreme court, supersedes Article 7, Sections 2 and 3. Act 205 of 1925, Section 1, increased the number of supreme court judges to seven. This section is cited in Citizens Bank v. Estate of Pettyjohn, 1984.

SECTION 2

The Supreme Court judges shall at stated times receive compensations for their services to be fixed by law. When the salary of the judges under this amendment to the Constitution shall have been established by law, such salary shall not thereafter be increased or diminished during their respective terms. Until otherwise provided by law, the judges of the Supreme Court shall each receive a salary of seven thousand five hundred dollars per annum.

This section is superseded by Amendment 43.

AMENDMENT 10: LOCAL BOND ISSUES FOR DEBTS ONLY

The fiscal affairs of counties, cities and incorporated towns shall be conducted on a sound financial basis, and no county court or levying board of agent of any county shall make or authorize any contract or make any allowance for any purpose whatsoever in excess of the revenue from all sources for the fiscal year in which said contract or allowance is made; nor shall any county judge, county clerk or other county officer, sign or issue any scrip, warrant or other certificate of indebtedness in excess of the revenue from all sources for the current fiscal year.

Provided, however, to secure funds to pay indebtedness outstanding at the time of the adoption of this amendment, counties, cities, and incorporated towns may issue interest-bearing certificates of indebtedness or bonds with interest coupons for the payment of which a county or city tax in addition to that now authorized, not exceeding three mills, may believed for the time as provided by law until such indebtedness is paid.

Where the annual report of any city or county in the State of Arkansas shows that scrip, warrants or other certificates of indebtedness had been issued in excess of the total revenue for that year, the officers of the county or city or incorporated town who authorized, signed or issued such scrip, warrants or other certificates of indebtedness shall be deemed guilty of a misdemeanor and upon conviction thereof, shall be fined in any. sum not less than five hundred dollars nor more than ten thousand dollars, and shall be removed from office.

This amended Article 12, Section 4. It was proposed by the General Assembly at the 1923 regular session and voted on at the general election on October 7, 1924. The amendment was declared adopted in Brickhouse v. Hill, 1925. This amendment, limiting legislative and taxing power, should be read in conjunction with Amendment 13, which prohibits state and local governments from lending credit, and Amendment 49, which provides localities with the option of issuing industrial development bonds to encourage new industry.

AMENDMENT 11: EIGHTEEN-MILL DISTRICT SCHOOL TAX

The General Assembly shall provide by the general laws for the support of common schools by taxes, which shall never exceed in any one year three mills on the dollar on the taxable property in the State, and by an annual per capita tax of one dollar, to be assessed on every male inhabitant of this State over the age of twenty-one years. Provided, that the General Assembly may, by general law, authorize school districts to levy by a vote of the qualified electors of such districts a tax not to exceed eighteen mills on the dollar in any one year for the maintenance of schools, the erection and equipment of school buildings and the retirement of existing indebtedness for buildings.

Provided, further, that no such tax shall be appropriated for any other purpose nor to any other district than that for which it is levied.

This amended Article 14, Section 3. It was proposed by the General Assembly at the 1925 regular session and was adopted at the general election on October 5, 1926. Article 14, Section 3, as amended by Amendment 11, was further amended by Amendment 40 (Arkansas State Highway Commission v. Coffelt, 1990).

AMENDMENT 12: COTTON MILLS TAX EXEMPT FOR SEVEN YEARS

All capital invested in a textile mill in this State for the manufacture of cotton and fiber goods in any manner shall be and is hereby declared to be exempt from taxation for a period of seven years from the date of the location of said textile mill.

This amendment was proposed by the General Assembly at the 1925 regular session and adopted at the general election on October 5, 1926. This amendment represents one of the state's first industrial development initiatives. It has been interpreted broadly to include limited-life unwoven products produced from rayon and polyester fibers and designed for single usage as disposable diapers as fiber goods that are entitled to this exemption (Casey v. Scott Paper Co., 1981).

AMENDMENT 13: MUNICIPAL IMPROVEMENT BONDS

Neither the State nor any city, county, town or other municipality in this State, shall ever lend its credit for any purpose whatever; nor shall any county, city, town or municipality ever issue any interest-bearing evidences of indebtedness, except such bonds as may be authorized by law to provide for and secure the payment of the indebtedness existing at the time of the adoption of the Constitution of 1874, and the State shall never issue any interest-bearing treasury warrants or scrip.

Provided, that cities of the first and second class may issue by and with the consent of the majority of the qualified electors of said municipality voting on the question at an election held for the purpose, bonds in sums and for the purpose approved by such majority at such election as follows:

> For the payment of any indebtedness existing at the time of the adoption of this amendment for the purpose of rights of way for construction of public streets, alleys, and boulevards within the corporate limits of such municipality; for the construction of, widening or straightening of streets, alleys and boulevards within the corporate limits of such municipality; for the purchase, development and improvement of public parks and flying fields located either within or without the corporate limits of such municipality; for the construction of sewers and comfort stations; for the purchase of fire fighting apparatus and fire alarm systems; for the purchase of street cleaning apparatus; for the purchase of sites for, construction of, and equipment of city halls, auditoriums, prisons, libraries, hospitals, public abattoirs, incinerators or garbage disposal plants; for buildings for the housing of fire fighting apparatus; for the construction of viaducts and bridges; and for the purpose of purchasing, extending, improving, enlarging, building, or construction of water works or light plants, and distributing systems therefor.

No bonds issued under the authority of this amendment shall bear a greater rate of interest than six per cent per annum payable either annually or semiannually; that is to say, the cost to the municipality for interest and discount, on each issue of bonds shall not exceed six per cent per annum, and no bonds issued under the authority of this amendment shall ever be sold except at public sale after twenty days' advertisement in some newspaper having a bona fide circulation in the municipality issuing such bonds.

In order to provide for the payment of the bonds issued under the provisions of this amendment, and interest thereof, a special tax not to exceed five mills be levied by municipalities on the real and personal taxable property therein. And any municipality issuing any bonds, shall before or at the time of doing so, levy a direct tax payable annually not exceeding the amount limited as above, sufficient to pay the interest on such bonds as the same matures, and also sufficient to pay and discharge the principal of all such bonds at their respective maturities; provided, that the above limitations of the rate of taxation shall not apply to bonds issued by any municipality for the purpose of acquiring, purchasing, extending, improving, enlarging, building or construction of water works and light plants, but the levy of the special tax of five mills authorized by this amendment having been exhausted, or the balance unlevied being insufficient to pay interest on and retire the proposed bonds, said municipality for the purpose of paying the principal and interest of such water works and light plant bonds, may, as far as required, levy and collect a special tax, in addition to the rate allowed by this amendment of not to exceed five mills on the dollar.

Said bonds shall be serial, maturing annually after three years from date of issue, and shall be paid off as they mature, and no bonds issued under the authority of this amendment shall be issued for a longer period than thirty-five years.

No municipality shall ever grant financial aid toward the construction of railroads or other private enterprises operated by any person, firm or corporation, and no money raised under the provisions of this amendment by taxation or by sale of bonds for a specific purpose shall ever be used for any other or different purpose.

It shall be the duty of the mayor and city council or other governing body established by law, to exercise supervision over the sale of any bonds, which may be voted by the people at an election held for that purpose and they shall expend economically the funds so provided for the specified purpose for which they were voted.

Said election shall be held at such times as the city council may designate by ordinance, which ordinance shall specifically state the purpose for which the bonds are to be issued, and if for more than one purpose, provisions shall be made in said ordinance for balloting on each separate purpose; which ordinance shall state the sum total of the issue, the date of maturity thereof and shall fix the date of election so that it shall not occur earlier than thirty days after the passage of said ordinance. Said election shall be held and conducted, and the vote thereof canvassed, and the result thereof declared under the law and in the manner now or hereafter provided for municipal elections, so far as the same may be applicable, except as herein otherwise provided. Notice of said election shall be given by the mayor by advertisement weekly for at least four times, in some newspaper published in said municipality and having a bona fide circulation therein; the last publication to be not less than ten days prior to the date of said election.

Qualified voters of said municipality only shall have a right to vote at said election. The result of said election shall be proclaimed by the mayor and the result as proclaimed shall be conclusive unless attacked in the courts within thirty days after the date of such proclamation. This amendment shall not repeal or affect any law relating to the organization of improvement districts.

This amendment shall be in force upon its adoption, and shall not require legislative action to put it into force and effect.

All provisions of this amendment shall be treated as mandatory, and all provisions of the Constitution or amendments thereto in conflict herewith are hereby repealed.

This amended Article 16, Section 1, and was itself repealed by Amendment 62, Section 11.

AMENDMENT 14: LOCAL ACTS BY LEGISLATURE PROHIBITED

The General Assembly shall not pass any local or special act. This amendment shall not prohibit the repeal of local or special acts.

This amendment was proposed by an initiative petition filed in the office of the secretary of state on May 28, 1926 (see Acts 1927, p. 1215). It was approved at the general election on October 5, 1926, and supersedes Article 5, Sections 24 through 26. This amendment prohibits the general assembly from passing local or special acts if they arbitrarily separate some person, place, or thing from those on which, except for such separation, it would operate, such as an act that applies to any division or subdivision of the state that is less than the whole (Board of Trustees v. City of Little Rock, 1988; Owen v. Dalton, 1988).

The legislature's statement that an act is general in application does not bound a court; rather, the court will look to the operation and effect of the legislation, and if that operation and effect is necessarily local, then the act is local, regardless of its form. On the other hand, if the legislature is to decide whether an act is local or special legislation, then this amendment serves no purpose and might just as well have not been adopted (Owen v. Dalton, 1988). Although a statute may ultimately affect less than all the state's territory, that does not necessarily render it local or special (City of Little Rock v. Waters, 1990).

Classification among geographical or political subdivisions is permitted if the General Assembly could have had a rational basis for it, and the fact that the classification includes only one city does not necessarily mean that it is local in the constitutional sense (Board of Trustees v. City of Little Rock, 1990). If the classifications are such that the legislation applies only to political subdivisions of a certain population, the legislation is local if the specific population has nothing to do with the subject matter of the law (Owen v. Dalton, 1988).

Statutes establishing or abolishing separate courts are not violative of this amendment since they relate to the administration of justice and are neither local nor special. Statutes designed to meet the judicial needs of an area on a nondiscriminatory basis are a part of a judicial system for the entire state and are not local or special within the meaning of this amendment, even though such statutes may apply only to individual counties, judicial districts, or divisions within districts (Littleton v. Blanton, 1984).

AMENDMENT 15: SALARIES OF STATE OFFICIALS

That the annual salaries of the State and District officers hereinafter mentioned, which shall be paid in monthly installments, shall be as follows:

For Govemor, the sum of $6,000; for Secretary of State, the sum of $4,000; for Treasurer of the State, the sum of $4,000; for Auditor of the State, the sum of $4,000;

for Attorney General, the sum of $5,000; for Judge of the Circuit Courts and Chancellors; each the sum of $3,600.

This amendment was proposed by the General Assembly at the 1927 regular session and was approved at the general election on November 6, 1928. It was superseded by Amendment 37 (Berry v. Gordon, 1964; also, Amendment 56).

AMENDMENT 16: TRIAL BY JURY

The right of trial by jury shall remain inviolate, and shall extend to all cases at law, without regard to the amount in controversy; but a jury trial may be waived by the parties in all cases in the manner prescribed by law; and in jury trials in civil cases, where as many as nine of the jurors agree upon a verdict, the verdict so agreed upon shall be returned as the verdict of such jury; provided, however, that where a verdict is returned by less than twelve jurors all the jurors consenting to such verdict shall sign the same.

This amendment to the Constitution of Arkansas shall be self-executing and requires no enabling act, but shall take and have full force and effect immediately upon its adoption by the electors of the State.

This amended Article 2, Section 7. It was proposed by the General Assembly at the 1927 regular session and adopted at the general election on November 6, 1928. This amendment prevents the legislature from giving the state claims commission exclusive jurisdiction of tort claims against state employees or officers for their unlawful acts (Grimmett v. Digby, 1979). The constitutional right to trial by jury does not secure the right in all possible instances because it extends only to the trial of issues of fact in civil and criminal causes (Jones v. Reed, 1979). A party is not entitled to trial by jury in contempt proceedings (Neel v. State, 1849).

AMENDMENT 17: CONSTRUCTION AND BUILDING TAX

The power and right is hereby vested in the qualified electors of each respective county in this State by a majority of said electors voting on the question, to authorize the construction, reconstruction, or extension of any County Court House, or County Jail, and to authorize the levy of a tax not to exceed one-half of one per cent on the dollar of the valuation of all properties in such county subject to taxation to defray the cost and expenses thereof, or to take up any indebtedness existing at the time of adoption hereof incurred in building, construction or extending any County Court House or Jail.

This amendment was repealed by Amendment 62, Section 11; see also Amendments 25 and 65.

AMENDMENT 18: TAX TO AID INDUSTRIES

It being most apparent that factories, industries and transportation facilities are necessary for the development of a community and for the welfare of its inhabitants, a special tax not exceeding five mills on the dollar of all taxable property in cities of the first class located in counties now or hereafter having not less than one hundred five thousand population, in addition to other taxes now provided by law, may be levied in such cities for the period that may be provided by law, when petitioned for by ten per cent of the owners of real property in such cities and on consent of a majority of the electors of such city voting on the question.

The proceeds of such tax shall be expended by a board of three commissioners, each of whom shall be a taxpayer in such city, said commissioners to serve for such terms as may be provided by law without compensation, except actual expenses. One of the commissioners shall be selected by a majority of the judges of the Supreme Court, sitting as a board, one by a majority of the judges of the Circuit, County and Chancery Courts of the county, sitting as a board, and one by a majority of the banks and trust companies located in such city whose representatives shall sit as a board. Where there are two such cities in such county and the tax herein provided for has been voted in each, one board of commissioners may be appointed for both cities if a majority of the boards having the appointive power deem best, and in that event a majority of the banks and trust companies in both cities shall appoint one commissioner, and the proceeds of the tax shall be expended for the benefit of both cities.

The proceeds of such tax may be expended as may be provided by law for the purpose of securing the location of factories, industries, river transportation and facilities therefor within and adjacent to such cities or other public purposes, exclusive of charities and those now within the powers of said city to perform, and the expenditures may also be made for advertising such cities and the State, or making secured loans to such factories and industries, or for any other public purpose that may be provided by law, connected with securing the location of such factories and industries and encouraging them.

The provisions of this amendment are separable, and if any should be held invalid, the remainder shall stand.

This amendment was proposed by initiative petition and approved at the general election on November 6, 1928. Section 5 of the implementing act was unconstitutional in attempting to strip the board of commissioners of all the authority vested in them by this amendment, to reduce them to no duties except the receipt and deposit the tax proceeds from the county treasurer, and to vest all the powers of the commissioners in the governing body of the city (McDonald v. Bowen, 1971).

The legislature can authorize the electorate to approve a continuing levy to support a long-term bond issue under this section (McDonald v. Bowen, 1971). This amendment does not purport to delegate the power of eminent domain to municipalities for the purpose of acquiring industrial sites or parks (City of Little Rock v. Raines, 1967).

AMENDMENT 19: TAX INCREASE RESTRICTIONS? PASSAGE OF LAWS

This amendment added five sections to Article 5, Sections 37 through 41. The amendment was proposed by the General Assembly at the 1933 regular session and adopted at the general election on November 6, 1934.

That Article 5 of the Constitution of the State of Arkansas be amended by adding thereto the following:

SECTION 37

Not less than a majority of the members of each House of the General Assembly may enact a law.

Majority vote, which is required in this section replaced the occasional quorum vote of the General Assembly with the enactment of a statute.

SECTION 38

None of the rates for property, excise, privilege or personal taxes, now levied shall be increased by the General Assembly except after the approval of the qualified electors voting thereon at an election, or in case of emergency, by the vote of three-fourths of the members elected to each House of the General Assembly.

This section has dictated the type of tax system that Arkansas has developed over the last sixty years. Since sales taxes were not then levied, they may be increased by a simple majority and, therefore, have been used extensively to fund all major educational reform initiatives of the last decade, including the funding of the Educational Excellence Trust Fund and the new Quality Standards Act.

SECTION 39

Excepting monies raised or collected for educational purposes, highway purposes, to pay Confederate pensions and the just debts of the State, the General Assembly is hereby prohibited from appropriating or expending more than the sum of Two and One-Half Million Dollars for all purposes, for any biennial period; provided, the limit herein fixed may be exceeded by the votes of three-fourths of the members elected to each house of the General Assembly.

Most appropriation bills require a three-fourths majority vote for passage. For example, an appropriation to support college senior classes in pharmaceutical education from the general fund was ruled to require a three-fourths majority (Humphrey v. Garrett, 1951).

SECTION 40

> In making appropriations for any biennial period, the General Assembly shall first pass the General Appropriation Bill provided for in Section 30 of Article 5 of the Constitution and no other appropriation bill may be enacted before that shall have been done.

These provisions, taken together, provide Arkansas, among all the states, with the most difficult procedures for increasing taxes and appropriating funds.

SECTION 41

> No expense shall be incurred or authorized for either House except by a bill duly passed by both Houses and approved by the Governor.

This section requires line-item appropriations and authorizes a line-item veto by the governor.

> The provisions of the Constitution of the State of Arkansas in conflict with this Amendment are hereby repealed insofar as they are in conflict herewith, and this Amendment shall be self-executing and shall take and have full effect immediately upon its adoption by the electors of the State.

This amendment does not require implementing legislation because it is selfexecuting.

AMENDMENT 20: ISSUANCE OF BONDS

> Except for the purpose of refunding the existing outstanding indebtedness of the State and for assuming and refunding valid outstanding road improvement district bonds, the State of Arkansas shall issue no bonds or other evidence of indebtedness pledging the faith and credit of the State or any of its revenue for any purpose whatsoever, except by and with the consent of the majority of the qualified electors of the State voting on the question at a general election or at a special election called for that purpose.
>
> This Amendment to the Constitution of Arkansas shall be self-executing and require no enabling act, but shall take and have full force and effect immediately upon its adoption by the electors of the State.

This amendment may be superseded by Amendment 65. It was proposed by the General Assembly at the 1933 regular session and was approved at the general election on November 6, 1934. This amendment does not repeal or supersede the initiative and referendum amendment (Matthews v. Bailey, 1939). The pledging of so-called state or public revenues is not prohibited by this amendment unless the pledge is for the payment of state bonds (McCarthur v. Smallwood, 1955).

The provisions of the real property transfer tax, authorizing state agencies to pledge portions of the tax collected for the payment of revenue bonds, violate this section (Borchert v. Scott, 1970). Revenues of school districts are not revenues of the state within the meaning of this section. Funds of the permanent school fund arising from sales of sixteenth section lands, which were set aside in the Land Ordinance of 1787, are revenues of the state and cannot be pledged as security for the payment of bonds (State ex rel. Attorney General v. State Board of Education, 1937).

While permanent school funds may be loaned so that interest will accrue, they may not be borrowed upon for the repayment (Walls v. State Board of Education, 1938). Act 280 of 1985, relating to water resource development, is unconstitutional as it violates this amendment (Reeves v. Young, 1988).

AMENDMENT 21: CRIMINAL PROSECUTIONS-SALARIES OF PROSECUTING ATTORNEYS

This amendment was proposed by the General Assembly at the 1935 session and adopted by popular vote at the general election on November 3, 1936.

SECTION 1

All offenses heretofore required to be prosecuted by indictment may be prosecuted either by indictment by a grand jury or information filed by the Prosecuting Attorney.

As long as its adoption was valid, a state constitutional amendment serves as the state constitution with regard to the subject matter it addresses (Guinn v. State, 1989). In one related case, a trial judge was held to have encroached on the prosecutor's constitutional duties and breached the separation of powers doctrine when he amended a charge from a felony to a misdemeanor over the state's objection, because the duty of charging an accused with a felony is reserved either to the grand jury or the prosecutor (State v. Brooks, 1990).

Acts of the grand jury are not binding on the prosecuting attorney (Orsini v. State, 1985). A circuit judge does not have the inherent right to appoint a special prosecutor if the incumbent is in office, unless he or she is being investigated for illegal activity (Venhaus v. Brown, 1985).

SECTION 2

The General Assembly of Arkansas shall by law determine the amount and method of payment of salaries of prosecuting attorneys.

This section may supersede Article 19, Section 23, with respect to salaries of prosecuting attorneys, which are paid for by the state even though the prosecutors are elected locally.

AMENDMENT 22: EXEMPTION OF HOMESTEADS FROM CERTAIN STATE TAXES

This amendment was adopted by popular vote at the general election on November 3, 1936.

SECTION 1

The homestead of each and every resident of the State, whether or not such resident be married or unmarried, male or female, shall be wholly exempt from all State taxes authorized or referred to in Section 8 of Article XVI of the Constitution of Arkansas in all cases where such homestead does not exceed the assessed valuation of One Thousand Dollars ($1,000.00). Where the assessed valuation of such homestead exceeds One Thousand Dollars ($1,000.00), this exemption shall apply to the first One thousand Dollars ($1,000.00) of such valuation.

This popular provision, which is administered by the revenue commissioner, is a political and legal takeoff on the old saying, "A man's home is his castle." This section refers exclusively to a property tax and does not prevent the selection of other objects of taxation or fixing of the rate (Baker v. Hill, 1929).

SECTION 2

Within a maximum limit of Two Thousand Five Hundred Dollars ($2,500.00) and a minimum limit of One Thousand Dollars ($1,000.00), the legislature is hereby authorized and empowered from time to time to fix the amount of the exemption hereby provided.

This section further establishes the legislature's premier position of power in the area of homestead exemptions.

SECTION 3

Within a maximum limit of Two Thousand Five Hundred Dollars ($2,500.00) and a minimum limit of One Thousand Dollars ($1,000.00), the legislature is hereby authorized and empowered from time to time to fix the amount of the exemption hereby provided.

(a) Fully and completely to replace or restore any and all funds which will or may be eliminated, diminished or otherwise affected hereby or here-under; but the legislature shall not, in order to accomplish that purpose, impose or levy any new form of tax;

In funding any revenue losses, legislators may not enact new taxes. This reflects the antitax spirit which was prevalent in Arkansas at that time.

(b) To enact, without unnecessary delay, all legislation necessary and sufficient to make this amendment in all respects effective and workable.

No delays were permitted in the implementation phase.

SECTION 4

Nothing herein shall ever be construed, applied or administered so as to impair any right of any holder of any bond, note or other obligation heretofore issued or assumed by the State and now outstanding; but this amendment shall in every respect be construed, applied and administered so as fully to protect all the legal rights of all such holders.

This section was added to protect banks and mortgage lenders from careless debtors who would seek to use this amendment to avoid paying off loans to state-chartered financial institutions.

SECTION 5

After and as soon as, and not before, the legislature shall have fulfilled the requirements of section three hereof, this amendment or any legislation enacted in pursuance of section 2, shall be in full force and effect.

This section provides the schedule for establishing the homestead exemption in order that one will always exist, no matter what the action taken by the legislature.

AMENDMENT 23: THE BOARD OF APPORTIONMENT

This amendment superseded Article 8. It was adopted at the general election held on November 3, 1936. Article 8, as amended by this amendment, was subsequently amended again by Amendment 45.

SECTION 1

A Board to be known as "The Board of Apportionment," consisting of the Governor (who shall be chairman), the Secretary of State and the Attorney General, is hereby created and it shall be its imperative duty to make apportionment of representatives and senators in accordance with the provisions hereof; the action of a majority in each instance shall be deemed the action of said Board.

This section establishes the authority for legislative reapportionment in the executive branch.

SECTION 2

The House of Representatives shall consist of one hundred members and each county existing at the time of any apportionment shall have at least one representative; the remaining members shall be equally distributed (as nearly as practicable) among the more populous counties of the State, in accordance with ratio to be determined by the population of said counties as shown by the Federal census next preceding any apportionment hereunder.

This section has been declared unconstitutional, falling far short of the "one man, one vote" test of Yancey v. Faubus, 1965; and Wells v. White, 1981. Multimember districts can be constitutional (Kelly v. Bumpers, 1962).

SECTION 3

The Senate shall consist of thirty-five members. Senatorial districts shall at all times consist of contiguous territory, and no county shall be divided in the formation of such districts. "The Board of Apportionment" hereby created shall, from time to time, divide the State into convenient senatorial districts in such manner as that the Senate shall be based upon the inhabitants of the State, each Senator representing, as nearly as practicable, an equal number thereof; each district shall have at least one Senator.

Providing that counties cannot be divided for senatorial districts is unconstitutional, since senators must represent people and not counties (Wells v. White, 1981). Reapportionment should be done only when there is a change in population (Bailey v. Abington, 1921).

SECTION 4

The Board shall make the first apportionment hereunder within ninety days from January 1, 1937, thereafter, on or before February 1 immediately following each Federal census, said Board shall reapportion the State for both Representatives and Senators, and in each instance said Board shall file its report with the Secretary of State, setting forth:

(a) the basis of population adopted for representatives; (b) the basis for senators; (c) the number of representatives assigned each county; (d) the counties comprising each senatorial district and the number of Senators assigned to each, whereupon, after thirty days from such filing date, the apportionment thus made shall become effective unless proceedings for revision be instituted in the Supreme Court within said period.

The format of the board documents is set in this section.

SECTION 5

Original jurisdiction (to be exercised on application of any citizen and taxpayer) is hereby vested in the Supreme Court of the State: (a) to compel by mandamus or otherwise the Board to perform its duties as here directed, and (b) to revise any arbitrary action of or abuse of discretion by the Board in making any such apportionment; provided, any such application for revision shall be filed with said Court within thirty days after the filing of the report of apportionment by said Board with the Secretary of State, if revised by the Court, a certified copy of its judgment shall be by the clerk forthwith transmitted to the Secretary of State, and thereupon be and become a substitute for the apportionment made by the Board.

The state supreme court has original and exclusive jurisdiction and monitors the entire process oflegislative apportionment and reapportionment (Rockefeller v. Smith, 1969).

SECTION 6

At the next general election for State and County officers ensuing after any such apportionment, senators and representatives shall be elected in accordance therewith and their respective terms of office shall begin on January 1 next following. At the first regular session succeeding any apportionment so made, the Senate shall be divided into two classes by lot, eighteen of whom shall serve for a period of two years and the remaining seventeen for four years, after which all shall be elected for four years until the next reapportionment hereunder.

This section provides for a staggering of senate terms so that only half the Senate will be up for election at each general election.

■ AMENDMENT 24: PROBATE COURTS

This amended Article 7, Sections 19, 34, and 35. It was proposed by the General Assembly at the regular session of 1937 and was adopted at the general election on November 8, 1938.

ARTICLE VII, SECTION 34

In each county the Judge of the court having jurisdiction in matters of equity shall be judge of the court of probate, and have such exclusive original jurisdiction in matters relative to the probate of wills, the estates of deceased person, executors, administrators, guardians, and persons of unsound mind and their estates, as is now vested in courts of probate, or may be hereafter prescribed by law. The judge of the probate court shall try all issues of the law and of facts arising in causes or proceedings within the jurisdiction of said court, and therein pending. The regular terms of the courts of probate shall be held at such times as is now or may hereafter be prescribed by law; and the General Assembly may provide for the consolidation of chancery and probate courts.

Consolidating the jurisdiction of the probate court with the chancery court was held not to substitute the circuit clerk for the county clerk as clerk of the probate court (Lewis v. Smith, 1939).

ARTICLE VII, SECTION 35

Appeals may be taken from judgments and orders of the courts of probate to the Supreme Court; and until otherwise provided by the General Assembly, shall be taken in the same manner as appeals from courts of chancery and subject to the same regulations and restrictions.

This section establishes the appellate jurisdiction from the chancery courts and provides that appeals may be de novo (Campbell v. Hammond, 1941).

ARTICLE VII, SECTION 19

The clerks of the circuit courts shall be elected by the qualified electors of the several counties for the term of two years, and shall be ex-officio clerks of the county and probate courts and recorder; provided, that in any county having a population exceeding fifteen thousand inhabitants, as shown by the last Federal census, there shall be elected a county clerk, in like manner as the clerk of the circuit court, and in such case the county clerk shall be ex-officio clerk of the probate court of such county until otherwise provided by the General Assembly.

Circuit clerks originally served as clerks for the chancery courts as well as for the circuit courts.

▪ AMENDMENT 25: COUNTY CONSTRUCTION TAX

Amendment No. 17, Section 1

The power and right is hereby vested in the qualified electors of each respective County in this State by a majority of the said electors voting on the question, to authorize the construction, reconstruction, or extension of any County Court House, County Jail, or County Hospital, and to authorize the levy of a tax not to exceed one-half of one percent on the dollar of the valuation of all properties in such County subject to taxation to defray the cost and expenses thereof, or to take up any indebtedness existing at the time of adoption hereof incurred in building, construction or extending any County Court House, Jail, or Hospital.

Capital improvements for counties, such as courthouses, jails, and hospitals, can be provided only by popular vote. This amendment, which amended Article 17, was repealed by Amendment 62, Section 11.

AMENDMENT 26; WORKMENS' COMPENSATION

ARTICLE V, SECTION 32

The General Assembly shall have power to enact laws prescribing the amount of compensation to be paid by employers for injuries to or death of employees, and to whom said payment shall be made. It shall have power to provide the means, methods, and forum for adjudicating claims arising under said laws, and for securing payment of same. Provided, that otherwise no law shall be enacted limiting the amount to be recovered for injuries resulting in death or for injuries to persons or property; and in case of death from such injuries the right of action shall survive, and the General Assembly shall prescribe for whose benefit such action shall be prosecuted.

This amended Article 5, Section 32. It was proposed by initiative petition and was adopted at the general election on November 8, 1938. The legislature may limit the amount of recovery only in cases where an employer-employee relationship existed (Baldwin v. Maner, 1954).

AMENDMENT 27: INDUSTRY TAX EXEMPTION

The Governor and the Agricultural and Industrial Commission (or the agency created by law to assist in the industrial development of Arkansas) may investigate and contract with the owners of any new manufacturing or processing establishment to be located in the State, or owners making addition or additions to any manufacturing or processing establishment already located in the State, for the exemption from State property taxation of any such new manufacturing or processing establishment, upon such terms and conditions as the Governor and the said Commission may deem to the best interest of the State; provided, that no exemption from taxes shall be granted under this amendment for a longer period than ten (10) calendar years succeeding the date of any such contract. Any such exemption shall "ipso facto" cease upon violation of the terms and conditions of any contract hereby made.

This amendment was proposed by initiative petition and approved at the general election on November 8, 1938. This was the state's first effort at encouraging new industrial locations by offering tax concessions. Cited in Holbert v. Helena-West Helena Industrial Development Corporation, 1956.

AMENDMENT 28: RULES FOR LAW PRACTICE

> The Supreme Court shall make rules regulating the practice of law and the professional conduct of attorneys at law.

This amendment was proposed by initiative petition and approved at the general election on November 8, 1938, with the leadership from the Arkansas Bar Association. The court has power to disbar an attorney in order to protect the courts and the public and to maintain the honor of the profession (Hurst v. Bar Rules Committee, 1941). This amendment grants the supreme court the exclusive power to regulate the practice of law and the professional conduct of attorneys. Thus, the right to decide whether an attorney who regularly practices before a court can be appointed to represent an indigent in a criminal case is a judicial question, not a legislative one. Consequently, the legislature invaded the province of the judicial branch of government in declaring that certain attorneys could not be appointed as counsel in a criminal case (Ball v. Roberts, 1987).

The Arkansas Supreme Court is affirmatively charged with the duty of making and, by implication, enforcing rules governing the practice of law and the conduct of lawyers (Sexton v. Arkansas Supreme Court Commission on Professional Conduct, 1989). It was ruled that the Supreme Court Committee on Professional Conduct did not exceed its proper function or become a court in its own right by suspending an attorney's license (Sexton v. Arkansas Supreme Court Commission on Professional Conduct, 1989).

AMENDMENT 29: VACANCIES

This amendment was proposed by initiative petition and approved at the general election on November 8, 1938.

SECTION 1

> Vacancies in the office of United States Senator, and in all elective state, district, circuit, county, and township office except those of Lieutenant Governor, Member of the General Assembly and Representative in the Congress of the United States, shall be filled by appointment by the Governor.

This section supersedes Article 7, Section 50, with respect to judicial officers other than municipal court officers, but does not supersede that section with respect to municipal courts. See Johnson County Board of Election Commissioners v. Holman, 1983. These vacancies are caused by death, resignation, removal, or abandonment of office (Justice v. Campbell, 1967).

SECTION 2

The Governor, Lieutenant Governor and Acting Governor shall be ineligible for appointment to fill any vacancies occurring or any office or position created, and resignation shall not remove such ineligibility. Husbands and wives of such officers, and relatives of such officers, or of their husbands and wives within the fourth degree of consanguinity or affinity, shall likewise be ineligible. No person appointed under Section 1 shall be eligible to appointment or election to succeed himself.

This section prohibits nepotism and attempts to prevent appointees from profiting politically from their appointments. Elaborate schemes have been devised to improve those political prospects and at the same time to come within this law. Spouses, for example, often run to succeed appointees, after which the ex-appointee, who may essentially run the office while the spouse is appointed, can run to succeed the spouse.

SECTION 3

No person holding office contrary to this amendment shall be paid any compensation for his services. Any warrant, voucher or evidence of indebtedness issued in payment for such services shall be void.

The enforcement of the amendment is by the public and involves no penalty other than the forfeiture of salary.

SECTION 4

The appointee shall serve during the entire unexpired term in the office in which the vacancy occurs if such office would in regular course be filled at the next general election if no vacancy had occurred. If such office would not in regular course be filled at such next general election the vacancy shall be filled as follows: At the next general election, if the vacancy occurs four months or more prior thereto, and at the second general election after the vacancy occurs if the vacancy occurs less than four months before the next general election after it occurs. The person so elected shall take office on the 1st day of January following his election.

When an incumbent resigns, the person appointed by the governor to serve out the preceding term is to serve until a successor can be elected at the next general election (McCraw v. Pate, 1973).

SECTION 5

Only the names of candidates for office nominated by an organized political party at a convention of delegates, or by a majority of all the votes cast for candidates for the office in a primary election, or by petition of electors as provided by law, shall be placed on the ballots in any election.

The legislature is free to allow a convention, primary, or petition by electors for the nomination of candidates. No political party is guaranteed a vested right in any one of the methods of nominating its candidates (Newton County Republican Central Committee v. Clark, 1958). Independent candidates have used only the petition process and Democratic candidates have used only the primary process. Republican candidates have used all the available methods. Neither this section nor Section 7–7-202, which establishes and implements the majorityvote primary runoff requirement, violate the Fourteenth or Fifteenth Amendments of the U.S. Constitution or the federal Voting Rights Act (Whitfield v. Democratic Party, 1988).

AMENDMENT 30: MUNICIPAL LIBRARY TAX

This amendment was proposed by initiative petition and adopted at the general election on November 5, 1940.

SECTION 1

Whenever 100 or more tax paying electors of any city, having a population of not less than 5,000, shall file a petition with the Mayor asking that an annual tax on real and personal property be levied for the purpose of maintaining a public city library and shall specify a rate of taxation not exceeding one mill on the dollar, the question as to whether such tax shall be levied shall be submitted to the qualified electors of such city at a general city election. Such petition must be filed at least thirty days prior to the election at which it will be submitted to the voters. The ballot shall be in substantially the following form:

For a ____________ mill tax on real and personal property to be used for maintenance of a public city library.

Against a ____________ mill tax on real and personal property to be used for maintenance of a public city library.

Cities cannot broaden the list of beneficiaries by municipal ordinance because this amendment only applies to libraries. The Firemen's Relief Pension Fund Act was declared unconstitutional because it attempted to extend coverage to firefighter retirement pay (McLaughlin v. Retherford, 1944).

SECTION 2

The Election Commissioners shall certify to the Mayor the result of the vote, and if a majority of the qualified electors voting on the question at such election vote in favor of specified tax, then it shall thereafter be continually levied and collected as other general taxes of such city are levied and collected. The result of the election shall be proclaimed by the mayor. The result so proclaimed shall be conclusive unless attacked in the courts within thirty days. The proceeds of any tax voted for the maintenance of a city public library shall be segregated by the city officials and used only for that purpose.

Municipalities must establish a separate library account (essentially a library trust fund) with special earmarked revenue.

SECTION 3

Whenever 100 or more tax paying electors of any city having a library tax in force shall file a petition with the Mayor asking that such tax be raised, reduced or abolished, the question shall be submitted to the qualified electors at a general city election. Such petition must be filed at least thirty days prior to the election at which it will be submitted to the voters. The ballot shall follow, as far as practicable, the form set forth in Section 1 hereof. The result shall be certified and proclaimed as provided in Section 2 hereof, and the result as proclaimed shall be conclusive unless attacked in the courts within thirty days. The tax shall be lowered, raised or abolished, as the case may be, according to the majority of the qualified electors voting on the question at such election; provided, however, that it shall not be raised to more than one mill on the dollar. If lowered or raised, the revised tax shall thereafter be continually levied and collected and the proceeds used in the manner and for the purposes as provided for in Section 2 hereof.

Unlike the county road tax, at the time of adoption this tax did not have to be reenacted every two years. Instead, it was to remain in effect until being repealed.

SECTION 4

Nothing herein shall be construed as preventing a coordination of the services of a city public library and a county public library.

Such coordination of library and information services has been increasingly encouraged and implemented throughout the state and has been increasingly made possible through technology such as personal computers, fax machines, and phone lines.

AMENDMENT 31: MUNICIPAL RETIREMENT TAX

This amendment was proposed by initiative petition and adopted at the general election on November 5, 1940.

SECTION 1

After consent of the majority of those voting on the question at any general or special election in cities of the first or second class, the cities may annually thereafter levy a tax on the assessed value of real and personal property, not to exceed two mills on the dollar, from which there shall be created a fund to pay Retirement Salaries and Pensions to policemen and firemen theretofore or thereafter earned, and pensions to the widows and minor children of such, as may be provided by law. The annual levy for the Policemen's Retirement Salary and Pension Funds shall not exceed one mill on the dollar, and the annual levy for the Firemen's Retirement Salary and Pension Fund shall not exceed one mill on the dollar. The manner of such levy of the tax, and the eligibility for the retirement salaries and pensions, the several amounts thereof, and when payable, shall be such as may be provided by laws.

This amendment, which was proposed by an initiative sponsored by the Arkansas Municipal Police Association and the Arkansas Firefighters Association, was patterned somewhat along the lines of the library tax. It allowed up to one mill for firefighter retirement funds and another one mill for police retirement funds to be levied by voters (Wright v. Story, 1989).

AMENDMENT 32: COUNTY OR CITY HOSPITAL TAX

This amendment was proposed by the General Assembly. It was filed in the Office of the Secretary of State on March 27, 1941, and was approved at the general election on November 3, 1942.

SECTION 1

Whenever in any county where there is located a public hospital owned by such county or by any municipal corporation therein, whether such hospital be operated by such county or municipal corporation or by a benevolent association as the agent or lessee of such county or municipal corporation, one hundred or more electors of such county shall file a petition with the county judge asking that an annual tax on real and personal property in such county be levied for the purpose of maintaining, operating and supporting such hospital and shall specify a rate of taxation not exceeding one mill on the dollar of the assessed value of real and personal property in the county. The question as to whether such tax shall be levied shall be submitted to the qualified electors of such county at a general election. Such petition must be filed at least thirty days prior to the election at which it will be submitted to the voters. The county judge upon the filing of such petition shall notify the county board of election commissioners thereof and the county board of election commissioners shall cause the question to be placed upon the ballots in substantially the following form:

FOR a ____________ mill tax on real and personal property to be used for maintenance, operation and support of a public hospital.

AGAINST a ____________ mill tax on real and personal property to be used for maintenance, operation and support of a public hospital.

A maintenance tax can be included in the proposal to acquire a hospital (Gamer V. Lowery, 1953).

SECTION 2

The election commissioners shall certify to the county judge the result of the vote and if a majority of the qualified electors voting on the question at such election vote in favor of the specified tax then it shall thereafter be continually levied and collected as other general taxes of such county are levied and collected. The result of the election shall be proclaimed by the county judge by publication for one insertion in some newspaper published and having bona fide circulation in such county. The result so proclaimed shall be conclusive unless attacked in the courts within thirty days and after the election it shall not be competent to attack the results thereof on the ground that any signers of the petition were not qualified electors. The proceeds of any tax so voted shall upon the settlement of the collecting officer be paid by the treasurer of the county to the treasurer of such hospital to be used by such treasurer in the maintenance, operation and support of such institution; provided that any county where there may be more than one hospital qualified to receive the proceeds of such tax, quorum court at its meeting for the purpose of adopting the county's budget, shall provide for the apportionment of the proceeds of said tax between the institutions so qualified according to their respective needs.

The apportionment of funds is left to local governing boards.

SECTION 3

Whenever one hundred or more electors of any county having a hospital tax in force shall file a petition with the county judge asking that such tax be raised, reduced or abolished, the question shall be submitted to the qualified electors at a general election. Such petition must be filed at least thirty days prior to the election at which it will be submitted to the voters. The Ballots shall follow, as far as practicable, the form set out in Section 1 hereof, and the results shall be certified and proclaimed as provided in Section 2 hereof and shall be conclusive in like manner. The tax shall be lowered, raised or abolished as the case may be, according to the majority qualified electors voting on the question at such election, provided, however, that it shall not be raised to more than one mill on the dollar. If lowered or raised the revised tax shall thereafter be continually levied and collected and the proceeds used in the manner and for the purposes provided in Section 2 hereof.

This provision was included to provide flexibility in case of decreased or increased public need or popular sentiment.

SECTION 4

The amendment shall be self executing and shall become a part of the constitution of the State of Arkansas when approved by a majority of the electors voting thereon at the next general election.

This provision is self-executing and requires no implementation legislation.

AMENDMENT 33: BOARDS AND COMMISSIONS

This amendment was proposed by initiated petition and adopted at the general election on November 3, 1942.

1. The term of office of members of the boards or commissions charged with the management or control of all charitable, penal or correctional institutions and institutions of higher learning of the State of Arkansas, now in existence or hereafter created, shall be five years when the membership is five in number, seven years when the membership is seven in number and ten years when the membership is ten in number. Such terms of office shall be arranged by the General Assembly to provide a membership with one term of office expiring every year from the effective date of this amendment. The unexpired terms of members serving on the effective date of this amendment shall not be decreased.

This amendment was drafted by Robert A. Leflar, distinguished professor of law emeritus at the University of Arkansas Law School in Fayetteville. He was prompted by the firing of J. William Fulbright as president of the University of Arkansas by Governor Homer Atkins in 1941 after his mother, Roberta Fulbright (publisher of the *Northwest Arkansas Times*) had endorsed Carl Bailey, Atkins's 1940 opponent in the Democratic gubematorial primary. It was passed by a very close vote in 1942 in an election that saw Atkins reelected as govemor and Fulbright elected to the U.S. House of Representatives, Ironically, Fulbright and Atkins opposed each other for the U.S. Senate in 1944. Fulbright won handily. This launched Fulbright's congressional career, which continued until his defeat in 1974 by then Govemor Dale Bumpers. Fulbright designed and passed the Fulbright Scholars program during that first term, which is of global significance today.

2. The board or commission of any institution, governed by this amendment, shall not be abolished nor shall the powers vested in any such board or commission be transferred, unless the institution is abolished or consolidated with some other State institution. In the event of abolition or consolidation, the new board or commission shall consist of a membership of five, seven or ten.

The basic assumption of this amendment is that governors will serve only the traditional two two-year terms. This represents the regular four-year tenure served by all Arkansas governors except for Orval Eugene Faubus, who was elected to six two-year terms; Jeff Davis, who was elected to three two-year terms; and Bill Clinton, who was elected to three two-year terms and two four-year terms; and three governors who served only one two-year term: John Martineau, Francis Cherry, and Frank White.

> **3.** The membership of any such board or commission now in existence shall not be increased or decreased in number after the effective date of this amendment nor shall the number of members of any such board or commission created after this amendment is in operation be increased or decreased subsequent to its creation.

This provision prevents the "stacking" of a board by extending the number of positions to allow a governor to appoint more than the allocated slots.

> **4.** The Governor shall have the power to remove any member of such board or commissions before the expiration of his term for cause only, after notice and hearing. Such removal shall become effective only when approved in writing by a majority of the total number of the board or commission, but without the right to vote by the member removed or by his successor, which action shall be filed with the Secretary of State together with a complete record of the proceedings at the hearing.
>
> An appeal may be taken to the Pulaski Circuit Court by the Governor or the member ordered removed, and the same shall be tried de novo on the record. An appeal may be taken from the circuit court to the Arkansas Supreme Court, which shall likewise be tried de novo.

This section gives added security to appointees, affording them some additional independence by forcing the governor to show cause, beyond politics, before removing any board member.

> **5.** Any vacancy arising in the membership of such board or commission for any reason other than the expiration of the regular term for which the member was appointed shall be filled by appointment by the Governor, subject to approval by a majority of the remaining members of the board or commission, and to be thereafter effective until the expiration of such regular term.

This section attempts to cover the process for the filling of vacancies.

AMENDMENT 34: LABOR UNION MEMBERSHIP

This amendment was proposed by initiated petition and approved at the general election on November 7, 1944.

SECTION 1

No person shall be denied employment because of membership in or affiliation with or resignation from a labor union, or because of refusal to join or affiliate with a labor union, nor shall any corporation or individual or association of any kind enter into any contract, written or oral, to exclude from employment members of a labor union or persons who refuse to join a labor union, or because of resignation from a labor union; nor shall any person against his will be compelled to pay dues to any labor organization as a prerequisite to or condition of employment.

This provision prohibits a closed union shop, is opposed by the Arkansas American Federation of Labor and Congress of Industrial Organizations (AFL-CIO). It has been discussed extensively but retained by each constitutional convention. A local union may serve as a bargaining agent for employees as long as union membership is not required (Williams v. Arthur J. Amey Co., 1966). The states are not empowered by the Taft Hartley Act to enact a right-to-work law prohibiting union-operated, exclusive hiring halls that do not discriminate between union members and nonmembers (Laborers' International Union of North America, Local 107 v. Kunco, Inc., 1973).

SECTION 2

The General Assembly shall have power to enforce this article by appropriate legislation.

Implementing legislation is up to the legislature. For statutory reference, see Section 11–3-301 et seq., right to employment.

AMENDMENT 35: GAME AND FISH COMMISSION

This amendment was proposed by initiative petition and approved at the general election on November 7, 1944 (see *Acts 1945*, p. 770).

SECTION 1

The control, management, restoration, conservation and regulation of birds, fish, game and wildlife resources of the State, including hatcheries, sanctuaries, refuges, reservations and all property now owned, or used for said purposes and the acquisition and establishment of same, the administration of the laws now and/or hereafter pertaining thereto, shall be vested in a Commission to be known as the Arkansas State Game and Fish commission, to consist of eight members. Seven of whom shall be active and one an associate member who shall be the Head of the Department of Zoology at the University of Arkansas, without voting power.

The commission has been given full and complete administrative power and authority to promulgate rules and regulations that are necessary for the conservation and preservation of all wildlife. This includes the power to establish a bag limit, to set the seasons in which to hunt and fish, to decide the penalty for violations, and to levy a reasonable and equitable license fee on all hunting dogs. This is to be done for regulatory purposes but not for revenue (Game and Fish Commission ex rel. Wright v. Casey, 1955; Chaffin v. Arkansas Game and Fish Commission, 1988).

SECTION 2

Commissioners shall have knowledge of and interest in wildlife conservation. All shall be appointed by the Governor. The first members of the Commission shall be appointed by the Governor for terms as follows: One for one year, one for two years, one for three years, one for four years, one for five years, one for six years, and one for seven years. Each Congressional District must be represented on the Commission.

The governor must make sure that at all times there is a resident of each congressional district on the commission (Drennen v. Bennett, 1959).

SECTION 3

Upon the expiration of the foregoing terms of the same Commission, a successor shall be appointed by the Governor for a term of seven years, which term of seven years shall thereafter be for each member of the Commission. No Commissioner can serve more than one term and none can succeed himself.

The prohibition against reappointment was designed to promote individual and political independence from the governor and the legislature.

SECTION 4

Each Commissioner shall take the regular oath of office provided in the Constitution and serve without compensation other than actual expenses while away from home engaged entirely on the work of the Commission.

No per diem was anticipated.

SECTION 5

A Commissioner may be removed by the Governor only for the same causes as apply to other Constitutional Officers, after a hearing which may be reviewed by the Chancery Court for the First District with right of appeal therefrom to the Supreme Court, such review and appeal to be without presumption in favor of any finding by the Governor or the trial court.

This provision of security for commissioners was intended to enhance their political independence (Rockefeller v. Hogue, 1969). For a fuller discussion, see Scott Stafford, "Separation of Powers and Arkansas Administrative Agencies: Distinguishing Judicial Power and Legislative Power," 7 *University of Arkansas Little Rock Law Journal* 279.

SECTION 6

Vacancies on the Commission due to resignation or death shall be filled by appointment of the Governor for the unexpired term within thirty days from date of such vacancy; upon failure of the Governor to fill the vacancy within thirty days, the remaining Commissioners shall make the appointment for the unexpired term. A Chairman shall be elected annually from the seven members of the Commission to serve one year.

This provision prohibits the governor from delaying the filling of any vacancy on the commission.

SECTION 7

The Commission shall elect an Executive Secretary, whose salary shall not exceed that of limitations placed on other constitutional departments; and other executive officers, supervisory personnel, office assistants, wardens, game refuge keepers, and hatchery employees, whose salaries and expenditures must be submitted to the Legislature and approved by an Act covering specific items in the biennial appropriation as covered by Article XVI, Section 4 of the Constitution.

Appropriations will govern the salary and number of staff members of the commission. From time to time, game and fish commissioners and directors seek special powers regarding salaries and the numbers of staff members on the basis that they have their own mandate for revenues and programs.

SECTION 8

No person shall be employed by the Commission who shall be related to any of the Commissioners or any other State officers within the third degree of relationship by blood or marriage. All employed personnel may make arrests for violation of the game and fish laws.

The fees, monies or funds arising from all sources by the operation and transaction of the said Commission and from the application and administration of the laws and regulations pertaining to birds, game, fish and wildlife resources of the State and the sale of property used for said purposes shall be expended by the Commission for the control, management, restoration, conservation and regulation of the birds, fish and wildlife resources of the State, including the purchases or other acquisitions of property for said purposes and for the administration of the laws pertaining thereto and for no other purposes. All monies shall be deposited in the Game Protection Fund with the State Treasurer and such monies as are necessary including an emergency fund shall be appropriated by the Legislature at each legislative session for the use of the Game and Fish Commission as hereto set forth. No monies other than those credited to the Game Protection Fund can be appropriated.

All money to the credit of or that should be credited to the present Game Protection Fund shall be credited to the new Game Protection Fund and any appropriation made by the Legislature out of the Game Protection Fund shall be construed to be for the use of the new Commission and out of the new Game Protection Fund.

The books, accounts and financial affairs of the Commission shall be audited by the State Comptroller as that department deems necessary, but at least once a year.

Resident hunting and fishing license, each, shall be one and 50/100 dollars annually, and shall not exceed this amount unless a higher license fee is authorized by an Act of Legislature.

The Commission shall have the exclusive power and authority to issue licenses and permits, to regulate bag limits and the manner of taking game and fish and furbearing animals, and shall have the authority to divide the State into zones, and regulate persons and manner of taking game and fish and fur-bearing animals therein, and fix penalties for violations. No rule or regulations shall apply to less than a complete zone, except temporarily in case of extreme emergency.

Said Commission shall have the power to acquire by purchase, gifts, eminent domain, or otherwise, all property necessary, useful or convenient for the use of the Commission in the exercise of any of its duties, and in the event the right of eminent domain is exercised in the same manner as now or hereafter provided for the exercise of eminent domain by the State Highway Commission. All laws now in effect shall continue in force until changed by the Commission. All contracts and agreements now in effect shall remain in force until the date of their expiration.

This amendment shall not repeal, alter or modify the provisions of any existing special laws under the terms of which a County Game Commission has been created.

The Commission shall be empowered to spend such monies as are necessary to match Federal grants under the Pittman-Robertson or similar acts for the propagation, conservation and restoration of game and fish.

This amendment shall become effective July 1, 1945.

This section prohibits nepotism, empowers game and fish officers to make certain arrests, and divests the legislature of all of its powers to conserve the wildlife resources of this state, except those powers that are expressly reserved, such as the power to make appropriations and to increase the cost of annual resident hunting and fishing licenses (Magruder v. Arkansas Game and Fish

Commission, 1987; Chaffin v. Arkansas Game and Fish Commission, 1988; Dennis v. State, 1989; A.R.Cr. P.12. State v. Henry, 1990).

AMENDMENT 36: VOTES OF MILITARY PERSONNEL

Any citizen of Arkansas, while serving in the armed forces of the United States, may vote in any election, without having paid poll tax, if otherwise qualified to vote in any such election.

This amendment was proposed by initiated petition and adopted at the general election on November 7, 1944 (see Acts 1945, p. 774). The poll tax exemption has been superseded by the voter registration system provided by Amendment 51.

AMENDMENT 37: STATE OFFICERS; COMPENSATION

SECTION 1

The Executive Department of this State shall consist of a Governor, Lieutenant Governor, Secretary of State, Treasurer of State, Auditor of State, Attorney General and Commissioner of State Lands, all of whom shall keep their offices at the seat of Government, and hold their offices for the term of two years and until their successors are elected and qualified.

SECTION 2

The annual salaries of such State Officers, which shall be paid in monthly installments, shall be as follows:

The Governor, the sum of $10,000.00; the Lieutenant Governor, the sum of $2,500.00; the Secretary of State, the sum of $5,000.00; the Treasurer of State, the sum of $5,000.00; the Auditor of State, the sum of $5,000.00; the Attorney General, the sum of $6,000.00; and for the Commissioner of the State Lands, the sum of $5,000.00.

SECTION 3

The members of the General Assembly shall receive as their salary the sum of twelve hundred ($1,200) dollars, except the Speaker of the House of Representatives, who shall receive his salary of thirteen hundred and fifty ($1,350) dollars, for each period of two (2) years; and in addition to such salary the members of the General Assembly shall receive five cents per mile for each mile traveled in going to and returning from the seat of government over the most direct and practicable route; and provided, further that when said members are required to attend an extraordinary session of the

General Assembly, they shall receive in addition to the salary herein provided, the sum of $6 per day for each day they are required to attend, and mileage, at the same rate herein provided.

SECTION 4

That the General Assembly of Arkansas shall by law determine the amount and method of payment of salaries and expenses of Circuit Judges and Chancellors of the various Circuit and Chancery districts; provided that the salary and expenses of any Circuit Judge or Chancellor shall not be less than $4,800.00 nor more than $7,200.00 per year.

SECTION 5

All parts and provisions of the Constitution of the State of Arkansas in conflict with this amendment, are hereby repealed, and this amendment shall take effect and be in operation on January 1, 1947.

This amendment was repealed by Amendments 43, 48, 56, and 63.

AMENDMENT 38: COUNTY LIBRARY TAX

This amendment was proposed by initiative petition and approved at the general election on November 5, 1946 (see *Acts 1947*, p. 1077).

SECTION 1

Whenever 100 or more tax paying electors of any county shall file a petition in the County Court asking that an annual tax on real and personal property be levied for the purpose of maintaining a public county library or a county library service or system and shall specify a rate of taxation not exceeding one mill on the dollar, the question as to whether said tax shall be levied shall be submitted to the qualified electors of such county at a general county election. Such petition must be filed at least thirty days prior to the election at which it will be submitted to the voters. The ballot shall be in substantially the following form:

FOR a ____________ mill tax on real and personal property to be used for maintenance of a public county library or county library service or system.

AGAINST a ____________ mill tax on real and personal property to be used for maintenance of a public county library or county library service or system.

This initiated amendment replaces the earlier county library tax provided in Amendment 30 (Weems v. Anderson, 1974). Counties with two districts are covered by statute, Section 13-2-403.

SECTION 2

The election commissioners shall certify to the County Judge the result of the vote. The County Judge shall cause the result of the election to be entered of record in the County Court. The result so entered shall be conclusive unless attacked in the courts within thirty days. If a majority of the qualified electors voting on the question at such election vote in favor of the specified tax, then it shall thereafter be continually levied and collected as other general taxes of such county are levied and collected; provided, however, that such tax shall not be levied against any real or personal property which is taxed for the maintenance of a city library, pursuant to the provisions of Amendment No. 30; and no voter residing within such city shall be entitled to vote on the question as to whether county tax shall be levied. The proceeds of any tax voted for the maintenance of a county public library or county library service or system shall be segregated by the county officials and used only for that purpose. Such funds shall be held in the custody of the County Treasurer. No claim against said funds shall be approved by the County Court unless first approved by the County Library board, if there is a county Library Board functioning under Act 24 of 1927, or similar legislation.

This provision establishes a library trust fund in each county having this tax by popular vote. Appropriations are then made by the county quorum court.

SECTION 3

Whenever 100 or more tax paying electors of any county having library tax in force shall file a petition in the County Court asking that such tax be raised, reduced or abolished, the question shall be submitted to the qualified electors at a general county election. Such petition must be filed at least thirty days prior to the election at which it will be submitted to the voters. The ballot shall follow, as far as practicable, the form set forth in Section 1 hereof. The result shall be certified and entered of record as provided in Section 2 hereof, and the result as entered of record shall be conclusive unless attacked in the courts within thirty days. The tax shall be lowered, raised or abolished, as the case may be, according to the majority of the qualified electors voting on the question at such election; provided, however, that it shall not be raised to more than one mill on the dollar. If lowered or raised, the revised tax shall thereafter be continually levied and collected and proceeds used in the manner and for the purposes as provided in Section 2 hereof.

This section allows the voters to repeal the tax.

SECTION 4

Nothing herein shall be construed as preventing the coordination of the services of a city public library and a county public library, or the coordination of the services of libraries of different counties.

This provision is identical to the final section of Amendment 30.

AMENDMENT 39: VOTER REGISTRATION

The General Assembly shall have power to enact laws providing for a registration of voters prior to any general, special, or primary election, and to require that the right to vote at any such election shall depend upon such previous registration. (See Amendment No. 51.)

This amendment was proposed by a senate joint resolution in the 1947 session and was approved at the general election on November 2, 1948. The amendment supersedes the clause in Article 3, Section 2, prohibiting voter registration. Prior to this amendment, the legislature was prohibited from passing a registration law or making registration a prerequisite to voting (Faubus v. Miles, 1964). This section, however, did not abolish the poll tax (Faubus v. Miles, 1964).

AMENDMENT 40: SCHOOL TAX MILLAGE

This amended Article 14, Section 3. It was proposed by a senate joint resolution, was filed in the Office of the Secretary of State on March 28, 1947, was adopted at the general election on November 2, 1948. (See notes to Article 14, Section 3.)

(Article XIV, Section 3) Section 1. Amendment No. 11. The General Assembly shall provide for the support of common schools by general law, including an annual per capita tax of one dollar, to be assessed on every male inhabitant of this State over the age of twenty-one years; and school districts are hereby authorized to levy by a vote of the qualified electors respectively thereof an annual tax for the maintenance of the schools, the erection and equipment of school buildings and the retirement of existing indebtedness, the amount of such tax to be determined in the following manner:

The Board of Directors of each school district shall prepare, approve and make public not less than sixty (60) days in advance of the annual school election a proposed budget of expenditures deemed necessary to provide for the foregoing purposes, together with a rate of tax levy sufficient to provide the funds therefore, including the rate under any continuing levy for the retirement of indebtedness. If a majority of the qualified voters in said school district voting in the annual school election shall approve the rate of tax so proposed by the Board of Directors, then the tax at the rate so approved shall be collected as provided by law. In the event a majority of said qualified electors voting in said annual school election shall disapprove the proposed rate of tax, then the tax shall be collected at the rate approved in the last preceding annual school election.

Provided, that no such tax shall be appropriated for any other purpose nor to any other district than that for which it is levied.

This amendment provides a financial safety net for schools in the sense that if voters defeat a millage proposal, it does not mean there will be no tax because the existing rate will remain in effect until it is replaced by a new levy. This amendment does not prohibit requiring schools to pay the cost of assessing and collecting taxes (Strawn v. Campbell, 1956). It was ruled that one ballot may contain the questions of a bond for a new school building and a tax for the retirement of existing debt (Johnson v. Gates, 1967).

AMENDMENT 41: COUNTY CLERK

The provisions for the election of a County Clerk upon a population basis are hereby abolished and there may be elected a County Clerk in like manner as a Circuit Clerk, and in such cases, the County Clerk may be ex-officio Clerk of the Probate Court of such county until otherwise provided by the General Assembly.

This amendment was proposed by House Joint Resolution 3. It was filed in the Office of the Secretary of State on March 20, 1951, and was approved at the general election on November 4, 1952. This amendment contained a preliminary paragraph that read "That the Constitution of the State of Arkansas be amended modifying Section 19 of Article 7, and Section 3 of Amendment No. 24 of said Constitution, so as to provide for the election of a County Clerk in all of the said counties of the State, as follow: . . ."

This amendment, abolishing the population requirement for the election of county clerks, requires enabling legislation since the word "may" is used in the amendment. Hence, a plaintiff who was elected county clerk in the 1952 election, a time at which the population of the county had declined to less than 15,000, was not entitled to take office (Huggins v. Wacaster, 1954).

AMENDMENT 42: HIGHWAY COMMISSION

This amendment was proposed by Senate Joint Resolution 7 in 1951. It was filed in the Office of the Secretary of State on March 20, 1951 and was approved at the general election on November 4, 1952.

SECTION 1

Commission Created—Members—Powers. There is hereby created a State Highway Commission which shall be vested with all the powers and duties now or hereafter imposed by law for the administration of the State Highway Department, together with all powers necessary or proper to enable the Commission or any of its officers or employees to carry out fully and effectively the regulations and laws relating to the State Highway Department.

This is the much-discussed Mack-Blackwell Amendment. It was adopted in 1952, during the Sid McMath administration. (McMath was defeated after an audit scandal in the highway department). Legislation that transferred the ministerial duties and powers of the Transportation Safety Agency and the Transportation Regulatory Board to a constitutional body, the Arkansas Highway Commission, was ruled to not violate the requirement of separation of powers. The General Assembly may enlarge the powers granted or may subsequently modify or remove them in favor of another agency; moreover, by its own terms, this section indicates that additional powers and duties may be provided for the State Highway Commission (Arkansas Motor Carriers Association v. Pritchett, 1990).

SECTION 2

Qualifications and Appointment of Members—Terms of Office of First Commission. Within ten days after the convening of the General Assembly of the State of Arkansas in the year 1953, the Governor, by and with the advice and consent of the Senate, shall appoint five persons who are qualified electors of the State to constitute the State Highway Commission for terms of two, four, six, eight and ten years respectively. The terms of the persons so appointed shall be determined by lot. The Commissioners to be appointed from the State at large; provided, however, that no two Commissioners shall be appointed from any single Congressional District.

In the event of rejection by the Senate of a person whose name has been so submitted, the Governor shall within five days after receipt of written notice from the Secretary of the Senate of such rejection submit the name of another appointee to fill such vacancy. In the event the Governor should within five days thereafter fail to appoint or fail to submit to the Senate for confirmation the name of any person to be appointed, the Senate shall proceed to make the appointment of its own choice.

This section, under which the Senate must confirm gubernatorial appointments to the commission, is designed to keep any governor from controlling the highway department by providing ten-year terms for commissioners (with five commissioners, one to be appointed every two years), while governors traditionally serve only four years.

SECTION 3

Terms of Office of Members. Upon the expiration of the foregoing terms of said Commissioners, a successor shall be appointed by the Governor in the manner provided for in Section 2 for a term of ten years, which term of ten years shall thereafter be for each member of the Commission.

No governor presumably would appoint more than two of the five commissioners. Only Governors Faubus and Clinton have appointed more. However, Governor Clinton had served ten years as governor before appointing all the members of the commission.

SECTION 4

Removal of Members—Hearing—Review and Appeal. A Commissioner may be removed by the Govemor only for the same causes as apply to other constitutional officers after a hearing which may be reviewed by the Chancery Court for the First District with right of appeal therefrom to the Supreme Court, such review and appeal to be without presumption in favor of any finding by the Govemor or the trial court and provided further, in addition to the right of confirmation hereinabove reserved to the Senate, the Senate may upon the written request of at least Five (5) of its members that a member or members of the Commission should be removed therefrom, proceed, when in session, to hear any and all evidence pertinent to the reasons for removal. The member or members whose removal is so requested shall be entitled to be heard in the matter and to be represented before the Senate by legal Counsel. These proceedings conducted by the Senate shall be public and a transcript of the testimony so heard shall be prepared and preserved in the journal of the Senate. The taking of evidence either orally or by deposition shall not be bound by the formal rules of evidence. Upon the conclusion of the hearing, the Senate, sitting as a body in executive session, may remove said member or members of the Commission by a majority vote conducted by secret ballot.

This section provides the strongest possible independence to this highway commission—more than any other highway department in the nation and any other administrative agency in Arkansas.

SECTION 5

Vacancies—Filling. Vacancies on the Commission due to resignations, death or removal shall be filled by appointment of the Govemor for the unexpired term within thirty days from the date of such vacancy. Upon failure of the Govemor to fill the vacancy within thirty days, the remaining Commissioners shall make the appointment for the unexpired term.

Candidates for these positions contact governors years in advance of the anticipated vacancies. This is by far the most sought-after gubernatorial appointment.

SECTION 6

The Commission shall appoint a Director of Highways who shall have such duties as may be prescribed by the Commission or by statute.

The director is hired by the commission rather than the governor, in contrast to other members of the cabinet. The present director, Maurice Smith of Birdeye, served as a highway commissioner in the past and as the Governor's Campaign Chairman in 1982.

AMENDMENT 43: JUDGES' SALARIES

The General Assembly shall by law determine the amount and method of payment of salaries and expenses of the judges of the Supreme Court, Circuit Courts, Chancery Courts, and Municipal Courts of Arkansas; provided such salaries and expenses may be increased but not diminished during the term for which such judges are elected; provided further that the salaries of Circuit and Chancery Judges shall be uniform throughout the state.

This amendment was proposed by initiative petition. It was filed in the Office of the Secretary of State on June 15, 1956, and was approved at the general election on November 6, 1956. This amendment supersedes Amendment 9, Section 2. It seeks to establish a state system of courts with some uniformity out of the somewhat chaotic judiciary system that had developed over time. "Arkansas' Judiciary: Its History and Structure," 18 *Arkansas Law Review* 152.

AMENDMENT 44: INTERPOSITION

This amendment was proposed by initiative petition. It was filed in the Office of the Secretary of State on July 3, 1956, and was approved at the general election on November 6, 1956. This amendment directly challenges the principle that the federal judiciary is supreme in the exposition of the law of the Constitution. It is unconstitutional under the supremacy clause of the U.S. Constitution, Article VI, clauses 2 and 3; and void ab initio, Dietz v. Arkansas, 1989.

SECTION 1

From and after the Adoption of this Amendment, the General Assembly of the State of Arkansas shall take appropriate action and pass laws opposing in every Constitutional manner the Un-Constitutional desegregation decisions of May 17, 1954 and May 31, 1955 of the United States Supreme Court, including interposing the sovereignty of the State of Arkansas to the end of nullification of these and all deliberate, palpable and dangerous invasions of or encroachments upon rights and powers not delegated to the United States nor prohibited to the States by the Constitution of the United States and Amendments thereto, and those rights and powers reserved to the States and to the People thereof by any department, commission, officer, or employee of such department or commission of the Government of the United States, or of any government of any Nation or Federation of nations acting upon the apparent authority granted them by or assumed by them from the Government of the United States. Said opposition shall continue steadfast until such time as such Un-Constitutional invasions or encroachments shall have abated or shall have been rectified, or the same shall be transformed into an Amendment to the Constitution of the United States and adopted by action of three-fourths of the States as provided therein.

This states' rights amendment was initiated by petition. It was the brainchild of then State Senators Jim Johnson of Crossett and Jerry Screeton of Hazen in response to the Little Rock Central High School crisis of 1957, in which President Dwight Eisenhower federalized the Arkansas National Guard to assist the integration of the school after Governor Faubus had declined to do so.

SECTION 2

The General Assembly shall enact laws to insure the administration and enforcement of the spirit and letter of this Amendment; and shall appropriate adequate fund to effect the same, including a proportionate share of such expenses as may be necessary for the maintenance of regional committees created among the States for the preservation of rights belonging to the States and the people thereof.

This section is an unconstitutional violation of the equal protection clause of the U.S. Constitution.

SECTION 3

The General Assembly shall enact such laws under the Police Powers reserved to the States as may be necessary to regulate health, morals, education, marriage, good order and to insure the domestic tranquility of the citizens of the State of Arkansas.

This section specifically was written to make segregation statutes—"Jim Crow laws"—legal, but it is itself unconstitutional (Garrett v. Faubus, 1959).

SECTION 4

No public official or employee of the State of Arkansas or of any political subdivision thereof shall have immunity from arrest, prosecution and trial for the violation of such penal laws as the General Assembly shall provide for the willful failure and refusal to carry out the clear mandates of this Amendment; and in addition to the penalties provided for by the General Assembly, shall automatically forfeit his or her office.

This section provides for the full force of this provision. The entire amendment was repealed by the voters at the 1990 election.

AMENDMENT 45: SENATORIAL DISTRICTS

This amended Article 8, as amended by Amendment 23, was proposed by initiative petition. It was filed in the Office of the Secretary of State on July 5, 1956, and was adopted at the general election on November 6, 1956.

SECTION 1

Board of Apportionment Created—Powers and Duties. A Board to be known as 'The Board of Apportionment,' consisting of the Governor (who shall be Chairman), the Secretary of State and the Attorney General is hereby created and it shall be its imperative duty to make apportionment of representatives in accordance with the provisions hereof; the action of a majority in each instance shall be deemed the action of said board.

This amendment supersedes Article 8 and Amendment 23 and seeks to preserve the existing senatorial districts, as well as incumbent senators.

SECTION 2

One Hundred Members in House of Representatives—Apportionment. The House of Representatives shall consist of one hundred members and each county existing at the time of any apportionment shall have at least one representative; the remaining members shall be equally distributed (as nearly as practicable) among the more populous counties of the State, in accordance with a ratio to be determined by the population of said counties as shown by the Federal census next preceding any apportionment hereunder.

This section is unconstitutional in its devotion to representing geography rather than population.

SECTION 3

Senatorial Districts—Thirty-Five Members of Senate. The Senate shall consist of thirty-five members. Senatorial district as now constituted and existing, as heretofore directed by the Supreme court of Arkansas in the case of Pickens v. Board of Apportionment, 220 Ark. 145, 246 S.W. 2d 556, shall remain the same and the number of Senators from district shall not be changed.

On or before February 1 immediately following each Federal census, said Board shall reapportion the State for Representatives, and in each instance said Board shall file its report with the Secretary of State, setting forth (a) the basis of population adopted for representatives; (b) the number of representatives assigned to each county; whereupon, after 30 days from such filing date, the apportionment thus made shall become effective unless proceedings for revision be instituted in the Supreme Court within said period.

This provision precluded the necessity of an enabling act. It was held unconstitutional in Yancey v. Faubus, 1965. However, it was held in Faubus v. Kinney, 1965, that the remainder of the amendment was not affected (see notes to Article 8).

Mandamus to Compel Board of Apportionment to Act. Original jurisdiction (to be exercised on application of any citizens and taxpayers) is hereby vested in the Supreme Court of the State (a) to compel (by mandamus or otherwise) the Board to perform its duties as here directed and (b) to revise any arbitrary action of or abuse of discretion by the Board in making such apportionment; provided any such application for revision shall be filed with said Court within 30 days after the filing of the report of apportionment by said Board with the Secretary of State; if revised by the Court, a certified copy of its judgment shall be by the clerk thereof forthwith transmitted to the Secretary of State, and thereupon be and become a substitute for the apportionment made by the Board.

This section assures that no delaying tactics could be used.

Election of Senators and Representatives. At the next general election for State and County officers ensuing after any such apportionment. Representatives shall be elected in accordance therewith, Senators shall be elected henceforth according to the apportionment now existing, and their respective terms of office shall begin on January 1 next following. Senators shall be elected for a term of four years at the expiration of their present terms of office.

The provisions of the Constitution of the State of Arkansas in conflict with this Amendment are hereby repealed, and this Amendment shall take effect and be in operation immediately upon its approval and adoption by the people of the State of Arkansas, being self-executing and requiring no enabling act.

This section precludes the necessity of implementation legislation.

AMENDMENT 46: HOT SPRINGS HORSE RACING

Horse racing and pari-mutuel wagering thereon shall be lawful in Hot Springs, Garland County, Arkansas, and shall be regulated by the General Assembly.

This amendment was proposed by initiative petition, was filed in the office of the Secretary of State on July 5, 1956, and was approved at the general election on November 6, 1956. This amendment was initiated by the people because gambling is otherwise prohibited by the State Constitution.

AMENDMENT 47: STATE AD VALOREM TAX PROHIBITION

This amendment was proposed by House Joint Resolution 1 in 1957. It was filed in the Office of the Secretary of State on March 27, 1957, and was approved at the general election on November 4, 1958.

SECTION 1

No ad valorem tax shall be levied upon property by the State.

This section abolishes the state property tax, but allows the state to give financial and technical assistance to political subdivisions to assist them in the collecting of taxes and the assessing of utility property by the Tax Division of the Public Service Commission, a state agency (Eamhart v. Heath, 1974). An excise tax on real estate transactions, if not based on value of property, is constitutional (Borchert v. Scott, 1970).

SECTION 2

All provisions in the Constitution of the State of Arkansas, or any amendment thereto, or in the statutes of the State of Arkansas in conflict herewith are hereby repealed.

This is a traditional provision.

AMENDMENT 48: COMPENSATION OF MEMBERS OF GENERAL ASSEMBLY

This amendment was repealed by Constitutional Amendment 56, Section 5.

SECTION 1

The members of the General Assembly shall receive as their salary the sum of Twelve Hundred ($1,200.00) Dollars per annum, except the Speaker of the House of Representatives, who shall receive his salary of Thirteen Hundred and Fifty ($1,350.00) Dollars per annum, with such salaries to be payable in equal monthly installments; and in addition to such salary the members of the General Assembly shall receive Twenty ($20.00) Dollars per day for each day the General Assembly is in regular session, and shall receive five cents per mile for each mile traveled in going to and returning from the seat of government over the most direct and practicable route; and provided, further, that when said members are required to attend an extraordinary session of the General Assembly, they shall receive in addition to salary herein provided, the sum of Six ($6.00) Dollars per day for each day they are required to attend, and mileage, at the same rate herein provided.

This severely outdated provision was amended in 1976 by Amendment 56. It resulted from a year-long study by the Eagleton Institute of Politics, Rutgers University. It was conducted in 1973–1974, under the director of Cal Ledbetter (Professor of Political Science, the University of Arkansas at Little Rock), who was also a state legislator at the time.

SECTION 2

All provisions of the Constitution of the State of Arkansas in conflict herewith are hereby repealed.

AMENDMENT 49: INDUSTRIAL DEVELOPMENT BONDS AUTHORITY

SECTION 1

Any city of the first or second class, any incorporated town, and any county, may issue, by and with the consent of the majority of the qualified electors of said municipality or county voting on the question at an election held for the purpose, bonds in sums approved by such majority at such election for the purpose of securing and developing industry within or near the said municipality holding the election, or within the county holding the election.

SECTION 2

Such bonds shall bear interest at a rate not to exceed six per centum (6%) per annum and shall be sold only at public sale after twenty (20) days advertisement in a newspaper having a bona fide circulation in the municipality or county issuing such bonds; provided, however, that the said municipality or county may exchange such bonds for bonds of like amount, rate of interest, and length of issue.

SECTION 3

To provide for the payment of such bonds, principal and interest, as they mature, the municipality or county may levy a special tax, payable annually, not to exceed five (5) mills on the dollar, in addition the legal rate permitted on the real and personal taxable property therein; provided, however, the municipality or county may, from time to time, suspend the collection of such annual levy when not required for the payment of its bonds; and provided further, however, that in no event shall the real and personal taxable property in any city or town be subject to a special tax in excess of five (5) mills for bonds issued hereunder.

SECTION 4

Such bonds shall be serial, maturing annually after three years from date of issue, and shall be paid as they mature, and no such bonds shall be issued for a period longer than thirty (30) years.

SECTION 5

The governing body of the municipality or the County Court of the county shall exercise jurisdiction over the sale or exchange of any such bonds voted by the electors at an election held for that purpose and shall expend economically the funds so provided.

SECTION 6

The election on the issuance of such bonds shall be held at such time as the governing body of the municipality may designate by ordinance, or as the County Judge of the county may designate by order, which ordinance or order shall state the sum total of the issue, the dates of maturities thereof and shall fix the date of election so that it shall not occur earlier than thirty (30) days after the passage of the said ordinance or the granting of said order. The said election shall be held and conducted, the vote thereof canvassed, and the result thereof declared under the law and in the manner now or hereafter provided for municipal elections when the election is held by a municipality, and in the manner now or hereafter provided for county elections when the election is held by a county, so far as the same may be applicable, except as herein otherwise provided. Notice of the election shall be given by the Mayor of the municipality or by the County Judge of the county by advertisement weekly for at least four times in some newspaper having a bona fide circulation in the said municipality or county, with the last publication to be not less than ten (10) days prior to the date of the said election. Only qualified electors of the said municipality or county shall have a right to vote at the said election; provided, however, that when an election is held by the county, if any city or town within such county has previously voted a levy of five mills under the provisions of this amendment which levy shall not have expired at the time of the election held by the county, then the electors of such city or town shall not be eligible to vote in the county election. The result of the said election shall be proclaimed by the Mayor of the municipality or by the County Judge of the county, and the result as proclaimed shall be conclusive, unless attacked in the courts within thirty (30) days after the date of such proclamation.

SECTION 7

All provisions of the Constitution, or amendments thereto, in conflict herewith are, to the extent of such conflict, hereby repealed.

This amendment was repealed by Amendment 62, Section 11, and Amendment 65.

AMENDMENT 50: THE PERMISSIVE VOTING MACHINE AMENDMENT

This amendment was proposed by initiative petition and adopted at the general election on November 6, 1962.

SECTION 1

Article III, Section 3, of the Constitution of the State of Arkansas is hereby repealed and following section is substituted therefor.

This amendment was a profoundly important step in reforming Arkansas elections. It was initiated by the people and supported by both political parties, as well as labor and business, and was spearheaded by the Arkansas League of Women Voters, led by Shirley McFarlin. (Walsh v. Campbell, 1966).

SECTION 2

All elections by the people shall be by ballot or by voting machines which insure the secrecy of individual votes.

The secret ballot, although taken for granted in many other states, was, before 1964, not generally the rule throughout Arkansas. A statute providing for absent voters does not violate the residence requirements of the Constitution, and the legislature may devise methods for conducting an election (Jones v. Smith, 1924).

SECTION 3

In elections by ballot every ballot shall be numbered in the order in which it is received, the number shall be recorded by the election officers on the list of voters opposite the name of the elector who presents the ballot, and the election officers shall be sworn or affirmed not to disclose how any elector voted unless required to do so as witnesses in a judicial proceeding or a proceeding to contest an election.

This provision, which was carried forward from previous constitutions, provides a system by which each vote may be checked for accuracy in case of a court-ordered recount in contested elections. However, voters cannot be forced to deposit ballots in a way that discloses their contents to bystanders (Jones v. Glidewell, 1890).

SECTION 4

Voting machines may be used to such extent and under such rules as may be prescribed by the General Assembly.

This provision specifically permits the use of voting machines, which were long held to be unconstitutional since only paper ballots were envisioned at the time of the drafting of the 1874 Constitution. Cited in Walsh v. Campbell, 1966.

AMENDMENT 51: VOTER REGISTRATION WITHOUT POLL TAX PAYMENT

This amendment was proposed by initiative petition and approved at the general election on November 3, 1964.

SECTION 1

Statement of Policy. The purpose of this Amendment is to establish a system of permanent personal registration as a means of determining that all who cast ballots in general, special and primary elections in this State are legally qualified to vote in such elections, in accordance with the Constitution of Arkansas and the Constitution of the United States.

Once election reform began in 1962 with the adoption of the previous voting machine amendment, the full force of public support lined up squarely behind an even more comprehensive change. See Walker v. State, 1967; Mears v. City of Little Rock, 1974.

SECTION 2

Definitions. As used in this Amendment, the terms:

a. "County Board of Registration" means the County Board of Election Commissioners in each of the several counties of this State.
b. "Permanent Registrar" means the County Clerk in each of the several counties of this state.
c. "Deputy Registrar" means the Deputy County Clerk or clerical assistants appointed by the County Clerk.
d. "Election" means any general, special or primary election held pursuant to any provisions of the Constitution or statutes of the State of Arkansas; provided, that this Amendment shall not apply to selection of delegates to party conventions by party committees or to selection of party committeemen by party conventions.

These definitions were necessary and were new in the letter and the spirit of the law. With the abolishment of the poll tax, a traditional registration was instituted.

SECTION 3

Application. No person shall vote or be permitted to vote in any election unless registered in a manner provided for by this Amendment.

No exceptions were allowed to this system, although some were made to the poll tax system.

SECTION 4

Permanent Registration. When a voter is once registered under the provisions of this Amendment, it is unnecessary for such voter again to register unless such registration is cancelled or subject to cancellation in a manner provided for by this Amendment.

This registration, unlike the annual poll tax, is permanent (Booth v. Smith, 1977).

SECTION 5

Duties of Registration Officials, (a) The registration of voters is to be under the supervision of the Permanent Registrar and at any other place or places within the county as are designated by the Permanent Registrar. The Permanent Registrar shall provide office and clerical facilities and may employ such clerical assistants which he may deem necessary to fulfill the duties imposed by this Amendment; provided, that all clerical assistants so employed shall have the qualifications required by law of eligible voters and shall be selected on the basis of competence and without reference to political affiliation.

These provisions have, over time, made the county clerks' offices the most prominent in the state in election administration.

(b) The State Auditor, from and after the effective date of this Amendment, shall provide a sufficient number of blank forms to each Permanent Registrar for the registration of the voters in each county. The forms shall be known as "Affidavits of Registration" and shall consist of looseleaf sheets of durable quality. All Affidavits of Registration shall be made and executed in quadruplicate, the original and each copy of a distinctively different color. Each form shall be printed at the top thereof with the word "Original," "Duplicate," "Triplicate" or "Quadruplicate," as the case may be, each to be followed immediately by the words "Affidavit of Registration." The forms shall be bound together in books or pads and each set of copies shall be capable of being detached from the book or pad and inserted and locked into the Registration Record Files. All forms in a quadruplicate set shall have an identical number, the sets being numbered in sequence.

This provision was included to inject some control and centralization over what had been seventy-five different processes in each of Arkansas's seventy-five counties.

(c) The State Board of Election Commissioners is authorized and, as soon as is possible after the effective date of this Amendment, directed to prescribe, adopt, publish and distribute:

(1) Such Rules and Regulations supplementary to this Amendment and consistent with this Amendment and other laws of Arkansas as are necessary to secure uniform and efficient procedures in the administration of this Amendment throughout the State;

(2) A Manual of Instruction for the information, guidance and direction of election officials within the State; and

(3) Detailed specifications of the Registration Record Files, the Affidavits of Registration and other registration forms, all of which shall be consistent with this Amendment and uniform throughout the State.

These provisions (cl-c3) have not been used up to now, but the state board of election commissioners is presently discussing each one, both formally and informally. The board of election commissioners does not have authority to revise the registration procedure so as to allow the oath to be administered by someone other than registrar and his or her deputies in completion of affidavit of registration (Faubus v. Fields, 1965).

SECTION 6

Affidavits of Registration, (a) The front of the Affidavit of Registration shall contain the name of the County in which issued and:

(1) The voter's name, including given name, middle name or initial (if any), and last name, and, in the case of a woman, the given name shall be preceded by the designation of "Miss" or "Mrs.";

(2) The legal residence of the voter, including street address and house number if house numbers are used, otherwise such a description of the voter's legal residence as makes its location possible for determination of the voter's proper precinct, and length of time during which the voter has resided at the above address. If the voter resides at a hotel, motel, apartment house, boarding house or institution, such additional information is to be included as is necessary to determine the exact location of the legal residence of the voter;

(3) Country or State and country of the voter's birth;

(4) If any voter is foreign bom, how his American citizenship was acquired, including the name of the court granting the same, the place and date thereof, and if naturalized through another person, the name of such person;

(5) The month, day and year of birth of the voter;

(6) If the voter cannot read or write, this must be indicated;
(7) If the voter is unable to make a mark or cross on the Affidavit of Registration or on a ballot, this must be indicated;
(8) Number or name of the voter's school district and number or name of the voter's precinct;
(9) The address in Arkansas where the voter was last registered, if any, and the name under which so registered; and
(10) The signature of the Permanent or Deputy Registrar who receive the voter's application to register.

Forms have been designed in compliance with all the provisions.

(b) The back of the Affidavit of Registration shall contain:
(1) signature. When registering the voter shall manually sign with ink or indelible pencil the original and all copies of the Affidavit of Registration, the signature to include given name, middle name or initial (if any), and last name. If the voter is unable to sign his name, the voter, witnessed by the Permanent or Deputy Registrar, may sign with a mark or cross. If the voter signs with a mark or cross or is unable to sign or make a mark or a cross, the Permanent or Deputy Registrar shall so indicate in the space provided for the voter's signature, and must write in said space the month and day of the voter's birth;
(2) affidavit. Immediately above the space for the signature on the original and all copies must be printed an affidavit in which the voter swears or affirms that he has all qualifications required by the law of this State to entitle him to vote and, thereafter, these words: "I, being duly sworn on oath (or affirmation), depose and swear (or affirm) to the best of my knowledge and belief that the statements hereon made by me are true and correct"; and
(3) record of voting. Immediately following the space for the signature of the voter on the Affidavit of Registration forms shall be printed a Record of Voting Form, which include as many blank spaces as may be possible, each blank space sufficient to include a stamped date and the signature or mark of the voter, substantially as follows:

RECORD OF VOTING

Date ____________

Signature

Date ____________

Signature

(et cetera for as many spaces as possible)

This safeguard of signature comparison has been touted as extremely crucial in insuring clean and honest elections. It is supported by the *Arkansas Gazette*, the League of Women Voters, and other reform-minded organizations.

> **(c)** The State Board of Election Commissioners may require blank spaces for additional information, including supplements to the Record of Voting Form.

The board has not used provision (c) but is discussing party registration as a possible future proposal. Act 828 of 1971 provides for the number or name of voter's school district and of voter's precinct to be included on the form. Requiring a title (Miss or Mrs.) for women discriminates against them and violates equal protection (Walker v. Jackson, 1975).

SECTION 7

Registration Record Files. (a) In each county, the Permanent Registrar shall provide three active Registration Record Files for all voters legally resident within that county:

(1) the Permanent Registration File which shall contain, securely fastened, all original copies of the Affidavits of Registration in alphabetical order for the whole county without regard to precincts or other districts;

(2) a Precinct Registration File which shall contain, securely fastened in binders suitable for locking, all duplicate copies of the Affidavits of Registration, arranged and bound by precinct; and

(3) a Precinct Registration File which shall contain, securely fastened in binders suitable for locking, all triplicate copies of the Affidavits of Registration, arranged and bound by precinct.

(b) The Affidavits of Registration within the Precinct Registration Files shall be arranged in alphabetical order; provided, that the Affidavits of Registration in all or in some of such Files may be arranged by street and street number or on some other appropriate basis, and shall be so arranged at the direction of the County Board of Registration.

(c) In each county, the Permanent Registrar shall provide an Inactive Registration File which shall contain, securely fastened, all cancelled original Affidavits of Registration, arranged in alphabetical order for the whole county without regard to precincts or other districts.

(d) The appropriate Precinct Registration File or Files containing the duplicate copies of Affidavits of Registration shall be delivered to the polling places and used in all elections; provided, that the appropriate Precinct Registration File or Files containing the duplicate copies of the Affidavits of Registration shall be delivered to the polling places of the majority political party for use at party primary elections of such party and the appropriate Precinct Registration File or Files containing the triplicate copies of the Affidavits of Registration shall be delivered to the polling places of the

minority political party for use at party primary elections of such party. Before being delivered to the appropriate County Board of Registration or other lawfully designated election officials for use at any election, the Affidavits of Registration in the precinct Registration Files shall be securely fastened and locked.
(e) The County Board of Registration or other lawfully designated election officials shall cause the appropriate Precinct Registration Files to be at the polling places on the date of elections, and shall return them at the close of the election to the office of the Permanent Registrar with the ballot boxes.

Registration record files are monumental collections that are outgrowing the capacity of most courthouses around the state.

SECTION 8

Spoiled Affidavits of Registration. The Permanent Registrar shall give a receipt to the State Auditor for all blank Affidavits of Registration issued to the county and shall be strictly accountable to the State Auditor for the blanks provided. The Permanent Registrar must account for each blank set of Affidavits of Registration, whether unused, spoiled or in the proper Registration Records Files. If for any cause a blank Affidavit of Registration is spoiled or mutilated, it shall be stamped or written across the face of all copies of the blank form and all copies of the form shall be retumed by the Permanent Registrar to the State Auditor. The State Auditor shall compile a record of the number of the spoiled or mutilated Affidavits of Registration, send a copy of such record to the Permanent Registrar, and then destroy the spoiled or mutilated Affidavits of Registration. By the first of June of each year the Permanent Registrar shall make an accounting of all Affidavits of Registration to the State Auditor.

County clerks cannot destroy any registration forms because they must account to the auditor of state for each one.

SECTION 9

Application to Register, **(a)** All persons may register who:

(1) are qualified electors and who have not previously registered;
(2) will become qualified electors during the twenty (20) day period immediately prior to the next election scheduled within the County; or
(3) are qualified electors but whose registration has been cancelled or is subject to cancellation in a manner provided for by this Amendment.

(b) Registration shall be in progress at all times except during the twenty (20) day period immediately prior to any election scheduled within the county, during which period registration of voters shall cease for that election, but registration during such period shall be effective for subsequent elections.

(c) The original, duplicate and triplicate copies of all Affidavits of Registration submitted as applications for registration to the Permanent Registrar shall be filed promptly in the active Registration Record Files unless the applicant lacks one or more of the qualifications required by law of voters of this State. The quadruplicate copy of all Affidavits of Registration shall be given to each applicant immediately upon the acceptance of his application. The Permanent and Deputy Registrars are empowered to administer oaths for purposes of executing the Affidavits of Registration.

(d) If the Permanent Registrar has any reason to doubt the qualifications of an applicant for registration, he shall submit such application to the County Board of Registration and such Board shall make a determination with respect to such qualifications and shall instruct the Permanent Registrar regarding the same.

(e) If any person eligible to register as a voter is unable to register in person at the Permanent Registrar's office by reason of sickness or physical disability, the Permanent or Deputy Registrar shall register the applicant at his place of abode within such county, if practicable, in the same manner as if he had appeared at the Permanent Registrar's office.

(f) Notwithstanding other provisions of this Amendment, all members of the armed forces of the United States and their spouses when residing with or accompanying them, who are otherwise eligible, may vote without registration by absentee ballot in accordance with the laws of this State.

(g) Any person whose registration status or voting eligibility is affected adversely by an administrative determination under this Amendment may appeal such adverse determination within five (5) days of receipt of notice thereof to the County Board of Registration. The County Board of Registration shall act on such appeal and render its decision within ten (10) days of its receipt. Within thirty (30) days after receipt of such decision, any aggrieved party may appeal further to the Circuit Court of the county.

These provisions in subsection (b), which were drafted during the Faubus administration, are intended to insure protection from political recrimination. Subsection (3) contains the most formal part of the process, the swearing in of each voter. The questioning of qualifications, mentioned in subsection (d), is rarely exercised but is provided for by this process. County clerks often make "house calls" to register disabled or elderly voters, per subsection (3), either in person or by a deputy. Subsection (f) provides the sole exemption from the registration process being done in person. The appeal process mentioned in part (g), a due process provision, helps engender support but is rarely used; it is a typical provision found in most states.

Persons who registered within the twenty-day cutoff period provided by this section for voter registration were not "qualified electors" for the purpose of determining whether a petition for the dissolution of a school district was signed by a majority of qualified electors (Pike County School District No. 1 v. Pike County Board of Education, 1969).

SECTION 10

Transfer and Change of Status, (**a**) Upon a change of legal residence within the county, any registered voter may cause his registration to be transferred to his new address by signing a mailed request to the Permanent Registrar, giving his present address and the address at which he was last registered, or by applying in person at the office of the Permanent Registrar. The Permanent Registrar shall strike through the last address and record the new address of the voter on the original, duplicate and triplicate copies of the Affidavit of Registration and upon the quadruplicate copy if it is presented for that purpose to the Permanent Registrar by the registered voter. The Permanent Registrar promptly shall make such appropriate changes in the Precinct Registration Files as necessitated by such change of address.
(**b**) Upon a change of legal residence to another county within the State of Arkansas, an eligible voter must register again and shall record his former address in the spaces provided for such purpose in the Affidavit of Registration.
(**c**) Upon a change of name by marriage or otherwise, an eligible voter must register again and shall record his former name in the spaces provided for such purpose in the Affidavit of Registration.

The change of address process, as described in subsection (a), was designed to be much easier than the initial registration process. Duplicate registrations could result from the provision contained in subsection (b), but the county clerks do exchange information. Increasing numbers have computerized lists of registered voters which they may share. Subsection (c) provides that it is advisable for voters to keep their voter registrations as up-to-date as possible.

SECTION 11

Cancellation of Registration, (**a**) It shall be the duty of the Permanent Registrar to cancel the registration of voters:

(**1**) Who have failed to vote in any election during four (4) successive calendar years immediately preceding the first of January of any years [year] and have not responded to the notice prescribed by Section 11(f) of this Amendment;
(**2**) Who have changed their residence to an address out the county;
(**3**) Who have died or changed their name;
(**4**) Who have been convicted of felonies and have not discharged their sentence or been pardoned; or
(**5**) Who are not lawfully qualified or registered electors of this State, or of the county.

(**b**) It shall be the duty of the Permanent Registrar of each county upon the registration of a person who has been registered previously in another county to notify promptly the Permanent Registrar of such other county of the new registration.

(c) It shall be the duty of the Director of the Bureau of Vital Statistics to notify promptly the Permanent Registrar in each county of the death of all residents of such county.

(d) It shall be the duty of the Circuit Clerk of each county upon the conviction of any person of a felony to notify promptly the Permanent Registrar of the county of residence of such convicted felon.

(e) Within ten (10) days following the receipt or possession of information requiring any cancellation of registration, other than under Section 11(a) (1) of this Amendment, the Permanent Registrar shall write or stamp the work "cancelled" across the face of such original Affidavit of Registration and note the date of the cancellation, the reason for the cancellation, and the signature of the persons cancelling in blank spaces provided thereon for such purposes. Such cancelled original Affidavit of Registration shall then be transferred to the Inactive Registration File and the duplicate and triplicate copies in the Precinct Registration Files shall then be destroyed.

(f) The Permanent Registrar shall, thirty (30) days before cancellation, notify all persons whose Affidavits of Registration are to be cancelled in accordance with Section 11(a) (1) of this Amendment. The notice may be either by publication or by first class mail. The notice by mail shall be as follows: "NOTICE OF IMPENDING CANCELLATION OF VOTER REGISTRATION. Notice is hereby given that due to your failure to vote in any election in this county during the preceding four (4) calendar years, under the laws of this State your voter registration will be cancelled unless you respond in person or by mail to this office within thirty (30) days after the date postmarked on the envelope of this notice that you are still a qualified voter and desire that your voter registration not be cancelled." Alternatively, the Permanent Registrar may publish a list of the names of all persons whose Affidavits of Registration are to be cancelled in accordance with Section 11(a) (1) of this Amendment. The list shall be published in a legal newspaper having a general circulation in the county. To assure proper identification, the name of the person's street or route and the name of the city, town or community in which the person lives shall be included. The following notice shall be given and shall be followed by the list of names: "NOTICE OF IMPENDING CANCELLATION OF VOTER REGISTRATION. Notice is hereby given that due to your failure to vote in any election in this county during the preceding four (4) calendar years, under the laws of this State your voter registration will be cancelled unless you respond in person or by mail to this office within thirty (30) days from the date of this notice that you are still a qualified voter and desire that your voter registration not be cancelled." When, in response to the notice, a qualified voter requests the Permanent Registrar not to cancel the voter registration, the voter registration shall not be cancelled under Section 11(a) (1) of this amendment unless the voter fails to vote in any election in the county during the succeeding four **(4)** calendar years after the date of the notice.

(g) The Permanent Registrar is authorized, and may be directed by the County Board of Registration, to determine by mail check, house to house canvass or any other reasonable means at any time within the whole or any part of the county whether active Record Registration Files contain the names of any persons not qualified by law to vote. Further, upon application based upon affidavits of one or more qualified voters by the Prosecuting Attorney for the county, the Circuit Judge of the county, for good cause shown, may order the Permanent Registrar to make sure determination or to cancel the registration of such unqualified persons. [As amended by Act 744 of 1977, Section 1; Act 11 of 1983, Section 1; and Act 800 of 1987, Section 1.]

Subsection (a) provides that the county clerk is responsible for keeping an up-to-date registry of eligible and active voters. The provision in subsection (b) was designed to cut down on duplicate registration and voting. The exchange of information among relevant agencies is mandated in subsection (c). The responsibility is specifically fixed with the clerk of the circuit court, subsection (d), with whom the convictions are rendered for the disqualification of voters due to criminal convictions. The requirement is not an absolute prerequisite to cancellation of a registration, but is one method by which a registrar may obtain information concerning the disqualification of a voter (Merritt v. Jones, 1976). This provision, subsection (e), establishes a process for deleting records for a disqualified voter. A statute, which was passed in 1989, revised this section (subsection [f]), requiring the specific use of first-class mail for notification of cancellation. This section, subsection (g), provides a relatively proactive position for County Clerks in enforcing voter registration provisions (see Act 744 of 1977 and Act 11 of 1983). This section was amended by two 1987 acts which conflict and cannot be codified together.

SECTION 12

Loss or Destruction of Affidavits of Registration. In the event any Registration Record File shall become lost or destroyed, or in the event that any Affidavit of Registration in any Registration Record File shall be mutilated or destroyed in any manner not authorized by this Amendment, the Permanent Registrar shall prepare, from the remaining Files, temporary copies of the Affidavits of Registration, if necessary for the conduct of any election. The Permanent Registrar shall send notice of such fact by first-class mail to any voter whose Affidavit has been lost, destroyed or mutilated in order that such voter may register again. The previous registration shall be cancelled at the time of the new registration, and in any event within sixty (60) days after mailing of such notice.

If a voter or a registrar makes a mistake on the affidavit, the voter must reregister.

SECTION 13

Signature Requirement, (a) No voter shall receive a ballot at any election until a judge of the election has stamped the date and until the voter, in the presence of such judge, has signed his name, including his given name, his middle name or initial (if any) and his last name in the first unused space on the Record of Voting Form.

(b) No registered voter shall receive a ballot for any election unless the signature of the person on the Affidavit of Registration or previous signature on the Supplement Record of Voting Form and his signature in the appropriate space on the Record of Voting Form thereto are deemed by the judges to be identical.

(c) No registered voter unable to sign his signature or unable to make his mark or cross in the appropriate space on the Record of Voting Form shall receive a ballot at any election unless the month and day of the person's birth, as then stated by him, conform to that entered in the space for the person's signature on the Affidavit of Registration by the Permanent or Deputy Registrar.

(d) Absentee voting shall be conducted in the same manner as now provided under the laws of the State; provided, that the Permanent Registrar shall determine that the signature on the application for absentee ballot is identical with the signature appearing on the voter's Affidavit of Registration before mailing or passing out an absentee ballot. The Permanent Registrar shall, upon permitting absentee voting in the manner hereinabove authorized, stamp in the first vacant and unused blank space in the Record of Voting Form the date of the forthcoming election and shall note thereafter the words "absentee ballot."

(e) Notwithstanding the foregoing provisions of this Section, if a voter presents himself at a polling place on the date of an election but no copy of his Affidavit of Registration can be located by the judges of the election in the Precinct Registration Files, such voter shall be permitted to vote when all of the following conditions are satisfied:

(1) The voter surrenders the quadruplicate copy of his Affidavit of Registration;

(2) the voter signs such quadruplicate copy in accordance with Section 13 (a), (b) and (c) of this Amendment;

(3) an election judge verifies the existence of an original Affidavit of Registration in the Permanent Registration File; and

(4) the original Affidavit of Registration reveals that the voter has presented himself at a precinct polling place where he is legally qualified to vote. The quadruplicate Affidavits of Registration so surrendered shall be returned to the Permanent Registrar with the Precinct Registration Files, and new registration shall thereupon be required in accordance with the procedure set out by Section 12 of this Amendment.

The signature comparison component of voter registration was designed to protect the integrity of the election process, as is stated in subsection (a). Subsection (**b**) seems to require an on-the-spot comparison and temporarily prevents a total computerizing of the process, as used in many other states, until technology provides an affordable scanning machine to compare signatures. Subsection (c) provides a safeguard for those who happen to be illiterate. Absentee ballots are protected by subsection (d). They must be applied for and may be picked up by someone other than the voter. The county clerk is the custodian of absentee ballots (Henley v. Goggin, 1966). An application for absentee ballot is required in order for a signature comparison to be made (Martin v. Hefley, 1976). Subsection (e), amended by Act 149 of 1973, covers the unlikely situation where a voter shows up at a polling place where his Affidavit of Registration cannot be located.

SECTION 14

Lists of Voters, (**a**) By the first day of June of each year, and at such other times as may be practicable, all Permanent Registrars shall, and at this discretion at other times may, print or otherwise duplicate and public lists of registered voters by precincts, and may distribute such lists free of cost, or, with the approval of the County Board of Registration, at a price necessary to cover cost of publication. A copy of the most current such list in each precinct shall be furnished the election officials at each precinct at the time the ballot boxes are delivered and such election officials shall post said list at a conspicuous place in the polling area.
(**b**) By the first day of June of each year, the Permanent Registrar shall certify to the State Auditor the total number of registered voters in the county. The State Auditor shall tabulate the total number of registered voters in the State and shall make such information available to interested persons upon request.

Many of the lists mentioned in subsection (a) are produced by computer and priced to cover the costs of printing and administrative distribution. Campaign organizations and marketing experts are the major markets for these lists. Traditionally, subsection (b) has meant that an annual report is expected.

Section 15. Penalties, (**a**) Any person who shall maliciously and intentionally destroy, steal, mutilate or unlawfully detain or obtain any Affidavits of Registration or any Registration Record Files shall be guilty of a felony, and upon conviction thereof shall be fined in the sum of not less than one hundred dollars ($100.00) nor more than one thousand dollars ($1,000.00) or be imprisoned in the State Penitentiary for a period of not less than one (**1**) year nor more than five (5) years, or both.
(**b**) Any public official or election official who wilfully violates any provision of this Amendment shall be guilty of a misdemeanor, and upon conviction thereof shall also be removed from such office.
(**c**) Any other person who wilfully violates any provision of this Amendment shall be guilty of a misdemeanor.

The penalty mentioned in subsection (a) is often discussed but never praised. The penalties mentioned in subsection (b) reflect the distrust prevalent at the time (1964), with allegations of burned ballots, contested results, stuffed boxes, and slow counts to swing elections. If any situation has not been covered, subsection (c) serves as a safety net.

SECTION 16

Severability. If any provision of this Amendment or the application thereof to any person or circumstance is held invalid, such invalidity shall not affect other provisions or applications of the Amendment which can be given effect without the invalid provision or application, and to this end the provisions of this Amendment are declared to be severable.

This section protects the amendment against certain supreme court rulings that might affect registrations.

SECTION 17

Effect on Other Laws. This Amendment supersedes and repeals the requirement of Amendment No. 8 that a poll tax receipt be presented prior to registration or voting, and further supersedes and repeals Act 19 of 1964 and all other laws or parts of laws in conflict herewith.

Specific repealers were included here to remove any doubts that the federal abolition of poll tax had been met, with the expectation of an onslaught of litigation.

SECTION 18

Appropriations. The General Assembly shall make such appropriations as may be required for the effectuation of this Amendment.

The legislature appropriates funds biennially to the state auditor for voter registration forms. Funds are also thus appropriated for a car for the auditor's office for a staff person to make deliveries to county clerks and to offer public education on the voter registration process.

SECTION 19

Amendment. The General Assembly may, in the same manner as required for amendment of laws initiated by the people, amend Sections 5 through 15 of this Amendment, so long as such amendments are germane to this Amendment and consistent with its policy and purposes.

The legislature, by a vote of two-thirds, can change these specific sections, as with an initiated statute, instead of a constitutional amendment. This section provides that the authority of state board of election commissioners is one of implementation rather than one of creation (Faubus v. Fields, 1965).

SECTION 20

Short Title. This Amendment shall be known as the "Arkansas Amendment for Voter Registration without Poll Tax Payment."

This registration is free, and as its drafters wanted to tout that fact in their campaign, they coined this title.

SECTION 21

Effective Date. This Amendment shall be in full force and effect from and after January 1, 1965; provided, that for any elections held before March 1, 1965, those voters who are registered lectors as of December 31, 1964, shall be permitted to vote in such election if otherwise qualified.

This section is strictly the schedule for the transition from the poll tax system to the new voter registration system.

AMENDMENT 52: COMMUNITY COLLEGE ENABLING ACT

SECTION 1

The General Assembly may by law provide for the establishment of districts for the purpose of providing community college instruction and technical training. The General Assembly shall prescribe the method of financing such community college and technical institutes, and may authorize the levy of a tax upon the taxable property in such district for the acquisition, construction, reconstruction, repair, expansion, operation, and maintenance of facilities therefor.

This amendment was proposed by initiative petition and adopted at the general election on November 3, 1964. The legislature has the authority to establish community colleges (Turner v. Woodruff, 1985). Voters have voted property taxes to fund colleges in Sebastian, Boone, Benton, Garland, St. Francis, Phillips, and Mississippi counties. The largest is Westark Community College in Forth Smith, and the newest is Northwest Community College in Bentonville.

SECTION 2

No such district shall be created and no such tax shall be levied upon the property in an established district except upon approval of a majority of the qualified electors of such proposed or established district voting thereon. Provided that any millage so approved by the electors of a district shall be a continuing levy until increased, reduced or repealed in such manner as may be provided by law, providing they shall ever remain a community college and shall never be extended into four-year institutions.

This section puts the voters in charge of the local property tax revenue levels, but unlike school districts, the question is not referred to the voters each year.

AMENDMENT 53: KINDERGARTEN

SECTION 1

Section 1 of Article 14 of the Constitution of Arkansas of 1874, is hereby amended to read as follows:

"SECTION 1

Free School System.—Intelligence and virtue being the safeguards of liberty and the bulwark of a free and good government, the State shall ever maintain a general, suitable and efficient system of free public schools and shall adopt all suitable means to secure to the people the advantages and opportunities of education. The specific intention of this amendment is to authorize that in addition to existing constitutional or statutory provisions the General Assembly and/or public school districts may spend public funds for the education of persons over twenty-one (21) years of age and under six (6) years of age, as may be provided by law, and no other interpretation shall be given to it."

This amended Article 14, Section 1, and was proposed by Senate Joint Resolution No. 4 in 1967. It was filed in the Office of the Secretary of State on March 8, 1967, and was approved at the general election on November 5, 1968. The original constitution provided only for publicly funded programs for first grade through high school. This section gives authority to the legislature to establish statewide kindergarten; however, enabling legislation for kindergartens was not passed by the legislature for more than twenty years after the amendment's adoption.

AMENDMENT 54: STATE PRINTING CONTRACTS

SECTION 1

The printing, stationery, and supplies purchased by the General Assembly and other departments of government shall be under contracts given to the lowest responsible bidder, below such maximum price and under such regulations as shall be prescribed by law. No member or officer of any department of government shall in any way be interested in such contracts.

SECTION 2

Section 15 of Article 19 of the Constitution of the State of Arkansas is hereby repealed.

This Amendment was proposed by Senate Joint Resolution No. 6 in 1973. It was filed in the Office of the Secretary of State on April 5, 1973, and was approved at the general election on November 5, 1974. Amendment 54, Section 2, repealed Article 19, Section 15. Act 760 of 1983, Section 1, read: "On the effective date of this Act, printing, stationery and supplies subject to Amendment 54 of the Arkansas Constitution shall be subject to the provisions of the Arkansas Preference Law, Act 482 of 1979 as amended."

This amendment was intended to clear up the scandal in the purchasing process generally, and in the area of printing contracts specifically. Act 760 of 1983 applied the Arkansas Preference Law, Act 482 of 1979, to state printing contracts. Moreover, the state may produce its own duplicating and printing without submitting a bid (Erxleben v. Horton Printing Co., 1984). The repealer in section 2 is traditionally included for ease in interpretation.

AMENDMENT 55: REVISION OF COUNTY GOVERNMENT

This amendment was proposed by House Joint Resolution No. 20 in 1973. It was filed in the Office of the Secretary of State on April 10, 1973, and was approved at the general election on November 5, 1974.

SECTION 1

(a) A county acting through its Quorum Court may exercise local legislative authority not denied by the Constitution or by law.
(b) No county may declare any act a felony or exercise any authority not relating to county affairs.
(c) A county may, for any public purpose, contract, cooperate, or join with any other county, or with any political subdivisions of the State or any other states or their political subdivisions, or with the United States.

This section changes the traditional interpretation of local powers from only those specifically granted (the Dillion Rule) to all that are not specifically denied. The enabling legislation for this amendment was Acts 1977, No. 742, now codified as Section 14–14–101 et seq (Venhaus v. Adams, 1988).

SECTION 2

(**a**) No county's Quorum Court shall be comprised of fewer than nine (9) justices of the peace, nor comprised of more than fifteen (15) justices of the peace. The number of justices of the peace that comprise a county's Quorum Court shall be determined by law. The county's Election Commission shall, after each decennial census, divide the county into convenient and single member districts so that the Quorum Court shall be based upon the inhabitants of the county with each member representing, as nearly as practicable, an equal number thereof.
(**b**) The Quorum Court may create, consolidate, separate, revise, or abandon any elective county office or offices except during the term thereof; provided, however, that a majority of those voting on the question at a general election have approved said action.

The quorum court is a real legislative body and is now of a workable size (the Pulaski County Quorum Court was in excess of four hundred justices of the peace at the time of adoption). Single-member districts were created. Changes in the administrative organization of the county offices can be made by vote of the people of the respective county, whereas previously, it would have required a statewide vote.

SECTION 3

The County Judge, in addition to other powers and duties provided for by the Constitution and by law, shall preside over the Quorum Court without a vote but with the power of veto; authorize and approve disbursement of appropriated county funds; operate the system of county roads; administer ordinances enacted by the Quorum Court; have custody of county property; hire county employees, except those persons employed by other elected officials of the county.

The powers of the county judge, before this amendment, were almost unlimited and extended to the executive, legislative, and judicial areas. This section makes the county judge the chief administrative officer of the county and allows the retention of the historic title, which is rooted in the judicial process. This section changed the duties of the county judge from those of an official who pays claims as a judicial officer to those of an officer who pays claims as an administrative officer (Venhaus v. Pulaski County Quorum Court, 1987).

SECTION 4

In addition to other powers conferred by the Constitution and by law, the Quorum Court shall have the power to override the veto of the County Judge by a vote of three-fifths of the total membership; fix the number and compensation of deputies and county employees; fill vacancies in elective county offices; and adopt ordinances necessary for the government of the county. The Quorum Court shall meet and exercise all such powers as provided by law.

The quorum court resembles the city council as an institution and in its function.

Section 5. Compensation of each county officer shall be fixed by the Quorum Court within a minimum and maximum to be determined by law. Compensation may not be decreased during a current term; provided, however, during the interim, from the date of adoption of this Amendment until the first day of the next succeeding month following the date of approval of salaries by the Quorum Court, salaries of county officials shall be determined by law. Fees of the office shall not be the basis of compensation for officers or employees of county offices. Per diem compensation for members of the Quorum Court shall be fixed by law.

The state legislature establishes a pay plan with a maximum and a minimum for each classification of county, based on population, through omnibus legislation in almost every biennial legislative session. The biggest debate is always over increasing the minimum, rather than the maximum, especially from those counties paying only the existing minimum for each official. The authority to establish both the number and compensation of all county employees includes deputy sheriffs and is clearly vested in the quorum court of each county pursuant to this section (Venhaus v. Adams, 1988).

SECTION 6

All County Officers shall be bonded as provided by law.

This section provides security for losses to taxpayers.

SECTION 7

Sections 1 and 4 of this Amendment shall be effective January 1, 1977, and all other provisions hereof shall be effective when this Amendment is adopted.

The amendment was adopted in 1974. It was implemented in 1977, after a two-year study by a county government study commission named by then Governor David Pryor.

SECTION 8

All parts of the Constitution of Arkansas in conflict with this Amendment are repealed.

This is the regular repealer.

AMENDMENT 56: ESTABLISH AND LIMIT SALARIES OF GOVERNOR AND OTHER STATE CONSTITUTIONAL OFFICERS, MEMBERS OF THE GENERAL ASSEMBLY AND MUNICIPAL OFFICERS

This amendment was proposed by Senate Joint Resolution No. 2 in 1975. It was filed in the Office of the Secretary of State on January 28, 1976, and was approved at the general election on November 7, 1976. Amendment 56, Section 5, repealed Article 19, Section 23, and Amendments 37 and 48.

SECTION 1

The Executive Department of this State shall consist of a Governor, Lieutenant Governor, Secretary of State, Treasurer of State, Auditor of State, Attorney General, and Commissioner of State Lands, all of whom shall keep their offices at the seat of government, and hold their offices for the term of two (2) years, and until their successors are elected and qualified.

This section is superseded by Section 1 of Amendment 63, which extends these terms of office to four years.

SECTION 2

The annual salaries of the officers of the Executive Department, which shall be paid in monthly installments, shall be as follows: the Governor, the sum of $35,000; the Lieutenant Governor, the sum of $14,000; the Secretary of State, the sum of $22,500; the Treasurer of State, the sum of $22,500; the Auditor of State, the sum of $22,500; the Attorney General, the sum of $26,500; and the Commissioner of State Lands, the sum of $22,500.

This section increases salaries from the previous $5,000 per year for all constitutional officers except the governor. The governor's salary was $10,000, the lowest in the nation, until this amendment was adopted in 1976. Now, the salary is once again the lowest in the nation at $35,000. See Amendment 6, Section 6, and Amendment 15, which were previously held superseded by Amendment 37 (Berry v. Gordon, 1964).

SECTION 3

The members of the General Assembly shall receive as their annual salary the sum of $7,500, except the President Pro Tempore of the Senate and the Speaker of the House of Representatives, who shall each receive the sum of $10,000 annually, with such salaries to be payable in equal monthly installments. Provided, that no member of the General Assembly shall be entitled to per diem, reimbursement for documented expenses and mileage unless authorized, and within the limitations, as provided by law.

An act appropriating expense money for these public officials for use in public relations work was found not to violate this section (Berry v. Gordon, 1964). Subsequently, the Internal Revenue Service has begun requiring that taxes be paid on these public relations funds. Then, after recent conviction of the state attorney general of theft by deception. Act 798 of 1991 requires that state vouchers be submitted to receive these funds.

SECTION 4

Municipal Officers. Compensation of municipal officers and officials shall be fixed by the governing body of the municipality, not to exceed limits which may be established by law.

The former salary limit of $5,000 was removed for municipal officials. Limits on salaries of county officials had been removed previously by Amendment 55.

SECTION 5

Article 19, Section 23; Amendment 37; and Amendment 48 to the Constitution of the State of Arkansas all other laws and constitutional provisions in conflict herewith are hereby repealed.

This is the regular repealer clause.

SECTION 6

This Amendment shall be in full force and effect from and after January 1, 1977.

This section indicates that no enabling act is required and that the amendment takes effect immediately.

AMENDMENT 57: EXEMPTION OR LOWERING OF INTANGIBLE PERSONAL PROPERTY TAX

This amendment was proposed by Senate Joint Resolution No. 4 in 1975. It was filed in the Office of the Secretary of State on January 29, 1976, and was approved at the general election on November 7, 1976.

SECTION 1

The General Assembly may classify intangible personal property for assessment at lower percentages of value than other property and may exempt one or more classes of intangible personal property from taxation, or may provide for the taxation of intangible personal property on a basis other than ad valorem.

Up to this time, uniform rates had not been allowed and all property, real and personal, had to be taxed on an ad valorem basis, that is, according to the value of the property.

SECTION 2

The provisions of this Amendment shall be in lieu of those provisions of Article 16, Section 5 of the Constitution of the State of Arkansas relating to the assessment and taxation of intangible personal property.

This is the specific repealer of Article 16, Section 5, and was replaced by Amendment 59.

AMENDMENT 58: CREATION OF A STATE COURT OF APPEALS

This amendment was proposed by Senate Joint Resolution No. 5 in 1977. It was filed in the Office of the Secretary of State on March 23, 1977, and was approved at the general election on November 7, 1978.

SECTION 1

The General Assembly is hereby empowered to create and establish a Court of Appeals and divisions thereof. The Court of Appeals shall have such appellate jurisdiction as the Supreme Court shall by rule determine and shall be subject to the general superintending control of the Supreme Court. Judges of the Court of Appeals shall have the same qualifications as Justices of the Supreme Court and shall be selected in the manner provided by law.

This amendment established a new appellate court to take some of the caseload of the supreme court and further established the supreme court as the administrative head of the judicial branch. A judicial department, headed by an executive director who is hired by the chief justice of the supreme court, provides technical assistance and staff support for the state judiciary.

This amendment entrusts to the Supreme Court complete responsibility for determining both the initial jurisdiction of the Court of Appeals and the extent to which its decisions are reviewable (Moose v. Gregory, 1979). The statute authorizing the court of appeals to sit in divisions of three and authorizing any of the divisions to affirm or reverse a case by a unanimous decision is a valid exercise of legislative authority as contemplated by this section (Citizens Bank V. Estate of Pettyjohn, 1984).

AMENDMENT 59: PROPERTY TAX RELIEF AND ROLLBACK

Article XVI of the Constitution of the State of Arkansas is hereby amended by adding thereto new Sections, to read as follows:

This amendment repealed Article 16, Section 5, and substituted a new section therefor, which appears as Article 16, Section 5, and added Article 16, Sections 14 through 16. The amendment was proposed by the General Assembly in 1979 and was adopted at the November 4, 1980 election. See Wells v. Riviere, 1980.

SECTION 14

(a) Whenever a county-wide reappraisal or reassessment of property subject to ad valorem taxes made in accordance with procedures established by the General Assembly shall result in an increase in the aggregate value of taxable real and personal property in any taxing unit in this State of ten percent (10%) or more over the previous year the rate of city or town, county, school district, and community college district taxes levied against the taxable real and personal property of each such taxing unit shall, upon completion of such reappraisal or reassessment, be adjusted or rolled back, by the governing body of the taxing unit, for the year for which levied as provided below. The General Assembly shall, by law, establish the procedures to be followed by a county in making a county-wide reappraisal or reassessment of property which will, upon completion, authorize the adjustment or rollback of property tax rates or millage, as authorized hereinabove. The adjustment or rollback of tax rates or millage for the "base year" as hereinafter defined shall be designed to assure that each taxing unit will receive an amount of tax revenue from each tax source no greater than ten percent (10%) above the revenues received during the previous year from each such tax source, adjusted for any lawful tax or millage rate increase or reduction imposed in the manner provided by law for the year for which the tax adjustment or rollback is to be made, and after making the following additional adjustments:

(i) by excluding from such calculation the assessed value of, and taxes derived from, tangible personal property assessed in the taxing unit, and all real and tangible personal property of public utilities and regulated carriers assessed in the taxing unit, and

These provisions ensured increased popular support as well as support from utilities and railroads.

(ii) by computing the adjusted or rollback millage rates on the basis of the reassessed taxable real property for the base year that will produce an amount of revenue no greater than ten percent (10%) above the revenues produced from the assessed value of real property in the taxing unit (after making the aforementioned adjustments for personal properties and properties of public utilities and regulated carriers noted above) from millage rates in effect in the taxing unit during the base year in which the millage adjustment or rollback is to be calculated. Provided, further, that in calculating the amount of adjusted or rollback millage necessary to produce tax revenues no greater them ten percent (10%) above the revenues received during the previous year, the governing body shall separate from the assessed value of taxable real property of the taxing unit, newly-discovered real property and new construction and improvements to real property after making the adjustments for personal property or property of public utilities and regulated carriers noted above, and shall compute the millage necessary to produce an amount of revenues equal to, but no greater than the base year revenues of the taxing unit from each millage source. Such taxing unit may elect either to obtain an increase in revenues equal to the amount of revenues that the computed or adjusted rollback millage will produce from newly-discovered real property and new construction and improvements to real property, or if the same be less than ten percent (10%), the governing body of the taxing unit may recompute the millage rate to be charged to produce an amount no greater than ten percent (10%) above the revenues collected for taxable real property during the base year.

Provided, however, that the amount of revenues to be derived from taxable personal property assessed in the taxing unit for the base year, other than personal property taxes to be paid by public utilities and regulated carriers in the manner provided hereinabove, shall be computed at the millage necessary to produce the same dollar amount of revenues derived during the current year in which the base year adjustment or rollback of millage is computed, and the millage necessary to produce the amount of revenues received from personal property taxes received by the taxing unit, for the base year shall be reduced annually as the assessed value of taxable personal property increases until the amount of revenues from personal property taxes, computed on the basis of the current year millage rates will produce an amount of revenues from taxable personal property equal to or greater than received during the base year, and thereafter the millage rates for computing personal property taxes shall be the millage rates levied for the current year.

Provided, however, that the taxes to be paid by public utilities and regulated carriers in the respective taxing units of the several counties of this State during the first five (5) calendar years in which taxes are levied on the taxable real and personal property as reassessed and equalized in each of the respective counties as a party of a statewide reappraisal program, shall be the greater of the following:

(1) the amount of taxes paid on property owned by such public utilities or regulated carriers in or assigned to such taxing unit, less adjustments for properties disposed of or reductions in the assessed valuation of such properties in the base year as defined below, or

This rather complicated process and provision limits property tax revenue increases even in the face of increased assessments by providing a 10 percent cap on increases, through a complicated rollback process.

(**2**) the amount of taxes due on the assessed valuation of taxable real and tangible personal property belonging to the public utilities or regulated carriers located in or assigned to the taxing unit in each county at millage rates levied for the current year.

As used herein, the term "base year" shall mean the year in which a county completes reassessment and equalization of taxable real and personal property as a part of a statewide reappraisal program, and extends the adjusted or rolled back millage rates for the first time, as provided in subsection (a) of this Section, for the respective taxing units in such county for collection in the following year.

(**i**) in the event the amount of taxes paid the taxing unit in a county in the base year, as defined herein, is greater than the taxes due to be paid to such taxing unit for the current year of any year of the second (2nd) period of five (5) years after the base year, the difference between the base year taxes and the current year taxes for any year of such five (5) year period shall be adjusted as follows:

Current year of second period of five (5) years—taxes shall be current year taxes to which shall be added the following percentage of the difference between the current year taxes and the base year taxes (if greater than current year taxes)

1st year—80% of difference
2nd year—60% of difference
3rd year—40% of difference
4th year—20% of difference
5th year and thereafter—current year's taxes only.

This section provides for a phase-in of new rates.

(**ii**) if the current year taxes of a public utility or regulated carrier equal or exceed the base year's taxes due a taxing unit during any year of the first ten (10) years after the based year, the amount of taxes to be paid to such taxing unit shall thereafter be the current year's taxes and the adjustment authorized herein shall no longer apply in computing taxes to be paid to such taxing unit.

Provided, that in the event the aforementioned requirement for payment of taxes by public utilities and regulated carriers, or any class of utilities or carriers for the ten (10) year period noted above, shall be held by court decision to be contrary to the Constitution or Statutes of this State or of the Federal Government, the General Assembly may provide for other utilities or classes of carriers to receive the same treatment provided or required under the court order, if deemed necessary to promote equity between similar utilities or classes of carriers.

Equity among classes of property is sought to provide equal protection of the laws clause.

(b) The General Assembly shall, by law, provide for procedures to be followed with respect to adjusting ad valorem taxes or millage pledged for bonded indebtedness purposes, to assure that the adjusted or rolled-back rate of tax or millage levied for bonded indebtedness purposes will, at all times, provide a level of income sufficient to meet the current requirements of all principal, interest, paying agent fees, reserves, and other requirements of the bond indenture.

This provision was necessary to maintain the state's excellent credit rating.

SECTION 15

(a) Residential property used solely as the principal place of residence of the owner thereof shall be assessed in accordance with its value as a residence, so long as said property is used as the principal place of residence of the owner thereof, and shall not be assessed in accordance with some other method of valuation until said property ceases to be used for such residential purpose.
(b) Agricultural land, pasture land, timber land, residential and commercial land, excluding structures thereon, used primarily as such, shall be valued for taxation purposes under the provisions of Section 5 of this Article, upon the basis of its agricultural, pasture, timber, residential or commercial productivity or use, and when so valued, such land shall be assessed at the same percentum of value and taxed at the same rate as other property subject to ad valorem taxes.
(c) The General Assembly shall enact laws providing for the administration and enforcement of this Section and for the imposition of penalties for violations of this Section, or statutes enacted pursuant thereto.

This is a typical section transferring much discretion to the legislature from the cities and counties as well as from the state constitution.

SECTION 16

The General Assembly, upon approval thereof by a vote of not less than three-fourths (3/4ths) of the members elected to each house, may provide that the valuation of real property actually occupied by its owner as a residence who is sixty-five (65) years of age, or older, may be exempt in such amount as may be determined by law, but no greater than the first Twenty Thousand Dollars ($20,000.00) in value thereof, as a homestead from ad valorem property taxes.

The legislature is authorized to enact a homestead exemption of up to $20,000. It did so in 1979 and increased it to $30,000 in 1981.

SECTION 17

The provisions of Section 5 of Article XVI of the Constitution of the State of Arkansas of 1874 are hereby repealed, and the following provisions are substituted in lieu thereof:

"SECTION 5

(a) All real and tangible personal property subject to taxation shall be taxed according to its value, that value to be ascertained in such manner as the General Assembly shall direct, making the same equal and uniform throughout the State. No one species of property for which a tax may be collected shall be taxed higher than another species of property of equal value, except as provided and authorized in Section 15 of this Article, and except as authorized in Section 14 of this Article. The General Assembly, upon the approval thereof by a vote of not less than three-fourths (3/4ths) of the members elected to each house, may establish the methods and procedures for valuation of property for taxation purposes, but may not alter the method of valuation set forth in Section 15 of this Article.
(b) The following property shall be exempt from taxation: public property used exclusively for public purposes; churches used as such; cemeteries used exclusively as such; school buildings and apparatus; libraries and grounds used exclusively for school purposes; and buildings and grounds and materials used exclusively for public charity.

Nothing in this Section shall affect or repeal the provision of Amendment No. 57 to the Constitution of the State of Arkansas pertaining to intangible personal property." (See also Amendment Nos. 12, 22 and 27.)

This section ensures that Amendment 57 stands and remains unaffected by this amendment, which deals with real property and tangible property rather than intangible personal property such as certificates of deposit, stocks, and bonds.

AMENDMENT 60: INTEREST RATE CONTROL

This amended Article 19, Section 13. It was proposed by House Joint Resolution No. 7 in 1981 and was filed in the Office of the Secretary of State on March 30, 1981, and was approved at the general election on November 2, 1982.

Section 13, Article XIX, of the Arkansas Constitution of 1874, is hereby amended to read as follows;

SECTION 13

(a) General loans: (i) The maximum lawful rate of interest on any contract entered into after the effective date hereof shall not exceed five percent (5%) per annum above the Federal Reserve Discount Rate at the time of the contract, (ii) All such contracts having a rate of interest in excess of the maximum lawful rate shall be void as to the unpaid interest. A person who has paid interest in excess of the maximum lawful rate may recover, within the time provided by law, twice the amount of interest paid. It is unlawful for any person to knowingly charge a rate of interest in excess of the maximum lawful rate in effect at the time of the contract, and any person who does so shall be subject to such punishment as may be provided by law.

(b) Consumer loans and credit sales: All contracts for consumer loans and credit sales having a greater rate of interest than seventeen percent (17%) per annum shall be void as to principal and interest and the General Assembly shall prohibit the same by law.

(c) Definitions: As used herein, the term: **(i)** "consumer loans and credit sales" means credit extended to a natural person in which the money, property, or service which is the subject of the transaction is primarily for personal, family or household purposes, **(ii)** "Federal Reserve Discount Rate" means the Federal Reserve Discount Rate on ninety-day commercial paper in effect in the Federal Reserve Bank in the Federal Reserve District in which Arkansas is located.

(d) Miscellaneous: (i) The rate of interest for contracts in which no rate of interest is agreed upon shal be six percent (6%) per annum, **(ii)** The provisions hereof are not intended and shall not be deemed to supersede or otherwise invalidate any provisions of federal law applicable to loans or interest rates including loans secured by residential real property, **(iii)** The provisions hereof revoke all provisions of State Law which establish the maximum rate of interest chargeable in the State or which are otherwise inconsistent herewith.

Before this amendment was adopted, Arkansas had the lowest and most strict usury law in the nation, limiting interest to 10 percent per year with the stiffest penalty of both interest and principal. The historic penalty on consumer loans and credit sales was retained, but the interest limit was increased by 7 percent. The definitions in part (c) were the original ones as established by court decisions. Part (d) is essentially the regular repealer, with a schedule for transition.

AMENDMENT 61: THREE-MILL COUNTY ROAD TAX

This amendment was proposed by Senate Joint Resolution No. 1 in 1981. It was filed in the Office of the Secretary of State on March 30, 1981, and was approved at the general election on November 2, 1982.

SECTION 1

County quorum courts may annually levy a county road tax not to exceed three (3) mills on the dollar on all taxable real and personal property within their respective counties. Revenues derived from the county road tax shall be used for the sole purpose of constructing and repairing public roads and bridges within the county wherein levied. The authority granted by this Amendment shall be in addition to all other taxing authority of the county quorum courts.

This amendment replaces the right of the people to vote on a road tax every two years. If not voted, the tax previously could not be collected, even if it had been inadvertently omitted and had no opposition.

SECTION 2

Amendment 3 to the Constitution of the State of Arkansas is hereby specifically repealed.

This is the regular repealer, which was included to prevent litigation.

AMENDMENT 62: LOCAL CAPITAL IMPROVEMENT BOND

With respect to the requirement for electoral approval of bond issues, this amendment may be superseded by Amendment 65. This amendment was proposed by House Joint Resolution No, 1 in 1983. It was filed in the office of the Secretary of State on March 29, 1983, and was approved at the general election on November 6, 1984. Amendment 62, Section 11, repealed Amendments 13, 17, 25, and 49.

SECTION 1

(a) The legislative body of a municipality or county, with the consent of a majority of the qualified electors voting on the question at an election called for that purpose, may authorize the issuance of bonds, to bear interest at a rate not to exceed two percent (2%) per annum above the Federal Reserve Rate at the time of the election authorizing the bonds, for capital improvements of a public nature, as defined by the General Assembly, in amounts approved by a majority of those voting on the question either at an election called for that purpose or at a general election. The General Assembly shall prescribe a uniform method of calling and holding such elections and the terms upon which the bonds may be issued. If more than one purpose is proposed, each shall be stated separately on the ballot. The election shall be held no earlier than thirty (30) days after it is called by the legislative body. The tax to retire the bonds may be an ad valorem tax on real and personal property. Other taxes may be authorized by the General Assembly or the legislative body to retire the bonds.

This section is superseded by Amendment 65.

(b) The limit of the principal amount of bonded indebtedness of the municipality or county which may be outstanding and unpaid at the time of issuance of any bonds secured by a tax on real or personal property, except for bonds issued for industrial development purposes pursuant to Section 2 hereof, shall be a sum equal to ten percent (10%) for a county or twenty percent (20%) for a municipality of the total assessed value for tax purposed of real and personal property in the county or municipality, as determined by the last tax assessment.

This is the traditional type of limiting section, and was designed to inspire public confidence and popular mandates.

(c) The municipality or county may, from time to time, suspend the collect of a levy, when not required for the payment of its bonds, subject to the covenants with the bondholders.

This subsection is a cutoff valve so that surplus funds will not build up once the debt has been paid. It gives the flexibility to take care of situations in which sufficient funds might become available from other sources.

SECTION 2

(a) In addition to the authority for bonded indebtedness set forth in Section 1, any municipality or county may, with the consent of the majority of the voters voting on the question at an election held for that purpose, issue bonds in sums approved by such majority at that election for the purpose of financing facilities for the securing and developing of industry within or near the county or municipality holding the election.

The purpose for the adoption of this provision is the people's principal concern to create jobs and thus prevent unemployment and loss of population (Hackler v. Baker, 1961). Tourism is not defined as an industry (Purvis v. City of Little Rock, 1984). A county may not undertake the construction of facilities covered by this section except in cases where it has the necessary funds on hand, unless the voters have approved (Woolard v. Thomas, 1964; Johnson v. Cummings, 1984).

(b) To provide for payment of principal and interest of the bonds issued pursuant to this Section, as they mature, the municipality or county may levy a special tax, not to exceed five (5) mills on the dollar of the taxable real and personal property therein. However, the municipality or county may, from time to time, suspend the collection of such annual levy when not required for the payment of its bonds. In no event shall any parcel of real and personal taxable property be subject to a special tax levied under the authority of this Section in excess of five (5) mills for bonds issued under this Section.

This subsection is almost identical to Section 1, subsection (c).

SECTION 3

The bonds described in Section 2 hereof shall be sold only at public sale after twenty (20) days advertisement in a newspaper having a bona fide circulation in the municipality or county issuing such bonds; provided, however, that the municipality or county may exchange such bonds for bonds of like amount, rate or interest, and length of issue.

This section establishes the system for the selling of the public bonds. The former section did not prohibit the county from issuing convertible bonds (Gamer v. Lowery, 1953).

SECTION 4

The maximum rate of any special tax to pay bonded indebtedness as authorized in Sections 1 and 2 hereof shall be stated on the ballot. After such bond issue has been approved by the electorate, the municipality or county may, prior to the issuance of the bonds, borrow funds on an interim basis, not to exceed three (3) years, and pledge to the payment thereof the tax approved by the voters.

This section provides maximum cash management capability for local finances.

SECTION 5

The special tax for payment of bonded indebtedness authorized in Sections 1 and 2 hereof shall constitute a special fund pledged as security for the payment of such indebtedness. The special tax shall never be extended for any other purpose, nor collected for any greater length of time than necessary to retire such bonded indebtedness, except that tax receipts in excess of the amount required to retire the debt according to its terms may, subject to covenants entered into with the holders of the bonds, be pledged as security for the issuance of additional bonds if authorized by the voters. The tax for such additional bonds shall terminate within the time provided for the tax originally imposed. Upon retirement of the bonded indebtedness, any surplus tax collections which may have accumulated shall be transferred to the general funds of the municipality or county.

A city cannot use surplus revenue derived from a tax that was levied to pay the principal and interest on bonds for the construction of one item for the construction of another until the first bonds have been paid off (City of West Memphis v. Jordan, 1948).

SECTION 6

The General Assembly may enact laws governing the conduct of elections authorized by this Amendment. Absent the enactment of such laws, such elections shall be held, called and conducted in accordance with the laws governing elections generally.

The results of such election shall be published in a newspaper of general circulation in the county or municipality **(as the case may be)** and any contest of such election or the tabulation of the votes therein shall be brought within thirty (30) days after such publication or shall be forever barred.

The clear expression of the people is all that is required in this bond process, but nothing can be done without it.

SECTION 7

The provisions of this Amendment shall be self-executing. The legislature does not have to implement this amendment.

SECTION 8

Taxes levied prior to the effective date of this Amendment shall continue in force until abolished, reduced, or increased as provided by law. All bonds and other evidences of indebtedness authorized prior to the effective date of this Amendment shall be governed by the Constitutional provision and laws in effect at the time of authorization.

This amendment does not affect any of the rest of a locality's revenue structure in any way.

SECTION 9

Whenever two or more cities of the First or Second Class, or incorporated towns, and/or one or more counties and the school districts therein, desire to join together in a combined effort to secure and develop industries within one or more of such cities, towns, or counties, and share in the increased revenues estimated to be received by the city, towns, or counties, and share in the increased revenues estimated to be received by the city, town, or county, or school district, in which the industry or industries are to be located, they may, upon adoption by the governing bodies of each such city, town, school district, or county, enter into a compact setting forth the terms by which each of the participating cities, towns, school districts, and counties is to share in the revenues to be derived from the location of an industrial plant within the compact area through the combined efforts of the various participating cities, towns, school districts, and counties. Upon adoption of such compact by the governing bodies of the participating cities, towns, school district, and/or counties, the county court of each of the counties involved shall cause a special election to be called within not more than forty-five (45) days from the date of the filing of such compact with the county court. At such special election, the qualified electors of each of the cities, towns, school districts, and counties shall vote on whether to approve the compact and the methods of sharing in increased revenues to be derived by the city, school district, and/or county in which the proposed industry is to be located among the various participating cities, towns, counties, and school districts. The ballot at such election shall be in substantially the following form:

"FOR the establishment of an industrial development compact and the sharing of revenues to be derived from additional taxes to be generated by new industries."

"AGAINST the establishment of an industrial development compact and the sharing of revenues to be derived from additional taxes to be generated by new industries."

Said election shall be conducted in accordance with the election laws of the State, and the results thereof tabulated and certified to the County Clerk in the manner now provided by law. If a majority of the qualified electors voting on the question vote in favor of the creation of the compact, and the sharing of revenues to be derived from new industries located in the compact area, and the said compact shall be implemented in accordance with the terms thereof. If a majority of the qualified electors voting on said issue vote against issue at said special election, no additional election on said issue may be held within one (1) year from the date of said election. The results of said election shall be proclaimed by the county court of each of the counties in which the county and/or cities and towns, or school districts, are located. The results of said election shall be conclusive unless attacked in the courts within thirty (30) days.

This section encourages localities to provide services and to combine service efforts among localities, such as public safety or emergency services, jointly.

SECTION 10

Notwithstanding any other evidence of legislative intent, it is hereby declared to be the controlling legislative intent that if any provisions of this Amendment, or the application thereof to any person or circumstances, is held invalid, the remainder of the Amendment and the application of such provision to persons or circumstances other than those to which it is held invalid, shall not be affected thereby.

The drafters knew there would surely be litigation, as there is on any revenue measure, and this section precludes some litigation by its comprehensive severability clause.

SECTION 11

All provisions of the Constitution of 1874, or Amendments thereto in conflict with this Amendment including, but not limited to Amendment Numbers 13, 17, 25 and 49, are hereby repealed.

This is the standard repealer.

AMENDMENT 63: FOUR-YEAR TERMS FOR STATE CONSTITUTIONAL OFFICERS

This amendment was proposed by initiative petition. It was filed in the Office of the Secretary of State on July 2, 1984, and was approved at the general election on November 6, 1984. This amendment probably supersedes Article 6, Section 1; Amendment 6, Section 1; and Amendment 56, Section 1.

SECTION 1

The Executive Department of this State shall consist of a Governor, Lieutenant Governor, Secretary of State, Treasurer of State, Auditor of State, Attorney General and Commissioner of State Lands, all of whom shall keep their offices at the seat of government, and hold their offices for the term of four (4) years, and until their successors are elected and qualified.

This amendment extends the terms of these officials from two to four years and does not limit succession.

SECTION 2

This Amendment shall take effect and be in operation on January 1, 1987, and the provisions of this Amendment shall be applicable to those officers elected at the 1986 General Election and thereafter.

This amendment, which was voted on in 1984, would require voters to reelect all these officials, so none of them will automatically receive a four-year term without first having to pass voter scrutiny again. This was a political move to prevent candidates who opposed incumbents from working against the amendment.

SECTION 3

All laws and constitutional provisions which conflict with this Amendment are hereby repealed.

This is the regular repealer.

AMENDMENT 64: MUNICIPAL COURT JURISDICTION AMENDMENT

This amendment was proposed by House Joint Resolution No. 6 in 1985. It was filed in the Office of the Secretary of State on April 6, 1985, and was adopted at the general election on November 4, 1986.

SECTION 1

Notwithstanding any provision of this Constitution to the contrary and in addition to jurisdiction now conferred on municipal courts, municipal courts shall have jurisdiction concurrent with circuit courts (a) in matters of contract where the amount in controversy does not exceed three thousand dollars ($3,000) excluding interest, (b) in suits for the recovery of personal property where the value of the property does not exceed three thousand dollars ($3,000), and (c) in all matters of damage to personal property where the amount in controversy does not exceed three thousand dollars ($3,000); provided that the General Assembly may by law increase or decrease the jurisdictional limit by a two-thirds vote of each house of the General Assembly.

This amendment established for the first time a viable local court system below the circuit and chancery court levels; Arkansas law, both constitutional and statutory, provides municipal courts with no authority to hear and decide actions concerning damages to land. Accordingly, a municipal court lacks jurisdiction of a trespass on land action, and because the municipal court has no jurisdiction, the circuit court acquires none on appeal (Miles v. Southern, 1988).

SECTION 2

This Amendment shall become effective on July 1, 1987, and shall apply to causes of action arising after November 1, 1986.

This schedule made possible a smooth transition for this new local judicial process.

AMENDMENT 65: REVENUE BONDS

This amendment was proposed by initiative petition. It was filed in the Office of the Secretary of State on July 4, 1986, and was adopted at the general election on November 4, 1986. Amendment 65, Section 6, provided, in part, that the provisions of the amendment are self-executing. This amendment may supersede Constitution, Article 16, Section 1, with respect to prohibitions against bond issuance, and Constitutional Amendments 20 and 62 with respect to requirements for electoral approval.

SECTION 1

Subject to the provisions of Section 2 hereof, any governmental unit, pursuant to laws heretofore or hereafter adopted by the General Assembly, may issue revenue bonds for the purpose of financing all or a portion of the costs of capital improvements of a public nature, facilities for the securing and developing of industry or agriculture, and for such other public purposes as may be authorized by the

General Assembly. Such bonds may bear such terms, be issued in such manner, and be subject to such conditions, all as may be authorized by the General Assembly; and the General Assembly may, but shall not be required to, condition the issuance of such bonds upon an election.

This section adds agriculture as an acceptable public purpose for the issuance of bonds. The issuance is no longer contingent upon a popular vote but rather requires legislative authorization.

SECTION 2

(a) No revenue bonds shall be issued by or on behalf of any governmental unit if the primary purpose of the bonds is to loan the proceeds of the bonds, or to lease or sell the facilities financed with the proceeds of the bonds, to one or more private business users for shopping centers or other establishments engaged in the sale of food or goods at retail.

The amendment was not designed for retail establishments such as shopping centers, grocery stores, or restaurants, so these uses are specifically prohibited.

(b) No revenue bonds shall be issued by or on behalf of any governmental unit without the consent of a majority of the qualified electors voting on the question at an election held in accordance with state law if the primary purpose of the bonds is to loan the proceeds of the bonds, or to lease or sell the facilities financed with the proceeds of the bonds, to one or more private business users for hotels or motels, rental or professional office buildings, or facilities for recreation or entertainment.

Other private purposes can be financed, but only by a vote of the people in the locality.

SECTION 3

(a) The term "revenue bonds" as used herein shall mean all bonds, notes, certificates or other instruments or evidences of indebtedness the repayment of which is secured by rents, user fees, charges or other revenues (other than assessments for local improvements and taxes) derived from the project or improvements financed in whole or in part by such bonds, notes, certificates or other instruments or evidences of indebtedness, from the operations of any governmental unit, or from any other special fund or source other than assessments for local improvements and taxes.

This section merely serves as a definitional guide for the application of the amendment.

(b) The term "governmental unit" as used herein shall mean the State of Arkansas; any special assessment or taxing district established under the laws of the State of

Arkansas; and any agency, board, commission, or instrumentality of any of the foregoing.

The bonding authority was extended by this amendment to the state and its agencies, as well as to cities and counties, which already had this authority under Amendment 62.

SECTION 4

This Amendment shall be the sole authority required for the authorization, issuance, sale, execution and delivery of revenue bonds authorized hereby; provided, however, that the rate of interest on revenue bonds shall not exceed the maximum authorized by Amendment No. 60 to the Constitution of the State of Arkansas or any similar provision hereafter adopted. Nothing herein shall be construed to impair the initiative and referendum powers reserved to the people under Amendment No. 7 to the Constitution of the State of Arkansas.

This section attempts to eliminate contradictions in the law.

SECTION 5

All laws, constitutional provisions, and parts thereof which conflict with this Amendment are hereby repealed to the extent of such conflict.

This is the standard repealer.

SECTION 6

This Amendment shall be in force and effect upon its adoption, and the provisions of this Amendment shall be self-executing.

The legislature is not required to implement this amendment.

AMENDMENT 66: JUDICIAL DISCIPLINE AND DISABILITY COMMISSION

(a) **Commission:** Under the judicial power of the State, a Judicial Discipline and Disability Commission is established and shall be comprised of nine persons: Three justices or judges, appointed by the Supreme Court; three licensed attorneys in good standing who are not justices or judges, one appointed by the Attorney General, one by the President of the Senate, and one by the Speaker of the House; and three members appointed by the Governor. The members appointed by the Governor shall not be justices or judges, retired justices or judges, or attorneys. Alternate members shall be selected and vacancies filled in the same manner.

(b) Discipline, Suspension, Leave and Removal: The Commission may initiate, and shall receive and investigate, complaints conceming misconduct of all justices and judges, and requests and suggestions for leave or involuntary disability retirement. Any judge or justice may voluntarily request that the Commission recommend suspension because of pending disciplinary action or leave because of a mental or physical disability. Grounds for sanctions imposed by the Commission or recommendations made by the Commission shall be violations of the professional and ethical standards governing judicial officers, conviction of a felony, or physical or mental disability that prevents the proper performance of judicial duties. Grounds for suspension, leave or removal from office shall be determined by legislative enactment.

(c) Discipline: If, after notice and hearing, the Commission by majority vote of the membership determines that grounds exist for the discipline of a judge or justice, it may reprimand or censure the judge or justice, who may appeal to the Supreme Court. The Commission may, if it determines that grounds exist, after notice and hearing, and by majority vote of the membership, recommend to the Supreme Court that a judge or justice be suspended, with or without pay, or be removed, and the Supreme Court, en banc, may take such action. Under this amendment, a judge who also has executive or legislative responsibilities shall be suspended or removed only from judicial duties. In any hearing involving a Supreme Court justice, all Supreme Court justices shall be disqualified from participation.

(d) Leave and Retirement: If, after notice and hearing, the Commission by majority vote of the membership determines that a judge or justice is unable because of physical or mental disability to perform the duties of office, the Commission may recommend to the Supreme Court that the judge or justice be granted leave with pay or be retired, and the Supreme Court, en banc, may take such action. A judge or justice retired by the Supreme Court shall be considered to have retired voluntarily as provided by law.

(e) Vacancies: Vacancies created by suspension, the granting of leave or the removal of a judge or justice, or vacancies created by disqualification of justices, shall be filled as provided by law.

(f) Rules: The Supreme Court shall make procedural rules implementing this amendment and setting the length of terms on the Commission.

(g) Cumulative Nature: This amendment is alternative to, and cumulative with, impeachment and address authorized by this Constitution.

This amendment was proposed by Senate Joint Resolution 5 in 1987 and was adopted at the 1988 general election. The provision of Rule 12F of the Rules of Procedure of the Arkansas Judicial Discipline and Disability Commission, which provides that the supreme court may bring before it any action or failure to act on the part of the commission with respect to a case before the commission, has to do with reviewing the commissioner's actions in deciding the cases before it. It is not indicative of a general supervisory power of the supreme court (**Commission on Judicial Discipline and Disability v. Digby, 1990**).

AMENDMENT 67: JURISDICTION OF MATTERS RELATING TO JUVENILES AND BASTARDY

The General Assembly shall define jurisdiction of matters relating to juveniles (persons under eighteen (18) years of age) and matters relating to bastardy and may confer such jurisdiction upon chancery, circuit or probate courts, or upon separate divisions of such courts, or may establish separate juvenile courts upon which such jurisdiction may be conferred, and shall transfer to such courts the jurisdiction over bastardy and juvenile matters now vested in county courts by Section 28 of Article 7 of this Constitution.

This amendment was proposed by Senate Joint Resolution 1 in 1987, and was adopted at the 1988 general election. After the state supreme court overruled the historic juvenile system, which centered on the county judges' position as the key authority, there remained no lawful juvenile system in place, but only an interim, makeshift substitute. The Juvenile Justice Study Commission, established by the governor and the legislature, drafted this amendment and led the efforts in support of its adoption in 1988. It is within the power of the legislature to transfer the jurisdiction of matters concerning juveniles in need of supervision and dependent-neglected juveniles to the probate court of each county (**Hutton v. Savage, 1989**).

AMENDMENT 68: PREVENT ABORTION FUNDING AND TO RESTRICT ABORTION

1. Public Funding. No public funds will be used to pay for any abortion, except to save the mother's life.
2. Public Policy. The policy of Arkansas is to protect the life of every unborn child from conception until birth, to the extent permitted by the Federal Constitution.

This amendment was proposed by initiative petition and was adopted at the 1988 general election. After several unsuccessful attempts, this brief amendment was adopted in 1990 to prohibit public funds from being expended on abortions. It affected primarily the Department of Correction, the Department of Human Services, and the University of Arkansas Medical Sciences Campus.

AMENDMENT 69: REPEAL AMENDMENT 44 TO THE CONSTITUTION

SECTION 1

Amendment 44 to the Arkansas Constitution is hereby repealed. This amendment repealed Amendment 44 (the Interposition Amendment). It was proposed by House Joint Resolution 1003 and was adopted at the November 6, 1990 general election. This widely supported repeal was intended to remove an unconstitutional provision, to improve the image of the state, and to signal a new era in racial understanding.

AMENDMENT 70: AN AMENDMENT TO PROHIBIT PUBLIC RELATIONS FUNDS FOR STATE EXECUTIVE AND LEGISLATIVE OFFICIALS AND TO GOVERN COMPENSATION AND EXPENSE REIMBURSEMENT FOR SUCH OFFICIALS

SECTION 1

(a) No official of the Executive Department shall be reimbursed by the State of Arkansas for any expenses except those reasonably connected to their official duties and only if such reimbursement is made for documented expenses actually incurred and from the regular budget appropriated for the official's office. Such restrictions on expense reimbursement are of a general application and also are intended specifically to prohibit the appropriation and use of public relations funds. The annual salaries of the Executive Department, which shall be paid in monthly installments, shall be as follows: the Governor, the sum of $60,000; the Lieutenant Governor, the sum of $29,000; the Secretary of State, the sum of $37,500; the Treasurer of State, the sum of $37,000; the Attorney General, the sum of $50,000; the Commissioner of State Lands, the sum of $37,500; and the Auditor of State, the sum of $37,500. Except as provided herein, such officials of the Executive Department shall not receive any other income from the State of Arkansas, whether in the form of salaries or expenses.
(b) The members of the General Assembly shall receive as their annual salary the sum of $12,500, except the President Pro Tempore of the Senate and the Speaker of the House of Representatives, who shall each receive the sum of $14,000 annually, with such salaries to be payable in equal monthly installments. Except as provided herein, no member of the General Assembly shall receive any other income for service in the General Assembly, whether in the form of salaries or expenses, including, but not limited to, public relations funds. Provided further, that no member of the General Assembly shall be entitled to per diem unless authorized by law, or to reimbursement for expenses or mileage unless authorized by law, documented, and reasonably related to their official duties.

SECTION 2

In addition to the three amendments to the Constitution allowed pursuant to Article 19 Section 22, either branch of the General Assembly at a regular session thereof may propose an amendment to the Constitution to change the salaries for the offices of Governor, Lieutenant Governor, Attorney General, Secretary of State, Treasurer of State, Commissioner of State Lands, and Auditor of State and for members of the General Assembly. If the same be agreed to by a majority of all members elected to each house, such proposed amendment shall be entered on the journals with the yeas and nays, and published in at least one newspaper in each county, where a newspaper is published, for six months immediately preceding the next general election for Senators and Representatives, at which time the same shall be submitted to the electors of the State for approval or rejection. if a majority of the electors voting at such election adopt the amendment the same shall become a part of this Constitution. Only one amendment to the Constitution may be referred pursuant to this section.

SECTION 3

The salaries of the Executive Department officials and members of the General Assembly provided for in Section 1 or 2 of this amendment or adjusted pursuant to this section may be increased annually through subsequent appropriations by the General Assembly by an amount not to exceed the average percentage increase in the Consumer Price Index for All Urban Consumers or its successor, as published by the United States Department of Labor, for the two years immediately preceding the year of the salary appropriation.

SECTION 4

The provisions of this amendment shall be effective on January 1, 1993.

SECTION 5

Section 2 and Section 3 of Amendment 56 to the Arkansas Constitution are hereby repealed.

SECTION 6

All constitutional provisions and laws or parts of laws in conflict with this amendment are hereby repealed.

SECTION 7

The popular name of this resolution shall be as follows: "An Amendment to Prohibit Public Relations Funds For State Executive and Legislative Officials and To Govern Compensation and Expense Reimbursement For Such Officials."

SECTION 8

The ballot title of this resolution shall be as follows:

"An amendment to the Constitution of Arkansas providing that officials of the Executive Department shall not receive reimbursement from the State for expenses except those reasonably connected to their official duties and only if reimbursement is made for documented expenses actually incurred and from the regular budget appropriated for the official's office; applying such restrictions generally, and specifically to prohibit the appropriation and use of public relations funds; setting the following annual salaries for executive officials: Governor, $60,000, Lieutenant Governor, $29,000, Secretary of State, $37,500, Treasurer of State, $37,000, Attorney General, $50,000, Commissioner of State Lands, $37,500, and Auditor of State, $37,500; except as provided, prohibiting such officials from receiving other income from the State, whether in the form of salaries or expenses;

Providing an annual salary of $12,500 for members of the General Assembly, except the President Pro Tempore of Senate and the Speaker of the House of Representatives, who shall receive $14,000; except as provided, prohibiting such officials from receiving other income for service in the General Assembly, whether in the form of salaries or expenses, including, but not limited to, public relations funds; providing that such officials shall not be entitled to per diem unless authorized by law or to reimbursement for expenses and mileage unless authorized by law, documented, and reasonably related to their official duties;

Allowing the General Assembly to refer one additional constitutional amendment at a regular session of the General Assembly to change the salaries for the offices of Governor, Lieutenant Governor, Attorney General, Secretary of State, Treasurer of State, Commissioner of State Lands, and Auditor of State and for members of the General Assembly;

Providing the salaries set forth in the amendment or subsequent amendments may be increased annually by General Assembly appropriation by an amount not to exceed the average percentage increase in the federal Consumer Price Index for All Urban Consumers for the two years immediately preceding the year of the salary appropriation;

Making the provisions of the amendment effective on January 1, 1993; repeal ing constitutional provisions and laws or parts of laws in conflict with the amendment; and for other purposes."

This amendment raises the salaries of state officials, last set in 1976 by Amendment 56, from $35,000 for the Governor; $14,000 for the Lieutenant Governor; $26,000 for the Attorney General; $22,500 for the Secretary of State, Treasurer of State, Auditor of State, and State Land Commissioner; and $7,500 for state legislators with $10,000 for the House Speaker and President Pro Tempore of the State Senate.

Also, this amendment allows the legislature to propose one salary amendment per regular session, in addition to the three amendments currently allowed by Article 19, Section 22.

Future salary increases for state officials may be made by the General Assembly, but are not to exceed the cost-of-living increase, as measured by the consumer price index of the two preceding years.

Public relations funds are eliminated by this amendment.

AMENDMENT 71: PERSONAL PROPERTY TAX AMENDMENT

SECTION 1

Items of household furniture and furnishings, clothing, appliances, and other personal property used within the home, if not held for sale, rental, or other commercial or professional use, shall be exempt from all ad valorem taxes levied by any city, county, school district, or other taxing unit in this state.

SECTION 2

In addition to the method established by law for assessing and collecting real and personal property taxes, the General Assembly may establish special procedures, in lieu thereof, for the assessment and collection of annual personal property taxes on motor vehicles, owned by individuals, at the time of issuance or renewal of the registration and the license there of. Personal property taxes collected on motor vehicles under such procedures shall be based on the assessed value of the vehicles determined at the time the tax is paid, computed at the rate of personal property taxes levied during the preceding November, in the manner provided by law, in the taxing units in which the owner of the motor vehicle resides, or in which the motor vehicle is regularly located and assessed, and the taxpayer shall not be required to pay ad valorem taxes upon such motor vehicle based on the assessment for the previous year. In no event may more than one year's personal property taxes be collected on the same vehicle in the same year. Personal property taxes collected on motor vehicles under such procedures shall be remitted to the counties in which due, for distribution, as revenues of the year in which collected, to the respective taxing units in the manner provided by law.

SECTION 3

The provisions of this amendment shall be in lieu of those provisions of Article 16, Section 5 of the Constitution of the State of Arkansas relating to the assessment and taxation of tangible personal property.

SECTION 4

This amendment shall be in effect from and after January 1, 1993.

This amendment exempts all personal property, except motor vehicles, from ad valorem property taxes levied by any city, county, school district, or other taxing unit and provides that the legislature may establish procedures for collecting property taxes on motor vehicles.

The amendment provides that taxes are collected in the same year they are assessed. Historically, these taxes were collected two years after assessment, with a resulting loss of revenue.

AMENDMENT 72: CITY AND COUNTY LIBRARY AMENDMENT

SECTION 1

Section 1 of Amendment 30 to the Arkansas Constitution is hereby amended to read as follows:

"SECTION 1

Petition for tax levy - Election. Whenever 100 or more taxpaying electors of any city, having a population of not less than 5,000, shall file a petition with the Mayor asking that an annual tax on real and personal property be levied for the purpose of maintaining and operating a public city library and shall specify a rate of taxation not to exceed five mills on the dollar, the question as to whether such tax shall be levied shall be submitted to the qualified electors of such city at a general or special election. Such petition must be filed at least thirty days prior to the election at which it will be submitted to the voters. The ballot shall be in substantially the following form:

For a ____________ mill tax on real and personal property to be used for maintenance and operation of a public city library.

Against a ____________ mill tax on real and personal property to be used for maintenance and operation of a public city library."

SECTION 2

Section 3 of Amendment 30 to the Arkansas Constitution is hereby amended to read as follows:

"SECTION 3

Raising, reducing or abolishing tax - Petition and election. Whenever 100 or more taxpaying electors of any city having a library tax in force shall file a petition with the Mayor asking that such tax be raised, reduced or abolished, the question shall be submitted to the qualified electors at a general or special election. Such petition must be filed at least thirty days prior to the election at which it will be submitted to the voters.

The ballot shall follow, as far as practicable, the form set forth in Section 1 hereof. The result shall be certified and proclaimed, as provided in Section 2 hereof, and the result as proclaimed shall be conclusive unless attacked in the courts within thirty days. Subject to the limitations of Section 5(e) hereof, the tax shall be lowered, raised or abolished, as the case may be, according to the majority of the qualified electors voting on the question of such election. If lowered or raised, the revised tax shall thereafter be continually levied and collected and the proceeds used in the manner and for the purposes as provided in Section 2 hereof."

SECTION 3

Amendment 30 to the Arkansas Constitution is hereby amended by inserting an additional section at the end thereof to read as follows:

"SECTION 5

Petition for tax levy - Election, **(a)** Whenever 100 or more taxpaying electors of any city, having a population of not less than 5,000, shall file a petition with the Mayor asking that an annual tax on real and personal property be levied for capital improvements to or construction of a public city library and shall specify a rate of taxation not to exceed three mills on the dollar, the question as to whether such tax shall be levied shall be submitted to the qualified electors of such city at a general or special election. Such petition must be filed at least thirty days prior to the election at which it will be submitted to the voters. The ballot shall be in substantially the following form:

For a ____________ mill tax on real and personal property to be used for capital improvements to or construction of a public city library.

Against a ____________ mill tax on real and personal property to be used for capital improvements to or construction of a public city library.

(b) The electors may authorize the governing body of the city to issue bonds as prescribed by law for capital improvements to or construction of the library and to authorize the pledge of all, or any part of, the tax authorized by this section for the purpose of retiring the bonds. The interest rate on any bonds shall not exceed the rate provided by this Constitution. The ballot submitting the question to the voters shall be in substantially the following form:

For a ____________ mill tax on real and personal property within the city, to be pledged to an issue or issues of bonds not the exceed $_____, in aggregate principal amount, to finance capital improvements to or construction of the city library and to authorize the issuance of the bonds on such terms and conditions as shall be approved by the city.

Against a ____________ mill tax on real and personal property within the city, to be pledged to an issue or issues of bonds not to exceed $_____, in aggregate principal amount, to finance capital improvements to or construction of the city library and to authorize the issuance of the bonds on such terms and conditions as they shall be approved by the city.

(c) The maximum rate of any special tax to pay bonded indebtedness, as authorized by paragraph (b) hereof shall be stated on the ballot.

(d) The special tax for payment of bonded indebtedness authorized in paragraph (b) hereof shall constitute a special fund pledged as security for the payment of such indebtedness. The special tax shall never be extended for any purpose, nor collected for any greater length of time than necessary to retire such bonded indebtedness, except that tax receipts in excess of the amount required to retire the debt according to its terms may, subject to covenants entered into with the holders of the bonds, be pledged as security for the issuance of additional bonds if authorized by the voters. The tax for such additional bonds shall terminate within the time provided for the tax originally imposed. Upon retirement of the bonded indebtedness, any surplus tax collections, which may have accumulated, shall be transferred to the general funds of the city, and shall be used for maintenance and operation of the public city library.

(e) Notwithstanding any other provision of this amendment, a tax approved by the voters for the purpose of paying the bonded indebtedness shall not be reduced or diminished, nor shall it be used for any other purpose than to pay principal of, premium or interest on, and the reasonable fees of a trustee or paying agent, so long as the bonded indebtedness shall remain outstanding and unpaid."

SECTION 4

Section 1 of Amendment 38 to the Arkansas Constitution is hereby amended to read as follows:

"SECTION 1

Petition for tax levy - Election. Whenever 100 or more tax paying electors of any county shall file a petition in the County Court asking that an annual tax on real and personal property be levied for the purpose of maintaining and operating a public county library or a county library service or system and shall specify a rate of taxation not to exceed five mills on the dollar, the question as to whether said tax shall be levied shall be submitted to the qualified electors of such county at a general or special election. Such petition must be filed at least thirty days prior to the election at which it will be submitted to the voters. The ballot shall be in substantially the following form:

FOR a ____________ mill tax on real and personal property to be used for maintenance and operation of a public county library or county library service or system.

AGAINST a ____________ mill tax on real and personal property to be used for maintenance and operation of a public county library or county library service or system."

SECTION 5

Section 3 of Amendment 38 to the Arkansas Constitution is hereby amended to read as follows:

"SECTION 3

Raising, reducing or abolishing tax - Petition and election. Whenever 100 or more tax paying electors of any county having library tax in force shall file a petition in the County Court asking that such tax be raised, reduced or abolished, the question shall be submitted to the qualified electors at a general or special election. Such petition must be filed at least thirty days prior to the election at which it will be submitted to the voters. The ballot shall follow, as far as practicable, the form set forth in Section 1 hereof. The result shall be certified and entered of record as provided in Section 2 hereof, and the result as entered of record shall be conclusive unless attacked in the courts within thirty days. Subject to the limitations of Section 5(e) hereof, the tax shall be lowered, raised or abolished, as the case may be, according to the majority of qualified electors voting on the question at such election. If lowered or raised, the revised tax shall thereafter be continually levied and collected on proceeds used in the manner and for the purposes as provided in Section 2 hereof."

SECTION 6

Amendment 38 to the Arkansas Constitution is hereby amended by inserting an additional section at the end thereof to read as follows:

"SECTION 5

Petition for tax levy - Election, (a) Whenever 100 or more tax paying electors of any county shall file a petition in the County Court asking that an annual tax on real and personal property be levied for the purpose of capital improvements to or construction of a public county library or a county library service or system and shall specify a rate of taxation not to exceed three mills on the dollar, the question as to whether said tax shall be levied shall be submitted to the qualified electors of such county at a general or special election. Such petition must be filed at least thirty days prior to the election at which it will be submitted to the voters. The ballot shall be in substantially the following form:

FOR a ____________ mill tax on real and personal property to be used for capital improvements to or construction of a public county library or county library service or system.

AGAINST a ____________ mill tax on real and personal property to be used for capital improvements to or construction of a public county library or county library service or system.

(b) The voters may authorize the County Court to issue bonds as prescribed by law for capital improvements to or construction of the library and to authorize the pledge of all, or any part of, the tax authorized in Section 1 of this Amendment for the purpose of retiring the bonds. The interest rate on any bonds shall not exceed the rate provided in this Constitution. The ballot submitting the question to the voters shall be in substantially the following form:

FOR a ____________ mill tax on real and personal property within the county, to be pledged to an issue or issues of bonds not to exceed $_____, in aggregate principal amount, to finance capital improvements to or construction of the county library or county library service or system, and to authorize the issuance of the bonds on such terms and conditions as shall be approved by the County Court.

AGAINST a ____________ mill tax on real and personal property within the county, to be pledged to an issue or issues of bonds not to exceed $_____, in aggregate principal amount, to finance capital improvements to or construction of the county library or county library service or system, and to authorize the issuance of the bonds on such terms and conditions as shall be approved by the County Court.

(c) The maximum rate of any special tax to pay bonded indebtedness, as authorized by paragraph (b) hereof shall be stated on the ballot.

(d) The special tax for payment of bonded indebtedness authorized in paragraph (b) hereof shall constitute a special fund pledged as security for the payment of such indebtedness. The special tax shall never be extended for any purpose, nor collected for any greater length of time than necessary to retire such bonded indebtedness, except that tax receipts in excess of the amount required to retire the debt according to its terms may, subject to covenants entered into with the holders of the bonds, be pledged as security for the issuance of additional bonds if authorized by the voters. The tax for such additional bonds shall terminate within the time provided for the tax originally imposed. Upon retirement of the bonded indebtedness, any surplus tax collections, which may have accumulated, shall be transferred to the general funds of the county, and shall be used for maintenance of the county library or county library service or system.

(e) Notwithstanding any other provision of this Amendment, a tax approved by the voters for the purpose of paying the bonded indebtedness shall not be reduced or diminished, nor shall it be used for any other purpose than to pay principal of, premium or interest on, and the reasonable fees of a trustee or paying agent, so long as the bonded indebtedness shall remain outstanding and unpaid."

This amendment allows voters of a local jurisdiction to increase their ad valorem tax rate up to 5 mills for libraries' operation and maintenance, instead of the historic one mill limit.

Additionally, voters in cities over 5,000 population may petition the mayor to submit the question to the electorate at a special or general election up to three mills for library capital improvements and construction.

This amendment grew out of the growing statewide commitment to excellence in educational opportunity and lifelong learning.

AMENDMENT 73: ARKANSAS TERM LIMITATION AMENDMENT

Summary: This amendment provides a limit of two (2) terms for the Governor, Lieutenant Governor, Secretary of State, Treasurer of State, Auditor of State, Attorney General and Commissioner of State Lands. It provides a limit of three (3) terms for State Representatives, and a limit of two (2) terms for State Senators. It also provides that persons having been elected three (3) or more terms as a member of the United States House of Representatives from Arkansas shall not be eligible to appear on the ballot for election to the United States House of Representatives from Arkansas. Lastly, it provides that any person having been elected to two (2) or more terms as a member of the United States Senate from Arkansas shall not be eligible to appear on the ballot for election to the United States Senate from Arkansas.

Preamble: The people of Arkansas find and declare that elected officials who remain in office too long become preoccupied with reelection and ignore their duties as representatives of the people. Entrenched incumbency has reduced voter participation and has led to an electoral system that is less free, less competitive, and less representative than the system established by the Founding Fathers. Therefore, the people of Arkansas, exercising their reserved powers, herein limit the terms of elected officials.

Section 1—Executive Branch, (a) The Executive Department of this State shall consist of a Governor, Lieutenant Governor, Secretary of State, Treasurer of State, Auditor of State, Attorney General, and Commissioner of State Lands, all of whom shall keep their offices at the seat of government, and hold their offices for the term of four years, and until their successors are elected and qualified.
(b) No elected officials of the Executive Department of this State may serve in the same office more than two such four year terms.

Section 2—Legislative Branch, (a) The Arkansas House of Representatives shall consist of members to be chosen every second year by the qualified electors of the several counties. No member of the Arkansas House of Representatives may serve more than three such two year terms.
(b) The Arkansas Senate shall consist of members to be chosen every four years by the qualified electors of the several districts. No member of the Arkansas Senate may serve more than two such four year terms.

Section 3—Congressional Delegation, (a) Any person having been elected to three or more terms as a member of the United States House of Representatives from Arkansas shall not be certified as a candidate and shall not be eligible to have his/her name placed on the ballot for election to the United States House of Representatives from Arkansas.

(b) Any person having been elected to two or more terms as a member of the United States Senate from Arkansas shall not be certified as a candidate and shall not be eligible to have his/her name placed on the ballot for election to the United States Senate from Arkansas.

Section 4—Severability. The provisions of this Amendment are severable, and if any should be held invalid, the remainder shall stand.

Section 5—Provisions Self-Executing. Provisions of this Amendment shall be self-executing.

Section 6—pplication, (a) This Amendment to the Arkansas Constitution shall take effect and be in operation on January 1, 1993, and its provisions shall be applicable to all persons thereafter seeking election to the offices specified in this Amendment.

(b) All laws and constitutional provisions which conflict with this Amendment are hereby repealed to the extent that they conflict with this amendment.

This term-limit amendment went into litigation immediately upon adoption. It provides for a limit of two terms for the seven state constitutional officers, each with four year terms; three terms for State Representatives; and two terms for State Senators.

Additionally, United States Representatives may not appear on the ballot for more than three terms, nor United States Senators for more than two terms.

BIBLIOGRAPHICAL ESSAY

Government, politics, history, and constitutional development in Arkansas have not generated much published commentary. Any bibliographical essay on the Constitution and government of Arkansas must begin with the flagship piece of literature, Henry M. Alexander's *Government in Arkansas*, which was last revised and published in 1963 (Little Rock, Ark.: Pioneer Press). (The League of Women Voters has published an updated, replacement version of this centerpiece.) The premier work on modem Arkansas politics is Diane D. Blair's *Arkansas Politics and Government* (University of Nebraska Press, 1988).

Any discussion of constitutional literature on the state of Arkansas must begin with the *Constitution of the State of Arkansas* (1992) with all amendments, a publication of the Secretary of State's office.

Other general and historical works of major significance include Marie Cash, "Arkansas Achieves Statehood," *Arkansas Historical Quarterly*, 2, no. 4 (December 1943); Orval Driggs Truman, Jr., "The Issues of the Powell Clayton Regime, 1868–1871," *Arkansas Historical Quarterly*, 8, no. 1 (Spring, 1949); Eugene G. Feistman, "Radical Disfranchisement in Arkansas, *1861–1868,*" *Arkansas Historical Quarterly*, 12, no. 2 (Summer 1953); William A. Russ, Jr., "The Attempt to Create a Republican Party in Arkansas during Reconstruction," *Arkansas Historical Quarterly*, 1, no. 3 (September 1942); Walter Nunn, "The Constitutional Convention of 1814," *Arkansas Historical Quarterly*, 28, no. 3 (Autumn 1968), an examination of 1874 convention and why the Constitution was written as it was; James H. Atkinson, "The Adoption of the Constitution of 1874 and the Passing of the Reconstruction Regime," *Arkansas Historical Quarterly*, 5, no. 3 (Fall 1946); Committee on Submission and Address to the People (1918), a proposed draft of the Constitution prepared by the 1917–1918 Convention with a brief explanation of major changes; *Report of the Committee of the Arkansas Bar Association on the New Constitution* (Little Rock: Arkansas Bar Association 1917), a section-by-section commentary by the Arkansas Bar Association on the first draft of the proposed constitution of the committees of the convention; Abe Collins, "Reminiscences of the Constitutional Convention of 1917–18," *Arkansas Historical Quarterly*, Vol. II (1946), a discussion of the major controversial issues and political conditions of the 1917–1918 Arkansas convention by a former delegate; and Arkansas Constitutional Revision Study Commission, "Comparison of Selected Provisions of Five Recent Constitutions, the 1885 Florida Constitution, and the 1874 Arkansas Constitution" (1967, 9 pp.), which includes a chart comparing seven constitutions. Also see State of Arkansas, *Arkansas Constitutional Revision Study Commission Transcripts* (6 vols., 1967), a complete record of debates and proceedings of full commission sessions plus committee reports; Walter Nunn, "The Commission Route to Constitutional Reform: The Arkansas Experience," *Arkansas Law Review*, 22, no. 2 (Summer 1968), a description of the operation of the Constitutional Revision Study Commission; Henry M. Alexander, Speech to the Constitutional Convention Seminar, Little Rock, Arkansas, February 8, 1964; Martin L. Faust, Speech to the Constitutional Convention Seminar, Little Rock, Arkansas, February 8, 1964; and Charles W. Joiner, Speech to the Constitutional Convention Seminar, Little Rock, Arkansas, February 8, 1964. (Transcriptions of all of these speeches can be found at the Arkansas History Commission in Little Rock.)

There was, by the early 1960s, a recognition by public officials, students of political science, and public administrators that the 1874 Constitution imposed many difficulties on the structure, operation, and finance of Arkansas government which could not be alleviated by the piecemeal approach of constitutional amendment. This recognition led to the gradual appearance of literature calling for a comprehensive constitutional revision. One of the first articles to appear was "A New Constitution for Arkansas?" *Arkansas Law Review and Bar Association Journal*, 17, no. 1 (1962–63) by Ralph C. Barnhart, which argued the need for change. Another work on constitutional change, an analysis of the 1874 Constitution entitled "Revision of the Arkansas Constitution" (1966), is an unpublished master's thesis done at the University of Kansas by Walter H. Nunn.

The movement for constitutional reform had the backing of Winthrop Rockefeller when he took office as governor in early 1967, and he persuaded the Arkansas General Assembly that same year to permit the establishment of a commission to study the need for a constitutional convention. The meeting of the Arkansas Constitutional Revision Study Commission was to result in a number of works. *Succession of the Office of Governor in the Several States* (1967), *The Office of Secretary of State in the Several States* (1967), and *Administrative Boards, Commissions, and Agencies* (1967) are reports that were done for the study commission by Kay G. Collett, who was Research Assistant and Director for the commission and the two contemporary constitutional conventions. As their titles indicate, the reports compared several states' practices in various areas with those of Arkansas. Another report done for the study commission was *The Holford Bonds Amendment: A Just or Unjust Debt?* (1967), by Walter H. Nunn, who served the commission as a Research Assistant and the constitutional convention as Research Director. His report concerned the need to place in any new constitutional document a statement forbidding payment on bonds on which the state had defaulted in the last century.

The Arkansas Constitutional Revision Study Commission prepared several works outlining its findings. Among these are *Alternative Procedures for Constitutional Revision to be Included in a New Constitution* (1967), *Revising the Arkansas Constitution* (1968), and *Analysis and General Recommendations* (1968).

The latter two form an excellent statement about why there was a need for change in the constitutional document and contain a proposed new document which could serve as the basis of discussion at the subsequent constitutional convention.

The meeting of both the constitutional study commission and the constitutional convention promoted the publication of articles and books attempting to give some perspective to the setting in which both were conducted. Walter Nunn, in "The Commission Route to Constitutional Reform: The Arkansas Experience," *Arkansas Law Review*, 22, no. 2 (1968), declared the establishment of a commission in preparation for a convention to be of value in the reform process. "Symposium—Comments of the Proposed Arkansas Constitution," *Arkansas Law Review*, 24, no. 2 (Spring 1970), was an overall title for eight articles that analyzed the proposed 1970 Constitution, with limited emphasis on the legal aspects of the change. One of the articles was done by Robert A. Leflar, who served as Chair of the constitutional commission and President of the constitutional convention. Leflar, Distinguished Professor Emeritus of Law and a former Dean of the University of Arkansas Law School, was a nationally and internationally recognized authority on the conflicts of law and torts. The *Proposed Arkansas Constitution of 1970 with Comments* (1970) by the Seventh Arkansas Constitutional Convention was the official convention publication. It took a section-by-section approach to comparing the old Constitution and the proposed new one in an effort to fully explain all changes to the electorate as well as to argue for the adoption of the proposed 1970 Constitution.

In an effort to analyze why the proposed Constitution of 1970 was rejected, Robert W. Meriwether, who was a member of the political science faculty at Hendrix College in Conway, Arkansas, a member of the constitutional study commission, a delegate to the constitutional convention, and Executive Director of Arkansas for the Constitution of 1970, wrote "The Proposed Arkansas Constitution of 1970," *Nebraska Law Review*, 50, no. 4 (1971). A much more comprehensive work, however, is *Politics in Arkansas: The Constitutional Experience* (1972) by Calvin R. Ledbetter, Robert Johnston, Walter Nunn, Kay Goss, Greg Wilson, L. Lynn Hogue, and Robert K. Walsh. This was an effort to describe the political and constitutional traditions of Arkansas, explain factors that caused the calling of a constitutional convention, and analyze how the proposed 1970 Constitution differs from the existing constitution. It also described what major changes could be expected and explored why the proposed 1970 document failed to meet with voter approval. This work attempts to apply the empirical approach to the constitutional revision movement in Arkansas, while a more traditional treatment of the constitutional revision movement is found in *Political Paradox: Constitutional Revision in Arkansas* (New York: National Municipal League, 1973), a book by Kay G. Collett and Walter H. Nunn, which provides a full history of the movement and defines many of the probable reasons for the failure of the proposed new constitutional document.

A useful source material relating to the Constitution of the state of Arkansas is "Amending the Arkansas Constitution by the Initiative Process" (1949), an unpublished master's thesis from the University of Arkansas by Robert Gibbs Reaves.

The Institute of Politics published a series of pamphlets regarding each of the articles of the proposed Constitution during 1979 and 1980. *The Proposed Constitution of 1980* was published by the eighth Arkansas Constitution and included a secion-by-section explanation of changes and a comparison of provisions.

LEGISLATIVE ARTICLE

The study of the legislative branch of Arkansas state government has not been undertaken on a wide-scale basis. *The Sometimes Governments: A Critical Study of the Fifty American State Legislatures* (The Rutgers University Press: New Brunswick, N.J., 1971) by John Burns was an effort to rank, according to various criteria, all the state legislatures in the United States. In 1971, the Arkansas legislature hired a consulting group from the Eagleton Institute of Politics at Rutgers University to do an in-depth study of its operation, which resulted in the publication of *Strengthening the Arkansas Legislature* (The Rutgers University Press: New Brunswick, N. J., 1972) under the direction of Ralph Craft, Project Coordinator. Many of the recommendations made in the report have been adopted by the Arkansas General Assembly; thus, the report's effect has been substantial, especially in terms of internal legislative operation. In addition, a master's thesis, "A Proposed Legislative Article for a New Arkansas Constitution" (1969) by Norman L. Hodges, Jr., provides an interesting summary of contemporary issues.

Comparative studies found in several journals relating either in part or in whole to the legislative branch of Arkansas state government are "The Southern Legislature and Legislation," *Journal of Politics*, 10, no. 2 (1948), by H. C. Nixon; "State Legislatures in Southern Politics," *Journal of Politics*, 26, no. 1 (1964), by Malcolm E. Jewell; "The Constitutionality of Legislative Councils," *Western Political Quarterly*, 8, no. 1 (1955), by David W. Smith; and "Urban and Rural Representation and State Legislative Apportionment," *Western Political Quarterly*, 17, no. 4 (1964), by John P. White and Norman C. Thomas. Another of these comparative works, which deals on a much more in-depth basis with each legislature involved, is "Power in American State Legislatures; Case Studies of the Arkansas, Louisiana, Mississippi, and Oklahoma Legislatures,"*Tulane Studies in Political Science*, vol. 11 (1967), edited by Alex B. Lacy, Jr., in which the chapter entitled "The Arkansas Legislature," written by Donald T. Wells, indicates the General Assembly has performed well as a representative body reflecting state attitudes but has failed dismally in solving the state's profound problems in finances, economic development, education and human services.

A comparative study of some importance in the Arkansas legislative reform has been Walter Nunn and Calvin W. Clark's *Recent and Proposed Changes in Compensation for Legislators in the Fifty States* (Kansas City, Mo.: Citizens Conference on State Legislatures, 1967, 29 pp.), a state-by-state survey of legislative compensation.

EXECUTIVE ARTICLE

One of the most influential works on the executive branch of Arkansas state government has been *Administrative Reorganization in Arkansas* (1968) by Max Milam. At the time when Milam prepared the work for then Governor Winthrop Rockefeller, he was Chairman of the Department of Political Science at the University of Arkansas. Subsequently, he was to serve as the Director of the State Department of Finance and Administration under both Governors Rockefeller and Dale Bumpers. In this latter position, Milam had the opportunity of overseeing the implementation of his proposal which was adopted, largely intact, by the state legislature after Bumpers took office.

The first intensive study of the Arkansas Governor's office ever done by a trained political scientist was Daniel R. Grant's "The Role of the Governor of Arkansas in Administration" (1948), an unpublished doctoral dissertation from Northwestern University. Grant examined the role of the Arkansas governor in administration. Grant, a native Arkansan, a renowned political scientist, and a longtime member of the political science faculty at Vanderbilt University, was subsequently President of Ouachita Baptist University in Arkadelphia, Arkansas. Material developed by Grant was utilized in *The Office of Governor in the South* (1951) and *The Office of Governor in the United States* (1956) by Coleman B. Ransone, Jr., both of which deal with how Arkansas Governors spend their working hours, including the type of visitors and the time allocated to each. *The Governors of Arkansas*, edited by Timothy P. Donovan and Willard B. Gatewood, Jr. (Fayetteville: The University of Arkansas Press, 1981) contains essays in political biography.

Kay G. Collett prepared three studies, published by the state, relating to the executive branch of government for the constitutional study commission in 1967. These are *Succession to the Office of Governor in Several States* (1967), *The Office of the Secretary of State in the Several States* (1967), and *Administrative Boards, Commissions, and Agencies* (1967). Later, the League of Women Voters of Arkansas prepared and published *The Executive Branch: A Study of the Constitution of Arkansas* (1968), by Kay G. Collett. There is a noticeable lack of material concerning the executive branch of Arkansas government, specifically in professional journals. The Governor of Arkansas is one of several discussed in "Southern Governors," *Journal of Politics*, 10, no. 2 (1948), by Cortez A. M. Ewing; "The Executive Veto in Southern States," *Journal of Politics*, 10, no. 4 (1948), by Frank W. Prescott; "Political Leadership in the Governor's Office," *Journal of Politics*, 26, no. 1 (1964), by Coleman B. Ransone, Jr.; "Southern

Governors and Political Change: Campaign Stances on Racial Segregation and Economic Development, 1950–69," *Journal of Politics*, 33, no. 3 (1971), by Earl Black; and "The Southern Governor—Challenge to the Strong Executive Theme," *Public Administration Review*, 19, no. 1 (1959), by Robert B. Highsaw. Finally, three articles of note from the *Arkansas Law Review* are "Administrative Law in Arkansas," 4, no. 1 (1950), by Reginald Parker; "Judicial Review of Administrative Agencies in Arkansas," 25, no. 4 (1972), by Zachary D. Wilson and Charles N. Games; and "An Ombudsman for Arkansas," 21, no. 3 (1967), by Richard S. Arnold.

"The Office of Governor" by Calvin R. Ledbetter, Jr., is one of the most comprehensive studies in this area. Other relevant studies include Arkansas Legislative Council Research Department, *Functions and Duties of the State Land Department* (1955, 38 pp.), which describes factors involved in a proposal to transfer functions and duties of the Arkansas Land Department from the state to the county level, and Arkansas Legislative Council Research Department, *State Printing Laws of Arkansas and the Various States* (1963, 21 pp.), which includes the judicial interpretations of Section 15 of Article 19 of the Arkansas Constitution on printing contracts and the laws of other states.

JUDICIAL ARTICLE

The judicial system and structure of the state of Arkansas is the area that has received the least study by political scientists. The only major study done on the Arkansas Supreme Court and undertaken in the 1950s was "The Arkansas Supreme Court; 1958–1959" (1961), a doctoral dissertation done at Northwestern University by Calvin R. Ledbetter, Jr.

Other sources include Arkansas Bar Association, "Interim Report of Committee on Jurisprudence and Law Reform—On the Constitution of Arkansas" (1963); League of Women Voters of Arkansas, *The Arkansas Courts: Problems of Reform* (1964, 23 pp.), a discussion of judicial problems of constitutional and statutory nature; and T. T. James McDonough, "The Juvenile Court and Judicial Reform in Arkansas," *Arkansas Law Review*, 22, no. 1 (Spring 1968), which includes implications of the *Gault* decision for judicial reform in Arkansas.

COUNTY GOVERNMENT

Another of the least professionally studied and publicly understood areas of Arkansas constitutional law concerns the county level. Existing studies include *The Government and Finance of Counties in Arkansas (1956)*, by Edward W. Reed and Henry M. Alexander (both professors at the University of Arkansas, the former of economics and the latter of political science); *A Comparative Analysis of the Cost of County Government in Arkansas* (1945), by the Arkansas Public Expenditure Council; *Summary of County Sales and Use Tax, 1963–66* (1967), by the Arkansas State Department of Revenues; and *The Organization and*

Function of State and Local Government in Arkansas (1947), by Henry M. Alexander.

Professional papers done at the University of Arkansas include "Political Party Organization in Pulaski County Arkansas: The Democratic and Republican County Committees" (1967), by Patrick F. O'Connor, and "The County Judge in Washington County, Arkansas" (1969), by G. David Garrison, which concludes that the county judges, although the most important and powerful county officers, devote their major efforts toward the construction and maintenance of county roads. Other studies are "Federal and State Aid and the Washington County Judge" (1969), by Gary R. Cheatham, and "Fundamentals of Local Solid Waste Management Practices: The City of Camden and Ouachita County, Arkansas" (1973), by Cy Carney III.

Professional literature does exist on Arkansas county government (although it is extremely limited and seriously dated), including "City and County Manager Plans in the South," *Journal of Politics, 2,* no. 3 (1949), by Robert B. Highsaw, the only journal article relating to Arkansas county government.

Other reference sources include Henry M. Alexander, *Local Government Revenue Sources: Pulaski County Metropolitan Area* (chs. 1, 2, and Summary only; Little Rock: Metropolitan Area Planning Commission, 1965), pp. 1–32, 55–60, pertaining to levels and uses of state and local government finance and property tax revenue; Henry M. Alexander, "County Government is YOUR Business," *Open Thinking on Public Affairs,* no. 10 (Fayetteville: University of Arkansas Agricultural Extension Service, 1965); League of Women Voters of Arkansas and Kay G. Collett, *County Government in Arkansas* (1966, 27 pp.), a discussion of development, structure, and the problems and potential of county government; Committee for a Two-Party System, *Report on the Study of State and County Government—State of Arkansas,* prepared by Peat, Marwick, Mitchell & Company (1964); Arkansas Legislative Council Research Department, *Public Defenders* (1967, 9 pp.), a discussion of the rights of indigent defendants to legal counsel in state courts, the public defender system, and federal and other programs under which funds for a public defender system are available; and Gretchen Knief Schenk, *Survey of the Arkansas Library Commission and the Public Libraries of Arkansas* (1964, 57 pp.), an evaluation of services, examination of special problems, and set of suggestions for the improvement of Arkansas libraries and the Arkansas State Library Commission.

MUNICIPAL GOVERNMENT

The area of municipal government has been studied more than county government, and most of the work is descriptive rather than analytical. Much of the work on Arkansas municipal government was done by the late Henry M. Alexander, whose works include *Municipal Home Rule: Explanation and Recommendations* (1967), a general review of municipal home rule with specific attention to Arkansas; *Comments on the City Manager Plan in the United States and in Arkansas* (1959); *The City Manager Plan in Arkansas* (1966), which was co-authored with Kay G. Collett as a follow-up to his previous work. *The City Manager Plan in Arkansas* (1961); and *The Little Rock City Government* (1951), which Alexander coauthored with Frank Cantrell analyzing the administrative, financial, personnel, and accounting procedures of Little Rock city government and recommending improvements. A more descriptive and comprehensive work done by Alexander in this area is entitled *Organization and Function of State and Local Government in Arkansas* (1947).

An interesting article concerning federal-local relationships in Arkansas during the period of the Little Rock School Crisis of 1957–1958 was written by Morton Grodzins: "Arkansas Small Town in the Year of Little Rock," in *The American System: A New View of Government in the United States* (1966), edited by Daniel J. Elazar.

The Arkansas Municipal League has published numerous materials relating to Arkansas cities, which are exquisitely descriptive in nature, including *Financing Arkansas Municipalities* (1969, 1951); *Franchise Taxes, Salary Schedules and Other Statistical Data on Arkansas Municipalities* (1953); *The Mayor: His Statutory Powers and Duties* (rev. ed., 1949); *A Civic Guide to Economy in Municipal Government* (1945); various editions of the *Handbook for Arkansas Municipal Officials* (1966); and Ralph L. Liverman's *Municipal Bond Financing in Arkansas* (1971).

Guidelines for Municipal Officials (1966), a manual concerned with municipal planning policy and procedure, and *Funding Community Services and Facilities* (1972) were prepared by the City Planning Division of the University of Arkansas. Other works on municipal government in Arkansas include two master's internship papers from the University of Arkansas political science program: "Fayetteville Revenue Sources: A Comparative Study" (1972), by Fred Kleinhauer, which examines the financial base of a medium-sized Arkansas city, and "Developmental Planning in Arkadelphia: A Study of Institutional Participation" (1973), by Jack Hoyt.

Other studies of limited areas of municipal government are Arkansas Legislative Council Research Department, *City Tort Immunity* (1968, 24 pp.), a history of sovereign immunity and a summary of statutory development designed to minimize the liability of cities for tort damages; Henry M. Alexander, "The Organization of Arkansas Municipalities," *Arkansas Historical Quarterly*, 1, no. 1 (March 1942); and Henry M. Alexander, *Municipal Finance in Arkansas* (Fayetteville: University of Arkansas College of Business Administration, 1955, 45 pp.), an appraisal of financial problems of Arkansas cities and recommendations for improvement.

The few articles in professional journals concerning municipal government in Arkansas discuss Arkansas as a southern state, but not as an individual body. These are "Trends in Municipal Govemment in the South," *Journal of Politics*, 10, no. 3 (1948), by Weldon Cooper; "City and County Manager Plans in the

South," *Journal of Politics*, 11, no. 3 (1949), by Robert B. Highsaw; and "Urban and Rural Representation and State Legislative Apportionment," *Western Political Quarterly*, 17, no. 4 (1964), by John P. White and Norman C. Thomas.

TAXATION AND FINANCE

The most extensive, and intensive, studies of taxation and finance in Arkansas govemment were done by the late Henry M. Alexander. Over a period of years, he wrote numerous works concerning various aspects of taxation and finance. Among these works are *The State Budget System of Arkansas* (1951); *Tax Differentials in South Central States* (1954); *Municipal Finance in Arkansas* (1955); and *Sources of Local Government Revenue in Arkansas for Community Services and Facilities* (1961).

Charles E. Venus succeeded Alexander as the most prolific contemporary writer on these areas, with works including *The Arkansas State Tax Structure* (1968) and, in collaboration with W. Richard McLean, *Status of State-Level General Property Taxes, 1972* (1972).

Comparative Analysis of the Arkansas Tax System (1950) and *Comparative Analysis of Arkansas State Expenditures* (1952), by Edward W. Reed, are two works that compare Arkansas to surrounding and southern states. The Arkansas Chamber of Commerce prepared a work entitled *A Policy Statement on State and Local Taxation in Arkansas* (1952), which set forth its views on the existing system and explained how, in some instances, it might be changed. Along with the Industrial Research Extension Center of the University of Arkansas College of Business Administration, the chamber issued a publication entitled *The Problems of Financing Urban Growth in Arkansas* (1960), which dealt with the severe restrictions placed on local taxation that are found in the Arkansas Constitution and ways in which the state legislature could help or hinder urban growth.

Other works include *Activity Budgeting: Cost Information Needed for the Program Budgets* (1970), by the Arkansas Planning Commission; *Taxes in Arkansas, A Survey* (1948), by the Arkansas Public Expenditure Council; *Digest of Arkansas Tax Law* (1945) and *Digest of Arkansas Tax Laws* (1952), by the Arkansas Resources and Development Commission; *Compilation of the Laws of Arkansas Relating to Assessment, Equalization, and Extension of Taxes Ad Valorem on Property* (1949) and *Schedules of Assessable Values for the Year 1950* (1950), by the Arkansas Tax Commission; *Special Study of Treasury Management and Investment* (1971), by the Arkansas Department of Finance and Administration; *Franchise Tax Law of the State of Arkansas, Act Number 304 of 1953* (1953), by the Arkansas State Revenue Department; *Income Tax Act of 1929, Income Tax Statutes and Regulations Effective March 1, 1968* (1968), which covered state income tax statutes and regulations in effect in early 1968, by the Arkansas Department of Revenues; *Your Tax Dollar, What Happens to It?* (1952) and *General Accounting Procedure for State Agencies for the Disbursement of Funds in the*

State Treasury (1965), by the Arkansas State Auditorial Department, Office of State Comptroller; *State Travel Regulations* (1963) and *How New State Tax Revenues Are Being Used; A Report to the People of Arkansas* (1958), by the Arkansas Office of the State Comptroller; and finally. *Taxes and Government in Arkansas* (1956), which was a report on the relative burden of state and local taxes and the relative level of public services in Arkansas, and *A Summary of Taxes in Arkansas* (1958), both by the Industrial Research and Extension Center, College of Business Administration, University of Arkansas.

Several other works on taxation and finance are *The Holford Bonds Amendment: A Just and Unjust Debt?* (1967), written by Walter Nunn for the Constitutional Revision Study Commission; *Capital Budgeting Proposal* (1970), by Ralph B. Shull; and an unpublished master's thesis from the University of Arkansas by James R. McKenzie entitled "Program Budgeting in Arkansas State Government: The Budget Expenditure Plan Experiment" (1975).

Other sources include Charles R. Gamer, James L. Sloan, and John Haley, "Taxpayers' Suits to Prevent Illegal Exactions in Arkansas," *Arkansas Law Review and Bar Association Journal*, 8, no. 2 (Spring 1954), an analysis of court decisions on Section 13, Article 16 of the Arkansas Constitution, on illegal exactions; Arkansas Legislative Council Research Department, *Tax Exempt Status of Industrial Development Revenue Bonds* (1968, 14 pp.), an explanation of current developments in federal legislation on this subject; Arkansas Legislative Council Research Department, *Feasibility of Adapting the State Income Tax Law to the Federal Internal Revenue Code* (1966, 18 pp.), shows differences between the Arkansas and federal income taxes and how other states have handled the matter; Public Service Commission, *Fifth Biennial Report of the Department of Assessment Coordination of the Arkansas Public Service Commission* (1965–66, 132 pp.), a resume of the work of the Arkansas Assessment Coordination Division and tables of the assessed value of all property in each county; Arkansas Economic Expansion Study Commission, *Accelerating Economic Growth in Arkansas* (1964, 186 pp.), which was authorized by the 1963 Arkansas General Assembly to appraise the Arkansas economy, identify any barriers to economic expansion, and make recommendations for accelerating economic growth; and Donald T. Jack, Jr., "Usury—Recent Arkansas Developments Analyzed," *Arkansas Law Review and Bar Association Journal*, 21, no. 2 (Summer 1967), a review of major Arkansas court decisions on usury and their significance.

■ TABLE OF CASES

A

Abram v. City of Fayetteville, 281 Ark. 63, 661 S.W. 2d 371 (1983), **43**
Adams v. Dixie School District #7, 264 Ark. 178 570 S.W. 2d 603 (1978), **132**
Adams v. Hale, 213 Ark. 589, 212 S.W. 2d 330 (1948), **97**
Alexander v. Alexander, 262 Ark. 612, 561 S.W. 2d 59 (1978), **82**
Alford v. State, 69 Ark. 436, S.W. 217 (1901), **83**
Allen v. Langston, 216 Ark. 77, 224 S.W. 2d 377 (1949), **150, 153**
Allen v. Smith, 282 Ark. 401, 669 S.W. 2d 5 (1984), **93**
American Party v. Brandon, 253 Ark. 123, 484 S.W. 2d 881 (1972), **72, 156**
Anderson v. State, 266 Ark. 192, 583 S.W. 2d 14 (1979), **72, 80**
Andres v. First Arkansas Development Finance Corp., 230 Ark. 594 324 S.W. 2d 97 (1959), **111**
Andrews v. Briggs, 203 Ark. 714, 158 S.W. 2d 269 (1942), **92**
AP&L v. Pottach (1986), **102**
Applegate v. Lumjung Luke, 173 Ark. 93, 291 S.W. 978 (1927), **41**
Arco Auto Carriers, Inc. v. State ex rel. Bennett, 232 Ark. 779, 341 S.W. 2d 15 (1960), **43**
Arkansas Association of County Judges v. Green, 232 Ark. 438, 338 S.W. 2d 672 (1960), **87**
Arkansas Gazette Co. v. Loft on, 269 Ark. 109, 598 S.W. 2d 745 (1980), **35**
Arkansas Highway Commission v. Partain, 192 Ark. 803, 103 S.W. 2d 53 (1937), **57**
Arkansas Highway Commission v. Stupenti, 222 Ark. 9, 257 S.W. 2d 37 (1953), **42**
Arkansas Louisiana Electric Coop v. Arkansas Public Service Commission, 210 Ark. 84, 194 S.W.2d 673 (1946), **102**
Arkansas Louisiana Gas Co. v. Burkley, 242 Ark. 662, 416 S.W. 2d 263 (1967), **102**
Arkansas Motor Carriers Association v. Pritchett, 303 Ark. 620, 798 S.W. 2d 918 (1990), **192**
Arkansas Power & Light v. Potlach (1986), **102**
Arkansas State Highway Commission v. Coffelt, 301 Ark. 112, 782 S.W. 2d 45 (1990), **160**
Arkansas Stove Company v. State, 94 Ark. 27, 125 S.W. 100 (1910), **101**
Arkansas Tax Commission v. Moore, 103 Ark. 48, 145 S.W. 199 (1912), **152**
Arkansas Uniform and Linen v. Institutional Service Corp., 287 Ark. 370, 700 S.W. 2d 358 (1985), **112**
ARKLA v. James, 15 Ark. App. 184, 692 S.W. 2d 761 (1985), **102**

B

B.D.T., Inc. v. Moore, 260 Ark. 581, 543 S.W. 2d 220 (1976), **113**
Bailey v. Abington, 201 Ark. 1072, 48 S.W. 2d 176 (1921), **171**
Bailey v. Henslee, 287 F. 2d 936, 368 U.S. 877, 82 S. Ct. 121 (1961), **37**
Baker v. Harris, 178 Ark. 1001, 13 S.W. 2d 33 (1929), **97**
Baker v. Hill, 180 Ark. 387, 21 S.W. 2d 867 (1929), **169**
Baldwin v. Maner, 224 Ark. 348, 273 S.W. 2d 28 (1954), **174**
Ball v. Roberts, 291 Ark. 84, 722 S.W. 2d 829 (1987), **175**
Bank of Blytheville v. State, 148 Ark. 504, 230 S.W. 550 (1921), **101**
Bank of Manila v. Wallace, 177 Ark. 190, 5 S.W. 2d 937 (1928), **101**

Bank of Mulberry v. Frazhier, 178 Ark. 28, 9 S.W. 2d 793 (1928), **94**
Bank of Sun Prairie v. Hovig, 218 F. Supp, 769 (W.D. Ark. 1963), **93**
Baskins v. Wylds, 39 Ark. 347 (1882), **75**
Bates v. City of Litt le Rock, 361 U.S. 516, 80 S. Ct. 412, 4 L. Ed. 2d 480 (1960), **34**
Baumgardner v. Hall, 256 Ark. 254, 506 S.W. 2d 534 (1974), **36**
Baxter v. Brooks, 29 Ark. 173 (1874), **64**
Beauman v. Wells, Fargo & Co. Express, 77 Ark. 152, 91 S.W. 13 (1905), **81**
Beaumont v. Faubus, 239 Ark. 801 394 S.W. 2d 478 (1965), **111**
Becker v. McCuen, 303 Ark. 482, 798 S.W. 2d 71 (1990), **150**
Becker v. Riviere, 277 Ark. 252, 641 S.W. 2d 2 (1982), **150**
Bell v. Crawford County, 287 Ark. 251, 697 S.W. 2d 910 (1985), **114**
Bell v. State, 120 Ark. 530, 180 S.W. 186 (1915), **75**
Belote v. Coffman, 117 Ark. 352, 175 S.W. 37 (1915), **75, 98**
Benham v. Davis, 196 Ark. 740, 119 S.W. 2d 743 (1938), **37**
Bennett v. Hope, 204 Ark. 147, 161 S.W. 2d 186 (1942), **100**
Bennett v. NAACP, 236 Ark. 750, 370 S.W. 2d 79 (1963), **38, 40**
Berry v. Gordon, 237 Ark. 547 and 865, 376 S.W. 2d 279 (1964), **56, 164, 220, 221**
Berry v. Hall, 232 Ark. 648, 339 S.W. 2d 433 (1960), **151**
Besharse v. Blytheville, 254 Ark. 382, 493 S.W. 2d 708 (1973), **100**
Biffle v. Priddy, 192 Ark. 608, 93 S.W. 2d 328 (1936), **75**
Birdson v. Turtle, (1889), **91**
Block v. Allen, 241 Ark. 970, 411 S.W. 2d 21 (1967), **52**
Blytheville v. Thompson, 254 Ark. 46, 491 S.W. 2d 769 (1973), **41**
Board of Education v. Ashdown School District, 156 Ark. 549, 247 S.W. 70 (1923), **127**
Board of Trustees v. City of Little Rock, 295 Ark. 585, 750 S.W. 2d 950 (1988), **163**
Board of Trustees v. City of Little Rock, 295 Ark. 585, 750 S.W. 2d 950 (1990), **163**
Booe v. Road Improvement District No. 4, 141 Ark. 140, 216 S.W. 508 (1919), **59**
Booth v. Smith, 261 Ark. 838, 552 S.W. 2d 19 (1977), **84, 126, 203**
Borchert v. Scott, 248 Ark. 1041, 460 S.W. 2d 28 (1970), **113, 168, 198**
Boshears v. Arkansas Racing Commission, 258 Ark. 741, 528 S.W. 2d 646 (1975), **34**
Boyd v. Bryant, 35 Ark. 69, 37 Am. R. 6 (1879), **51, 59**
Bradley v. Galloway, 279 Ark. 231, 651 S.W. 2d 445 (1983), **153, 156**
Bradley Lumber Co. v. Cheney, 226 Ark. 857, 295 S.W. 2d 765 (1956), **58**
Brandt v. St. Vincent Infirmary, 701 S.W. 2d 103 (1985), **34**
Brenneman v. State, 264 Ark. 460, 573 S.W. 2d 47 (1978), **37**
Brewster v. Johnson, 260 Ark. 450, 541 S.W. 2d 306 (1976), **52**
Brick v. Simoneti, 279 Ark. 446, 652 S.W. 2d 23 (1983), **126**
Brickhouse v. Hill, 167 Ark. 513, 268 S.W. 865 (1925), **158, 160**
Brodie v. Fitzgerald, 57 Ark. 445, 22 S.W. 29 (1893), **113**
Brown v. State, 718 S.W. 2d 937 (1986), **71**
Burns v. Britt, 281 Ark. 225, 663 S.W. 2d 715 (1984), **76**

C

Cabot v. Morgan, 228 Ark. 1084, 312 S.W. 2d 333 (1958), **84**
Cain v. Woodruff County, 89 Ark. 456, 117 S.W. 768 (1909), **86**
Cairo T. and S.R.R. v. Arkansas Short Line, 172 Ark. 317, 288 S.W. 715 (1926), **117**
Camden v. Arkansas Power and Light Company, 145 Ark. 205, 224 S.W. 444 (1920), **40**
Campbell v. Hammond, 203 Ark. 130, 156 S.W. 2d 75 (1941), **173**
Campbell v. Geheb, 258 Ark. 225, 523 S.W. 2d (1975), **92**

Carl Lee v. State, 102 Ark. 122, 143 S.W. 909 (1912), **79**
Carpenter v. Logan, 281 Ark. 184, 662 S.W. 2d 808 (1984), **82**
Carpenter v. Paragould, 198 Ark. 454, 128 S.W. 2d 980 (1939), **153**
Casey v. Scott Paper Co., 272 Ark. 312, 613 S.W. 2d 821 (1981), **160**
Central Coal and Coke Company v. Graham, 129 Ark. 550, 196 S.W. 940 (1917), **75**
Central Manufacturer's Mutual Insurance Co. v. Friedman, 213 Ark. 9, 209 S.W. 2d 102 (1948), **127**
Chaffin v. Arkansas Game and Fish Commission, 296 Ark. 431, 757 S.W. 2d 950 (1988), **184, 187**
Champion v. State, 110 Ark. 44, 160 S.W. 878 (1913), **36**
Chaney v. Bryant, 259 Ark. 294, 532 S.W. 2d 741 (1976), **150**
Charisse v. Eldred, 252 Ark. 101, 477 S.W. 2d 480 (1972), **126**
Cheney v. St. Louis S.W. Ry., 239 Ark. 870, 394 S.W. 2d 731 (1965), **151**
Chicago, R.I. and P. Ry. v. Langley, 78 Ark. 207, 94 S.W. 58 (1906), **84**
Chicago, R.I. and P.R.R. v. State, 86 Ark. 412, 111 S.W. 456 (1908), **40**
Chicot County v. Davies, 40 Ark. 200 (1882), **58**
Chism v. Martin, 57 Ark. 83, 20 S.W. 809 (1892), **66, 74**
Chism v. Tucker, 101 Ark. 112, 141 S.W. 2d 503 (1911), **48**
Choctaw, O. and G. Ry. v. State, 73 Ark. 373, 84 S.W. 502, 92 S.W. 26 (1904), **119**
Citizens Bank v. Estate of Pettyjohn, 282 Ark. 222, 667 S.W. 657 (1984), **159**
City of Fayetteville v. S & H, Inc., 261 Ark. 148, 547 S.W. 2d 94 (1977), **42**
City of Little Rock v. Parish, 36 Ark. 166 (1880), **99**
City of Little Rock v. Quindley, 61 Ark. 622, 33 S.W. 1053 (1896), **58**
City of Little Rock v. Raines, 241 Ark. 1071, 411 S.W. 2d 486 (1967), **166**
City of Little Rock v. Waters, 303 Ark. 363, 797 S.W. 2d 426 (1990), **163**
City of North Little Rock v. Gorman, 264 Ark. 150, 568 S.W. 2d 481 (1978), **154**
City of West Memphis v. Jordan, 212 Ark. 739, 208 S.W. 2d 164 (1948), **231**
Clark v. Campbell, 514 Federal Supplement 1300 (1981), **80**
Clark v. Hambleton, 235 Ark. 467, 360 S.W. 2d 486 (1962), **128**
Clinton v. Taylor, 284 Ark. 238, 681 S.W. 2d 238 (1984), **61**
Cloverleaf Development v. Provence, 273 Ark. 12, 616 S.W. 2d 16 (1981), **92**
Cobb v. Hammock, 82 Ark. 584, 102 S.W. 382 (1907), **87**
Cobb v. State, 265 Ark. 527, 579 S.W. 2d 612 (1979), **79**
Cockrell v. Dobbs, 238 Ark. 348, 381 S.W. 2d 756 (1964), **75**
Cole v. State, 84 Ark. 473, 106 S.W. 673 (1907), **68**
Coleman v. Sherrill, 189 Ark. 843, 75 S.W. 2d 248 (1934), **150**
Combs v. Gray, 170 Ark. 956, 281 S.W. 918 (1926), **158**
Commissions on Judicial Discipline and Disability v. Digby, 303 Ark. 24, 792 S.W. 2d 594 (1990), **238**
Cope v. Collins, 37 Ark. 649 (1881), **114**
Cotham v. Coffman, 111 Ark. 108, 163 S.W. 1183 (1914), **128**
Cottrell v. Faubus, 233 Ark. 721, 347 S.W. 2d 52 (1961), **60**
Coulter v. Dodge, 197 Ark. 812, 125 S.W. 2d 115 (1939), **132**
Cox v. State, 72 Ark. 94, 78 S.W. 756 (1904), **70**
Craig v. Sims, 160 Ark. 269, 255 S.W. 1 (1923), **48**
Craig v. Waterworks Improvement District, 84 Ark. 390, 105 S.W. 867 (1907), **133**
Crawford County v. Van Buren, 201 Ark. 798, 146 S.W. 2d 914 (1941), **81**
Crittenden County v. Williford, 283 Ark. 289, 675 S.W. 2d 631 (1984), **87**
Crowley v. Thombrough, 226 Ark. 768, 296 S.W. 2d 62 (1956), **151**
Cude v. State, 237 Ark. 927, 377 S.W. 2d 816 (1964), **43**

Curlin v. Harding Drain Improvement District, 221 Ark. 412, 253 S W 2d 345 (1952), **133**
Curry v. State, 279 Ark. 153, 649 S.W. 2d 833 (1983), **63**
Czech v. Baer, 283 Ark. 365, 677 S.W. 2d 833 (1984), **151**
Czech v. Munson, 280 Ark. 486, 678 S.W. 2d 766 (1984), **156**

D

Dabbs v. State, 39 Ark. 353 (1882), **35**
Darden v. State, 80 Ark. 295, 97 S.W. 449 (1906), **36**
Datsun 280ZX v. Bentley (1982), **42**
Davies v. Gaines, 48 Ark. 370, 3 S.W. 184 (1886), **59**
Davis v. Merritt, 252 Ark. 659, 480 S.W. 2d 924 (1972), **79**
Dennis v. State, 26 Ark. App. 294, 764 S.W. 2d 466 (1989), **187**
Dickinson v. Cliboum, 125 Ark. 101, 187 S.W. 909 (1916), **60**
Dickinson v. Johnson, 117 Ark. 582, 176 S.W. 116 (1915), **58, 68**
Dickinson v. Page, 20 Ark. 377, 179 S.W. 1004 (1915), **68**
Dietz v. Arkansas, (1989), **194**
Diffee v. State, 78 S.W. 2d 94 (1986), **37**
Dingle v. City of Eureka Springs, 242 Ark. 382, 413 S.W. 2d 641 (1967), **153**
Drainage District v. Rolfe, 110 Ark. 374, 161 S.W. 1034 (1913), **74**
Drennen v. Bennett, 230 Ark. 330, 322 S.W. 2d 585 (1959), **184**
Dupree v. Alma School District No. 30, 279 Ark. 340, 651 S.W. 2d 90 (1983), **34**
Duncan v. State, 267 Ark. 41, 588 S.W. 2d 432 (1979), **37**
Durden v. Sebastian Company, 73 Ark. 305, 83 S.W. 1048 (1904), **77**

E

Eagle v. Beard, 33 Ark. 497 (1878), **105**
Emhart v. Heath, 369 F. Supp. 259, **198**
Edwards v. State, 12 Ark. 122 (1851), **68**
Equalization Board v. Landowners, 51 Ark. 516, 11 S.W. 822 (1889), **131**
Erxleben v. Horton Printing Co., 283 Ark. 272, 675 S.W. 2d 638 (1984), **217**
Evans v. Wheatley, 197 Ark. 997, 125 S.W. 2d 101 (1939), **53**
Exchange Bank and Trust v. Mathews, 267 Ark. 415, 591 S.W. 2d 354 (1979), **92**
Ex parte Anthony, 5 Ark. 358 (1844), **72**
Ex parte Dame, 162 Ark. 382 (1923), **38**
Ex parte Hawkins, 61 Ark. 321, 33, S.W. 106 (1895), **42**
Ex parte James, 27 Ark. 349 (1871), **75**
Ex parte King, 141 Ark. 213, 217 S.W. 465 (1919), **71**
Ex parte Levy, 204 Ark. 657, 163 S.W. 2d 529 (1942), **72**
Ex parte Levy, 43 Ark. 42 (1884), **41**
Ex parte Martin, 13 Ark. 198 (1853), **42**
Ex parte Snoddy, 44 Ark. 221 (1905), **73**
Ex parte Turner, 40 Ark. 548 (1883), **75**

F

Farmers Coop v. Stevens 260 Ark. 735, 543 S.W. 2d 920 (1976), **93**
Farrell v. State, 111 Ark. 180, 163 S.W. 768 (1914), **125**
Faubus v. Fields, 239 Ark. 241, 388 S.W. 2d 558 (1965), **204, 215**

Faubus v. Kinney, 239 Ark. 443, 389 S.W. 2d 887 (1965), **197**
Faubus v. Miles, 237 Ark. 947, 377 S.W. 2d 601 (1964), **46, 190**
Faulkner v. Woodard, 203 Ark. 254, 156 S.W. 2d 243 (1941), **48**
Federal Express v. Skelton, 265 Ark. 187, 578 S.W. 2d 1 (1979), **103**
Ferrell v. Keel, 105 Ark. 380, 151 S.W. 269 (1912), **57, 74, 151**
Ferstle v. McCuen, 296 Ark. 504, 758 S.W. 2d 398 (1988), **149, 150**
Fife v. State, 31 Ark. 455 (1876), **37**
Files v. Hill, 268 Ark. 106, 594 S.W. 2d 836 (1980), **46**
Fikes v. State, 221 Ark. 81, 251 S.W. 2d 1014 (1952), **36**
First National Bank v. Roberts, 242 Ark. 912, 416 S.W. 2d (1967), **34**
Fitzhugh v. Ford, 230 Ark. 531, 323 S.W. 2d 559 (1959), **103**
Fletcher v. Bryant, 243 Ark. 864, 422 S.W. 2d 698 (1968), **67**
Flora v. White, 692 F. 2d 53 (1982), **125**
Foreman v. Marianna, 43 Ark. 324 (1884), **77**
Fort Smith Light and Traction Co. v. Board of Imps, 169 Ark. 690, 276 S.W. 1012 (1925), **99**
Franklin v. State, 267 Ark. 311, 590 S.W. 2d 28 (1979), **42**
Franklin Electric v. Heath, 261 Ark. 269, 547 S.W. 2d 755 (1977), **103**
Freeze v. Jones, 260 Ark. 193, 539 S.W. 2d 425 (1976), **57**
French v. State, 256 Ark. 298, 506 S.W. 2d 820 (1974), **79**
Froman v. State, 232 Ark. 697, 339 S.W. 2d 601 (1960), **36**
Fulkerson v. Refunding Board, 201 Ark. 957, 147 S.W. 2d 980 (1940), **152**
Futtrell v. Oldham, 107 Ark. 386, 155 S.W. 502 (1913), **66, 67**

G

Gaines v. McCuen, 296 Ark. 513, 758 S.W. 2d 403 (1988), **150**
Game and Fish Commission ex rel. Wright v. Casey, 225 Ark. 149, 279 S.W. 2d 819 (1955), **184**
Gamer v. Lowery, 221 Ark. 571, 254 S.W. 2d 680 (1953), **180, 213**
Garrett v. Faubus, 230 Ark. 445, 323 S.W. 2d 877 (1959), **195**
Gentry v. Harrison, 194 Ark. 916, 110 S.W. 2d 497 (1937), **152**
Gerard v. State, 237 Ark. 287, 372 S.W. 2d 635 (1963), **39**
Gipson v. Brown, 706 S.W. 2d 369 (1986), **43**
Gipson v. Crawfis, 225 Ark. 903, 286 S.W. 2d 336 (1956), **112**
Gipson v. Ingram, 215 Ark. 812, 223 S.W. 2d 595 (1949), **60, 112**
Gipson v. Morely, 217 Ark. 560, 233 S.W. 2d 79 (1961), **34**
Gipson v. Morley, 217 Ark. 560, 233 S.W. 2d 79 (1950), **41, 42**
Glover v. Henry, 231 Ark. 111, 328 S.W. 2d 382 (1959), **53, 65, 70**
Godwin v. Godwin, 268 Ark. 364, 596 S.W. 2d 695 (1980), **40**
Goodwin v. Cross Country School District, No. 7, 394 Fed. Supp. 417 (1973), **107**
Goodwin v. State, 235 Ark. 457, 360 S.W. 2d 490 (1962), **111**
Gosnell v. State, 52 Ark. 228, 12 S.W. 392 (1889), **41**
Govan v. Jackson, 32 Ark. 553 (1877), **35, 48**
Gower v. Looney, 199 Ark. 272, 133 S.W. 2d 451 (1939), **131, 147**
Graham v. Nix, 102 Ark. 277, 144 S.W. 214 (1912), **106**
Graham v. State, 253 Ark. 462, 486 S.W. 2d 678 (1972), **37**
Gray v. Hodges, 107 Ark. 272, 154 S.W. 506 (1913), **133**
Griffin v. Rhoton, 85 Ark. 89, 107 S.W. 2d 380 (1913), **79**
Grigsby v. Mabry, 583 F. Supp. 629 (E.D. Ark. 1983), **36**
Grimmett v. Digby, 267 Ark. 192, 589 S.W. 2d 579 (1979), **39, 164**

Grimmett v. State, 251 Ark. 270a, 476 S.W. 2d 217 (1972), **39**
Guinn v. State, 27 Ark. App. 260, 771 S.W. 2d 290 (1989), **168**

H

Hackler v. Baker, 233 Ark. 690, 346 S.W. 2d 677 (1961), **230**
Haile v. State, 38 Ark. 564 (1882), **35**
Hailey v. Carter, 221 Ark. 20, 251 S.W. 2d 826 (1952), **151, 157**
Halbert v. Helena-West Helena Industrial Development Corp., 226 Ark. 620, 291 S.W. 2d 802 (1956), **101**
Hall v. Thompson, 283 Ark. 26, 669 S.W. 2d 905 (1984), **115**
Hammond Packing Company v. State, 12 U.S. 322, 29 S. Ct. 370, 53 L. Ed. 530 (1908), **39**
Hanson v. Hodges, 109 Ark. 479, 160 S.W. 392 (1913), **152**
Hargett v. Hill, Fontaine & Co., 101 Ark. 510, 142 S.W. 1137 (1911), **94**
Harrison v. Harrison, 239 Ark. 756, 394 S.W. 2d 128 (1965), **40**
Hart v. Wimberly, 173 Ark. 1083, 296 S.W. 39 (1927), **94**
Hartford Fire Insurance v. State, 76 Ark. 303, 89 S.W. 2d 42 (1905), **41**
Harvey v. Ridgeway, 248 Ark. 35, 450 S.W. 2d 281 (1970), **54**
Havis v. Philpot, 115 Ark. 250, 170 S.W. 1005 (1914), **34**
Helena v. Arkansas Utilities Company, 208 Ark. 442, 186 S.W. 2d 783 (1945), **120**
Helena Water Co. v. Helena, 140 Ark. 597, 216 S.W. 26 (1919), **120**
Henderson v. Gladesh, 198 Ark. 217, 128 S.W. 2d 257 (1939), **45**
Hendricks v. Block, 80 Ark. 333, 97 S.W. 63 (1906), **100**
Hendricks v. Hodges, 122 Ark. 82, 182 S.W. 538 (1916), **51**
Henley v. Goggin, 241 Ark. 348, 407 S.W. 2d 732 (1966), **213**
Herrington v. State, 697 S.W. 2d 899 (1985), **39**
Hester v. Bourland, 80 Ark. 145, 95 S.W. 992 (1906), **76**
Hickenbottom v. McCain, 207 Ark. 485, 181 S.W. 2d 226 (1944), **127**
Hicks v. State, 225 Ark. 916, 287 S.W. 2d 12 (1956), **79**
Highway Commission v. Nelson Brothers, 191 Ark. 629, 87 S.W. 2d 394 (1935), et al, **57**
Highway Commission v. Wilkinson, 12 Ark. App. 28, 670 S.W. 2d 462 (1984), **57**
Hill v. Bush, 192 Ark. 181, 90 S.W. 2d 490 (1936), **91**
Hogins v. Bullock, 92 Ark. 67, 121 S.W. 1064 (1909), **70**
Holbert v. Helena-West Helena Industrial Development Corporation, 226 Ark. 620, 291 S.W. 2d 802 (1956), **174**
Holman v. Dierks, 217 Ark. 677, 233 S.W. 2d 392 (1950), **100**
Holmes v. Cheney, 234 Ark. 503, 352 S.W. 2d 943 (1962), **115**
Holmes v. Morgan, 52 Ark. 99, 12 S.W. 201 (1889), **87**
Hooker v. Parkin, 235 Ark. 218, 357 S.W. 2d 534 (1962), **61**
Hosto v. Brickell, 265 Ark. 147, 577 S.W. 2d 401 (1979), **39**
Howard v. State, 37 Ark. 265 (1881), **37**
Howard County v. Rotenberry, 286 Ark. 29, 688 S.W. 2d 937 (1985), **55**
Hudson v. Higgins, 175 Ark. 585, 399 S.W. 1000 (1927), **61**
Hudson v. Higgins, 175 Ark. 585, 299 S.W. 1000 (1928), **60**
Huggins v. Wacaster, 223 Ark. 390, 266 S.W. 2d 58 (1954), 77, **191**
Hughes v. Jackson, 213 Ark. 243, 210 S.W. 2d 312 (1948), **82**
Humphrey v. Garrett, 218 Ark. 418, 236 S.W. 2d 569 (1951), **167**
Hunter State Bank v. Mills, 90 Ark. 10, 117 S.W. 760 (1909), **40**
Hurst v. Bar Rules Committee, 202 Ark. 1101, 155 S.W. 2d 697 (1941), **175**
Hutcheson v. Pitts, 170 Ark. 248, 278 S.W. 639 (1926), **86**

Hutton v. McCleskey, 132 Ark. 391, 200 S.W. 2d 1032 (1918), **38**
Hutton v. Savage, 298 Ark. 256, 769 S.W. 2d 394 (1989), **239**

I

In re Pitchford, 265 Ark. 752 (1979), **38**
In re Powers, (1962), **92**
Inman v. Kelley, 229 Ark. 149, 313 S.W. 2d 796 (1958), **112**
Irby v. Barrett, 204 Ark. 682, 163 S.W. 2d 512 (1942), **54**

J

J. W. Black Lumber Company v. Arkansas Department of Pollution Control and Ecology, 717 S.W. 2d 807 (1986), **40**
Jackson v. Munson, 288 Ark. 57, 701 S.W. 2d 378 (1986), **115**
Jackson v. Ozment, 283 Ark. 100, 671 S.W. 2d 736 (1984), **59, 71**
Jackson v. Smith, 236 Ark. 419, 366 S.W. 2d 278 (1963), **76**
Jackson v. State, 101 Ark. 473, 142 S.W. 1153 (1912), **151, 157**
Jeffery v. Jackson County Court, 251 Ark. 1071, 476 S.W. 2d 805 (1972), **74, 76**
Jeff rey v. Trevathan, (1949), **128**
Jewett v. McConnell, 112 Ark. 291, 165 S.W. 954 (1914), **73, 141**
Jobe v. Urquhart, 102 Ark. 470, 143 S.W. 121 (1912), **60**
John Watkins, "Access to Public Records under Arkansas Freedom of Information Act," 37 *Arkansas Law Review* 741, **55**
John Watkins, "Open Meetings under the Arkansas Freedom of Information Act," 38 *Arkansas Law Review* 268, **55**
Johnson v. Cummings, 281 Ark. 229, 663 S.W. 2d 168 (1984), **230**
Johnson v. Gates, 242 Ark. 631 415 S.W. 2d 329 (1967), **191**
Johnson v. Munger, 260 Ark. 613, 542 S.W. 2d 753 (1976), **153**
Johnson County v. Holman, 280 Ark. 128, 655 S.W. 2d 408 (1983), **87**
Johnson County Board of Election Commissioners v. Holman, 280 Ark. 128, 655 S.W. 2d 408 (1983), **175**
Jones v. Cheney, 253 Ark. 926, 489 S.W. 2d 785 (1973), **40**
Jones v. Clark, 278 Ark. 119, 644 S.W. 2d 257 (1983), **65, 70, 132**
Jones v. Glidewell, 53 Ark. 161, 13 S.W. 723 (1890), **201**
Jones v. Reed, 267 Ark. 237, 590 S.W. 2d 6 (1979), **35, 164**
Jones v. State, 154 Ark. 288, 242 S.W. 377 (1922), **69**
Jones v. State, 230 Ark. 18, 320 S.W. 2d 645 (1959), **37**
Jones v. Smith, 165 Ark. 425, 264 S.W. 950 (1924), **201**
Justice v. Campbell, 241 Ark. 802, 410 S.W. 2d 601 (1967), **126, 175**

K

Kansas City, F.S. and M.R.R. v. Becker, 67 Ark. 1, 153 S.W. 406 (1899), **120**
Keith v. State, 49 Ark. 439, 5 S.W. 880 (1887), **75**
Kelly v. Bumpers, 340 F. Supp. 568 (E.D. Ark. 1962), **171**
Kemp v. Simmons, 244 Ark. 1052, 428 S.W. 2d 59 (1968), **153**
Kennedy v. Kennedy, 205 Ark. 650, 169 S.W. 2d 876 (1943), **47**
Kerr v. East Central Arkansas Housing Authority, 208 Ark. 625, 187 S.W. 2d 189 (1945), **111**
Kirst v. Street Improvement District #120, 86 Ark. 1, 109 S.W. 526 (1908), **133**

Kozal v. State, 264 Ark. 587, 573 S.W. 2d 323 (1978), **36**
Krumpen v. Taylor, 183 Ark. 1046, 40 S.W. 2d 775 (1931), **101**

L

Laborers' International Union of North America, Local 107 v. Kunco, Inc., 472 F.2d 456 (8th Cir. 1973), **183**
Laman v. Harrill, 233 Ark. 967, 349 S.W. 2d 814 (1961), **59**
Lane v. State, 217 Ark. 428, 230, S.W. 2d 480 (1950), **37**
Lee v. Grubbs, 269 Ark. 205, 599, S.W. 2d 715 (1980), **82**
Lee v. Watts, 243 Ark. 957, 423 S.W. 2d 557 (1968), **85**
Legislative Research Bureau v. Mackrell, 212 Ark. 40, 204 S.W. 2d 893 (1947), **112**
Leonard v. State, 170 Ark. 41, 278 S.W. 654 (1926), **40**
Leonard v. State, 278 S.W. 654 (1926), **40**
Leprarie v. City of Hot Springs, 124 Ark. 346, 187 S.W. 422 (1916), **51**
Lewis v. Conlee, 258 Ark. 715, 529 S.W. 2d 132 (1975), **153**
Lewis v. Smith, 198 Ark. 244, 129 S.W. 2d 229 (1939), **173**
Little Rock v. Community Chest, 204 Ark. 562, 163 S.W. 2d 522 (1942), **100**
Little Rock v. Katzenstein, 52 Ark. 107, 12 S.W. 198 (1889), **133**
Little Rock and F. S. Ry. v. Hanniford, 49 Ark. 291, 5 S.W. 294 (1887), **119**
Little Rock and Fort Smith R. R. v. Barber, 39 Ark. 491 (1882), **61**
Little Rock and Fort Smith R. R. v. Barker, 39 Ark. 491 (1882), **78**
Little Rock and Fort Smith R. R. v. Worthen, 46 Ark. 312 (1885), **63**
Littleton v. Blanton, 281 Ark. 395, 665 S.W. 2d 239 (1984), **163**
Loftin v. Watson, 32 Ark. 415 (1877), **57**
Longstreth v. Cook, 215 Ark. 72, 220 S.W. 2d 433 (1949), **129**
Lucas v. Futtrell, 84 Ark. 540, 106 S.W. 667 (1907), **127**, **130**
Lumber Co. v. Biddle, 87 Ark. 587, 113 S.W. 796 (1908), **99**, **101**
Luxora v. Jonesboro L.C. & F.R.R., 83 Ark. 275, 103 S.W. 60 SC 1907, **100**

M

Mackey v. McDonald, 255 Ark. 978, 504 S.W. 2d 726 (1974), **115**
Magruder v. Arkansas Game and Fish Commission, 293 Ark. 39, 732 S.W. 2d 849 (1987), **186–187**
Mann v. City of Heber Springs, 239 Ark. 969, 395 S.W. 2d 557 (1965), **39**
Maples v. Road Improvement District No. 2, 137 Ark. 177, 208 S.W. 577 (1919), **76**, **77**
Maroney v. Universal Leasing Co., 263 Ark. 8, 562 S.W. 2d (1978), **80**
Martin v. Bratton, 223 Ark. 159, 264 S.W. 2d 635 (1954), **81**
Martin v. Hefley, 259 Ark. 484, 533 S.W. 2d 521 (1976), **213**
Martin v. State, 213 Ark. 507, 211 S.W. 2d 116 (1948), **42**
Martindale v. Honey, 259 Ark. 416, 533 S.W. 2d 198 (1976), **54**
Matthews v. Bailey, (1939), **168**
Matthews v. Rodgers, 279 Ark. 328, 651 S.W. 2d 453 (1983), **77**
Maxwell v. State, 216 Ark. 393 (1950), **37**
May v. Edwards, 258 Ark. 871, 529 S.W. 2d 647 (1975), **53**
May v. State, 254 Ark. 194, 492, S.W. 2d 888, cert. denied, 414 U.S. 1024, 94 S. Ct. 448, 38 L. #d. 2d 315 (1973), **44**
McAllister v. Forrest City Improvement District #11, 274 Ark. 372, 626 S.W. 2d 194 (1981), **133**
McArthur v. Smallwood, 225 Ark. 328, 281 S.W. 2d 428 (1955), **50**, **115**

McConnell v. Arkansas Brick and Manufacturing Co., 70 Ark. 568, 69 S.W. 559 (1902), **57**
McCraw v. Pate, 254 Ark. 357, 494 S.W. 2d 94 (1973), **126, 176**
McDonald v. Bowen, 250 Ark. 1049, 468 S.W. 2d 765 (1971), **165**
McEachin v. Martin, 193 Ark. 787, 102 S.W. 2d 864 (1937), **78**
McFarlin v. Kelly, 246 Ark. 1237, 442 S.W. 2d 183 (1969), **39**
McFerrin v. Knight, 265 Ark. 658, 580 S.W. 2d 463 (1979), **153**
McGehee v. MidSouth Gas Co., 235 Ark. 50, 357 S.W. 2d 282 (1962), **71**
McLaughlin v. Retherford, 207 Ark. 1094, 184 S.W. 2d 461 (1944), **177**
McMinn v. Little Rock, 275 Ark. 458, 631 S.W. 2d 288 (1982), **42**
Means v. Terral, 145 Ark. 443, 225 S.W. 601 (1920), **70**
Mears v. City of Little Rock, 256 Ark. 359, 508 S.W. 2d 750 (1974), **202**
Mears v. Hall, 263 Ark. 827, 569 S.W. 2d 91 (1978), **77**
Mears v. Little Rock School District, 268 Ark. 30, 593 S.W. 2d 42 (1980), **134**
Meeks v. State, 80 Ark. 579, 98 S.W. 378 (1906), **40**
Memphis and L. R. R.R. v. Adams, 46 Ark. 159 (1885), **92**
Merritt v. Jones, 259 Ark. 380, 533 S.W. 2d 497 (1976), **211**
Miles v. Southern, 297 Ark. 274, 760 S.W. 2d 868 (1988), **235**
Miller v. Tatum, 170 Ark. 152, 279 S.W. 1002 (1926), **75**
Miller v. Witcher, 160 Ark. 479, 254 S.W. 1063 (1923), **51**
Mississippi County v. Green, 200 Ark. 204, 138 S.W. 377 (1940), **81**
Missouri Pacific Railroad v. Conway County Bridge District, 134 Ark. 292, 204 S.W. 630 (1918), **36**
Missouri Pacific Railroad v. United Brick and Clay Workers Union, 218 Ark. 707, 238 S.W. 2d 945 (1951), **118**
Missouri Pacific Railroad v. W. S. Fox & Sons, 251 Ark. 247, 472 S.W. 2d 726 (1971), **103**
Mitchell v. Hopper, 153 Ark. 515, 241 S.W. 10 (1922), **67, 68**
Mohr v. Mohr, 206 Ark. 1094, 178 S.W. 2d 502 (1944), **47**
Monroe v. Green, 71 Ark. 527, 76 S.W. 199 (1903), **55, 67**
Moose v. Gregory, 267 Ark. 86, 590 S.W. 2d 662 (1979), **222**
Morgan v. State, 273 Ark. 252, 618 S.W. 2d 161 (1981), **106**
Morley v. Berg, 216 Ark. 562, 226 S.W. 2d 559 (1950), **70**
Mueller v. Coffman, 132 Ark. 45, 200 S.W. 136 (1918), **125**

N

Nall v. Kelley, 120 Ark. 277, 179 S.W. 486 (1915), **131**
Neel v. State, 9 Ark. 259 (1849), **35, 164**
Nethercutt v. Pulaski County Special School District, 248 Ark. 143, 450 S.W. 2d 777 (1970), **74**
Newton v. Edwards, 203 Ark. 18, 155 S.W. 2d 591,(1941), **86**
Newton County Republican Central Committee v. Clark, 228 Ark. 965, 311 S.W. 2d 774 (1958), **177**
Noble v. Davis, 204 Ark. 156, 161 S.W. 2d 189 (1942), **41**
North Little Rock Transportation Company v. City of North Little Rock, 207 Ark. 976, 184 S.W. 2d 52 (1944), **41**

O

O'Kane v. McClean Bottom Lance & Drainage District #3, 211 Ark. 938, 203 S.W. 2d 392 (1947), **131**

Oliver v. Southern Trust Co., 138 Ark. 381, 212 S.W. 77 (1919), **60**
Oliver v. State, 268 Ark. 579, 594 S.W. 2d 261 (1980), **38**
Orsini v. State, 286 Ark. 5, 371 S.W. 2d 518 (1963), **168**
Osborne v. State, 237 Ark. 5, 371 S.W. 2d 518 (1963), **68**
Owen v. Dalton, 296 Ark. 351, 757 S.W. 2d 921 (1988), **163**
Ozan Lumber Co. v. Buddie, 87 Ark. 587 (1908), **101**
Ozark Coal Co. v. Pennsylvania Anthracite R. R., 97 Ark. 495, 134 S.W. 634 (1911), **42**

P

Paragould v. Milner, 114 Ark. 334, 170 S.W. 78 (1914), **102**
Parker v. Laws, 249 Ark. 632, 460 S.W. 2d 337 (1970), **115**
Parker v. Murry, 221 Ark. 554, 254 S.W. 2d 468 (1953), **70**
Pamell v. State, 203 Ark. 652, 176 S.W. 2d 902 (1942), **36**
Patton v. Vaughan, 39 Ark. 211 (1882), **80**
Pearis v. State, 227 Ark. 230, 297 S.W. 2d 775 (1957), **40**
Peel v. Kelley, 268 Ark. 90, 594 S.W. 2d 11 (1980), **84, 85**
Pendergrass v. Sheid, 241 Ark. 908, 411 S.W. 2d 5 (1967), **54**
Perkins v. DuVal, 31 Ark. 236 (1876), **60**
Person v. Williams-Echols Dry Goods Co., 113 Ark. 467, 169 S.W. 233 (1914), **91**
Peterson v. Culpepper, 72 Ark. 230, 79 S.W. 783 (1904), **50**
Peterson v. Culpepper, 72 Ark. 230, 79 S.W. 783 (1906), **126**
Pettigrew v. Washington County, 43 Ark. 33 (1884), **77, 82**
Petty v. Clarke, 256 Ark. 412, 507 S.W. 2d 700 (1974), **83**
Peugh v. Oliger, 233 Ark. 281, 345 S.W. 2d 610 (1961), **38, 39**
Phillips Petroleum Corp. v. Jenkins, 297 U.S. 629, 56 S. Ct. 611 (1936), **102**
Philyaw v. State Indictment, 704 S.W. 2d 608 (1986), **37**
Pickens v. Board of Apportionment, 220 Ark. 145, 246 S.W. 2d 556, **196**
Piggott v. Woodard, 261 Ark. 406, 549 S.W. 2d 278 (1977), **41**
Pike County School District No. 1 v. Pike County Board of Education, 247 Ark. 14, 444, S.W. 2d 75 (1969), **208**
Pitcock v. State, 91 Ark. 527, 121 S.W. 742 (1909), **57**
Poe v. State, 251 Ark. 35, 470 S.W. 2d 818 (1971), **34**
Post-Conviction Relief in Arkansas, 24 Ark. L. Rev. 57, **38**
Powell v. Durden, 61 Ark. 21, 31 S.W. 740 (1895), **114**
Powell v. Hays, 83 Ark. 448, 104 S.W. 177 (1907), **57, 69**
Price v. Edmonds, 231 Ark. 332, 330 S.W. 2d 82 (1959), **115**
Protas v. Modem Investment Corporation, 198 Ark. 300, 128 S.W. 2d 360 (1939), **102**
Pryor v. Lowe, 258 Ark. 188, 523 S.W. 2d 199 (1975), **33, 44**
Puckett v. Puckett, 709 S.W. 2d 82 (1986), **80**
Pulaski County v. Horton, 224 Ark. 864, 276 S.W. 2d 706 (1955), **82**
Pulaski County Municipal Court v. Scott, 272 Ark. 115, 612 S.W. 2d 297 (1981), **71**
Pulaski v. Reeve, 42 Ark. 54 (1883), **105**
Purcell v. Jones, 242 Ark. 168, 412 S.W. 2d 284 (1967), **56, 69**
Purdy v. Glover, 199 Ark. 63, 132 S.W. 2d 821 (1939), **132**
Purvis v. City of Little Rock, 282 Ark. 101, 669 S.W. 2d 900 (1984), **230**

Q

Quattlebaum v. Davis, 265 Ark. 588, 579 S.W. 2d 599 (1949), **153**

R

Ragan v. Venhaus, 711 S.W. 2d 467 (1986), **134**
Railey v. Magnolia, 197 Ark. 1047, 126 S.W. 2d 273 (1939), **152**
Rainwater v. Haynes, 244 Ark. 1191, 428 S.W. 2d 254 (1968), **107**
Ralls v. Mittlesteadt, 268 Ark. 741, 596 S.W. 2d 349 (1980), **57**
Rambo v. Hall, 195 Ark. 502, 112 S.W. 2d 951 (1938), **136**
Randolph v. Abbott, 84 Ark. 341, 105 S.W. 576 (1907), **83**
Rawleigh Co. v. Castleberry, 201 Ark. 980, 147 S.W. 2d 734 (1941), **91**
Ray v. Mountain Home, 228 Ark. 885, 311 S.W. 2d 163 (1958), **111**
Reaves v. Jones, 257 Ark. 210, 515 S.W. 2d 201 (1974), **54, 55**
Rector v. Board of Imp., 50 Ark. 116, 6 S.W. 519, **133**
Reed v. Bradford, 141 Ark. 201, 217 S.W. 11 (1919), **83**
Reed v. Jones, 261 Ark. 550, 551 S.W. 2d 191 (1977), **61**
Reese v. Steel, 73 Ark. 66, 83 S.W. 355 (1904), **75**
Reeves v. Been, 217 Ark. 67, 228 S.W. 2d 609 (1950), **106, 108**
Reeves v. Young, 295 Ark. 506, 749 S.W. 2d 327 (1988), **168**
Reitzhammer v. Desha Road Improvement District, No. 2, 139 Ark. 168, 213 S.W. 733 (1919), **57**
Reynolds v. Holland, 35 Ark. 56 (1879), **105**
Rhodes v. Stuttgart, 192 Ark. 822, 95 S.W. 2d 101 (1936), **100**
Ricarte v. State, 717 S.W. 2d 488 (1986), **56**
Rice v. Palmer, 78 Ark. 432, 96 S.W. 396 (1906), **87**
Rice v. State, 204 Ark. 236, 161 S.W. 2d 401 (1942), **80**
Rich v. Walker, 237 Ark. 586, 374 S.W. 2d 476 (1964), **153**
Rideway v. Catlett, 238 Ark. 323, 379 S.W. 2d 277 (1964), **53**
Riviere v. Hardegree, 278 Ark. 167, 644 S.W. 2d 176 (1983), **79**
Riviere v. Wells, 270 Ark. 206, 604 S.W. 2d 560 (1980), **50**
Roberts v. Lowe, 231 Ark. 886, 333 S.W. 2d 897 (1960), **35**
Roberts v. Wilcoxin, 36 Ark. 355 (1880), **94**
Rockefeller v. Hogue, 246 Ark. 712, 439 S.W. 2d 805 (1969), **185**
Rockefeller v. Matt hews, 249 Ark. 341, 459 S.W. 2d 110 (1970), **64, 106**
Rockefeller v. Smith, 246 Ark. 819, 440 S.W. 2d 580 (1969), **172**
Roemild v. Jones, 239 F. 2d 492 (1957), **41**
Rogers v. State, 72 Ark. 565, 82 S.W. 169 (1904), **58**
Rogers v. State, 264 Ark. 258, 570 S.W. 2d 268 (1978), **79**
Rogers v. State, 711 S.W. 2d 461 (1986), **86**
Rogers C. Mears, Jr. v. Hall, 263 Ark. 827, 569 S.W. 2d 91 (1978), **64**
Ross Drainage District v. Clark County, 153 Ark. 175, 239 S.W. 740 (1922), **130**
Rowe v. Gose, 240 Ark. 722, 401 S.W. 2d 745 (1966), **93**
Rowe v. Housing Authority, 220 Ark. 698, 249 S.W. 2d 551 (1952), **100**
Rowland v. State, 213 Ark. 780, 213 S.W. 2d 370 (1948), **78**
Roy v. Recker, 225 F. Supp. 743 (1963), **101**
Ruff v. Womack, 174 Ark. 971, 298 S.W. 222 (1927), **103**
Russell v. Jacoway, 33 Ark. 191 (1878), **106**
Russ v. Camden, 256 Ark. 214, 506 S.W. 2d 529 (1974), **39**

S

Samples v. Grady, 207 Ark. 724, 182 S.W. 2d 875 (1944), **115**
Saunders v. City of Little Rock, 262 Ark. 256, 556 S.W. 2d 874 (1977), **42**

Scaramuzza v. McLeod, 207 Ark. 855, 183 S.W. 2d 55 (1944), **106**
Scherz v. Peoples National Bank, 214 Ark. 796, 218 S.W. 2d 86 (1949), **36**
School District v. West Hartford Special School District, 102 Ark. 261, 143 S.W. 895 (1912), **59**
Scott v. Dunaway, 228 Ark. 943, 311 S.W. 2d 305 (1958), **129**
Scott v. McCuen, _______ Ark_______, 709 S.W. 2d 77 (1906), **157**
Scott County Bank v. McCraw, 58 Bankr. 175 (Bankr. W. D. Ark. 1985), **93**
Scott Stafford, "Separation of Power and Legislative Power," 7 University of Arkansas Little Rock Law Journal 279, **110**
Sexton v. Arkansas Supreme Court Commission on Professional Conduct, 299 Ark. 439, 774
S.W. 2d 114 (1989) cert. denied _______ U.S_______, 110 S. Ct. 1782, 108 L.Ed. 2d 783 (1990), **175**
Shepherd v. City of Little Rock, 183 Ark. 244, 35 S.W. 2d 361 (1931), **58**
Sherrill v. Faulkner, 200 Ark. 1006, 142 S.W. 2d 229 (1940), **114**
Shofner v. Dowell, (1925), **100**
Shuffield v. Raney, 226 Ark. 3, 287 S.W. 2d 588 (1956), **129**
Shuman v. Phillips, 53 Ark. 37, 13 S.W. 510 (1890), **82**
Simpson v. Fuller, 281 Ark. 471, 665 S.W. 2d 269 (1984), **39**
Sims v. Weldon, 165 Ark. 13, 263 S.W. 42 (1924), **69**
Smalley v. Fort Smith, 239 Ark. 39, 386 S.W. 2d 944 (1965), **106**
Smith v. Askew, 48 Ark. 82, 2 S.W. 349 (1886), **76**
Smith v. Page, 192 Ark. 342, 91 S.W. 2d 281 (1936), **128**
Smith v. Ridgeview Baptist Church, Inc., 257 Ark. 139, 514 S.W. 2d 717 (1974), **58**
Smith v. Scott, 92 Ark. 143, 122 S.W. 501 (1909), **94**
Smith v. State, 262 Ark. 239, 555 S.W. 2d 569 (1977), **68**
Smith v. State, 48 Ark. 148, 2 S.W. 661 (1886), **72**
Smithee v. Garth, (1878), **58**
Southeast Arkansas Freight Lines v. Arkansas Corp. Comm., 204 Ark. 1023, 166 S.W. 2d 262 (1942), **117, 120**
Southwestern Bell v. Arkansas Public Service Commission, 267 Ark. 550, 593 S.W. 2d 434 (1980), **37**
Spa Kennel Club v. Dunaway, 241 Ark. 51, 406 S.W. 2d (1966), **62**
Sparks v. Day, 61 Ark. 570, 33 S.W. 1073 (1896), **93**
Special School District v. Sebastian County, 277 Ark. 326, 641 S.W. 2d 702 (1982), **114**
Speer v. Wood, 128 Ark. 183, 193 S.W. 785 (1917), **46, 80, 109**
St. Louis Southwestern Railway v. O'Neal, 163 *Ark.* 193, 259 S.W. 393 (1924), **84**
St. Louis I.M.&S. Railway v. Fort Smith & Van Buren Railway., 104 Ark. 344, 148 S.W. 531 (1912), **117**
St. Louis I.M.&S. Railway v. Pitcock, 82 Ark. 441, 101 S.W. 725 (1907), **121**
St. Louis National Bank v. Marion County, 72 Ark. 27, 79 S.W. 791 (1903), **114**
Stafford v. Cook, 159 Ark. 438, 252 S.W. 597 (1923), **87**
Stain v. Stain, 286 Ark. 140, 689 S.W. 2d 566 (1985), **80**
Stanley v. Gates, 179 Ark. 886, 19 S.W. 2d 1000 (1929), **40**
Stanley v. Snyder, 43 Ark. 429 (1884), **92**
Stames v. Sadler, 237 Ark. 325, 372 S.W. 2d 585 (1963), **54, 112**
State v. Bass, 224 Ark. 976, 277 S.W. 2d 479 (1955), **129**
State v. Brooks, 301 Ark. 257, 783 S.W. 2d 368 (1990), **168**
State v. Buzzard, 4 Ark. 18 (1842), **35**
State v. Cadle, 19 Ark. 613 (1858), **37**
State v. Devers, 34 Ark. 188 (1879), **74**
State v. George, 250 Ark. 968, 470 S.W. 2d 593 (1971), **78**

State v. Henry, 304 Ark. 339, 802 S.W. 2d 448 (1990), **187**
State v. Hutt, 2 Ark. 282 (1840), **50, 86**
State v. Leatherman, 38 Ark. 81 (1881), **73**
State v. Margay Oil Corporation, 167 Ark. 614, 269 S.W. 63 (1925), **101**
State v. Martin, 60 Ark. 343, 30 S.W. 421 (1895), **75**
State v. Moore, 76 Ark. 197, 88 S.W. 881 (1905), **61, 97**
State v. Sloan, 66 Ark. 575, 53 S.W. 47 (1899), **60**
State v. Wardlaw, 43 Ark. 73 (1884), **79**
State v. Williams, 97 Ark. 243, 133 S.W. 1017 (1911), **36**
State v. Ziegenbein, 282 Ark. 162, 666 S.W. 2d 698 (1984), **152**
State Bank v. Curran, 10 Ark. 142 (1849), **50**
State ex rel. Hebert v. Hall, 228 Ark. 500, 308 S.W. 2d 828 (1958), **67**
State ex rel. Attorney General v. State Board of Education, 195 Ark. 222, 112 S.W. 2d 18 (1937), **168**
State ex rel. Evans v. Wheatly, 197 Ark. 997, 125 S.W. 2d 101 (1939), **54**
State ex rel. Gray v. Hodges, 107 Ark. 272, 154 S.W. 506 (1913), **53, 133**
State ex rel. Hebert v. Hall, 1958, **67**
State ex rel. Murphy v. Townsend, 72 Ark. 180, 79 S.W. 782 (1904), **127**
State ex rel. Purcell v. Jones, 242 Ark. 168, 412 S.W. 2d 284 (1967), **56, 69**
State ex rel. Robinson v. Jones, 194 Ark. 445, 108 S.W. 2d 901 (1937), **48**
State ex rel. Williams v. Karston, 208 Ark. 703, 187 S.W. 2d 327 (1945), **63**
Stokes v. Stokes, 271 Ark. 300, 613 S.W. 2d 372 (1981), **93**
Storey v. Brewer, 232 Ark. 552, 339 S.W. 2d 112 (1960), **86**
Strawn v. Campbell, 226 Ark. 449, 291 S.W. 2d 508 (1956), **191**
Stuart v. Stuart, 280 Ark. 546, 660 S.W. 2d 162 (1983), **94**
Sulcer v. Northwestern National Insurance Co., 263 Ark. 583, 566 S.W. 2d 397 (1978), **92, 93**
Sumpter v. Duffie, 80 Ark. 369, 97 S.W. 435 (1906), **132**
Sweeney v. Sweeney (1980), **34**
Swepston v. Barton, 39 Ark. 549 (1882), **53**
Swindler v. State, 267 Ark. 418, (1979), **37**

T

Tanner v. State, 259 Ark. 243, 532 S.W. 2d 168 (1976), **68**
Taylor v. Governor, 1 Ark. 21 (1837), **40, 53**
Taylor v. State, 284 Ark. 103, 670 S.W. 2d 797 (1984), **37**
Taylor, Cleveland and Company v. Pine Bluff, 34 Ark. 603 (1879), **115**
Tedford v. Mears, 258 Ark. 450, 526 S.W. 2d 1 (1975), **115**
Teeter Motor Co. v. First National Bank, 260 Ark. 764, 543 S.W. 2d 938 (1976), **42**
Texas and Pacific Railway v. Stephens, 192 Ark. 115, 90 S.W. 2d 978 (1936), 78
Thomas v. Sitton, 213 Ark. 816212 S.W. 2d 710 (1948), **126**
Thompson v. Sanford, 281 Ark. 365, 663 S.W. 2d 932 (1984), **39**
Thompson v. Younts, 282 Ark. 524, 669 S.W. 2d 471 (1984), **153**
Tindall v. Searan, 192 Ark. 173, 90 S.W. 2d 476 (1936), **150, 153**
Tinkle v. State, 230 Ark. 966, 328 S.W. 2d 111 (1959), **68**
Titan Oil and Gas v. Shipley, 257 Ark. 278, 517 S.W. 2d 210 (1975), **76**
Town and Country v. Godwin, 233 Ark. 307, 344 S.W. 2d 338 (1961), **101**
Townsend v. Helena, 244 Ark. 228, 424 S.W. 2d 856, cert, denied, 393 U.S. 917, 89 S. Ct. 244, 21 L.Ed. 2d 203 (1968), **154**
Townsend v. Timmons, 44 Ark. 482 (1884), **84**

Tuggle v. Tribble (1928), **59**
Turner v. Woodruff, 286 Ark. 66, 689 S.W. 2d 527 (1985), **111, 215**

U

Umberger v. Westmoreland, 218 Ark. 632, 238 S.W. 2d 495 (1951), **82**
Union Carbide and Carbon Corp. v. White River Distributors, Inc., 224 Ark. 558, 275 S.W. 2d 455 (1955), **35**

V

Vance v. Johnson, 238 Ark. 1009, 386 S.W. 2d 240 (1965), **106**
Van Hook v. McNeil Monument Company, 101 Ark. 246, 142 S.W. 154 (1911), **87**
Vault v. State, 256 Ark. 343, 507 S.W. 2d 111 (1974), **37**
Veasy v. Joshlin, 257 Ark. 422, 516 S.W. 2d 596 (1974), **36**
Venable v. State, 260 Ark. 201, 538 S.W. 2d 286 (1976), **37**
Venhaus v. Adams, 295 Ark. 606, 752 S.W. 2d 20 (1988), **217, 219**
Venhaus v. Brown, 286 Ark. 229, 691 S.W. 2d 141 (1985), **79, 168**
Venhaus v. Pulaski Count Quorum Court, 291 Ark. 558, 726 S.W. 2d 668 (1987), **218**
Venhaus v. State ex rel. Loft on, 285 Ark. 23, 684 S.W. 2d 252 (1985), **50**
Vinsant v. Knox (1871), **57**

W

W. E. Tucker Oil Co. v. Portland Bank, 285 Ark. 453, 688 S.W. 2d 293 (1985), **50**
Wade v. Brocato, 192 Ark. 826, 95 S.W. 2d 94 (1936), **121**
Wade v. Homer, 115 Ark. 250, 170 S.W. 1005 (1914), **44, 58**
Wadkins v. Merchants Bank, 96 Ark. 465, 132 S.W. 218 (1910), **84**
Wait v. Hall, 196 Ark. 508, 118 S.W. 2d 853 (1938), **157**
Walls v. State Board of Education, 195 Ark. 955, 116 S.W. 2d 354 (1938), **110, 130**
Walker v. Jackson, 391 F. Supp. 1395 (1975), **206**
Walker v. Noll, 92 Ark. 148, 122 S.W. 488 (1909), **82**
Walker v. State, 35 Ark. 386 (1880), **75**
Walker v. State, 241 Ark. 300, 408 S.W. 2d 905 (1966, appeal dismissed), 386 U.S. 682, 87 S. Ct. 1325, 18 L.Ed. 2d 403, rehearing denied, 387 U.S. 926, 87 S. Ct. 2027, 18 L.Ed. 2d 987 (1967), **202**
Walsh v. Campbell, 240 Ark. 1034, 405 S.W. 2d 264 (1966), **201, 202**
Walther v. Walther, 233 Ark. 155, 343 S.W. 2d (1961), **47**
Ward School Bus Manufacturing, Inc., v. Fowler, 261 Ark. 100, 547 S.W. 2d 394 (1977), **72**
Watson v. State DF&A, 283 Ark. 287, 675 S.W. 2d 368 (1984), **91**
Weber v. Pryor, 259 Ark. 153, 531 S.W. 2d 708 (1976), **85**
Weems v. Anderson, 257 Ark. 376, 516 S.W. 2d 895 (1974), **188**
Welech v. State, 283 Ark. 281, 675 S.W. 2d 641 (1984), **77**
Wells v. Heath, 274 Ark. 45, 622 S.W. 2d 163 (1981), **60**
Wells v. Purcell, 267 Ark. 456, 592 S.W. 2d 100 (1979), **50, 56, 69**
Wells v. Riviere, 269 Ark. 156, 599 S.W. 2d 375 (1980), **115, 223**
Wells v. White, 274 Ark. 197, 623 S.W. 2d 187 (1981), **105, 171**
Wessell Brothers Foundry Drilling Co. v. Crossett Public School District, 287 Ark. 415, 701 S.W. 2d 99 (1985), **78**
West v. State, 255 Ark. 668, 501 S.W. 2d 771 (1973), **79**

Whaley v. Northern Road Improvement District, 152 Ark. 573, 240 S.W. 2d 1 (1922), **43**
White v. Reagen, 25 Ark. 622 (1869), **126**
Whitfield v. Democratic Party, 686 F. Supp. 1365 (E.D. Ark. 1988), **177**
Williams v. Arthur J. Amey Co., 240 Ark. 157, 398 S.W. 2d 515 (1966), **183**
Williams v. Douglas, 251 Ark. 555, 473 S.W. 2d 896 (1971), **53, 54**
Williams v. State, 47 Ark. 230, 1 S.W. 149 (1886), **86**
Williams v. State, 175 Ark. 752, 2 S.W. 2d 36 (1927), **79**
Williams v. Swann, 220 Ark. 906, 251 S.W. 2d 111 (1952), **92**
Williamson v. Lockhart, 636 F. Supp. 1298 (E.D. Ark. 1986), **36**
Wilson v. State, 33 Ark. 557 (1878), **35**
Wirges v. Roberts, 240 Ark. 138, 398 S.W. 2d 518 (1966), **76**
Wood v. Keith, 60 Ark. 425, 30 S.W. 756 (1895), **79**
Woods v. State, 278 Ark. 271, 644 S.W. 2d 937 (1983), **77**
Woolard v. Thomas, 238 Ark. 162, 381 S.W. 2d 453 (1964), **230**
Wright v. Johnson, 5 Ark. 687 (1844), **38**
Wright v. Story, 298 Ark. 508, 760 S.W. 2d 16 (1989), **179**

Y

Yancey v. Faubus, 238 F. Supp. 290 (E.D. Ark. 1965), **171, 197**
York v. State, 91 Ark. 582, 121 S.W. 1070 (1909), **78**
Young v. Energy Transportation Systems, 278 Ark. 146, 644 S.W. 2d 266 (1983), **102**

INDEX

Abortion, 44, 239
Adjournments during session of legislature, 64
Agricultural property, taxation on, 170
Agriculture, Mining and Manufacture, 91
Amendments to the State constitution, 19–23 (table), 141–245
- effective dates of, 154
- initiative process, 126–127, 129
- mechanisms for submission and approval of, 128, 131
- publication of proposed, 128
- record of votes on, 128
- separate consideration of proposed, 128
- submission to people, 128

Appeals, 77
Appellate jurisdiction of Supreme Court, 218
Appointment power of governor, 66, 172
Apportionment, 85
Appropriation, definition of, 56
Appropriation bills, 145
- debt limit on, 54–55
- item veto for, 64
- single, annual, 54

Article I–XIX. *See specific title of each article*
Assembly, right of, 30
Attainder, bill of, 36
Attorney General, selection of, 124, 192
Auditor, state, 49, 59–60, 66, 106

Bail, 32–33
"Ballot propositions," voting on, 48, 137
Banks, 111
Bicameral legislature, 49
Bill of rights. *See* Declaration of Rights
Bills
- of attainder, 40
- limitations on enactment of, 57

Blacks, suffrage for, 45, 140
Bond issue, 145, 229–30
Bond issues, 145–46, 148, 159–60, 219
Borrowing, 100
Boundaries, 31–32

Capital punishment
- bail and, 37
- cruel and unusual punishment and, 37
- right to appeal in case of, 37

Chief Justice of Supreme Court, 71, 143
Children, 199
Civil cases, right to jury trial in, 35
Civil liberties, declaration of rights, 33–44
Clemency, executive, 68
Clerk of Supreme Court, 71
Clinton, Bill, 65, 182
Collective bargaining rights, 183, 184
Commissions
- as executive department, 69
- granted by governors, form of, 63, 65, 82, 127

Compensation
- just, 42, 44
- for legislators, 53, 54, 141, 170, 199, 242. *See also* Salaries

Confrontation of witnesses, right to, 37
Constitutional Conventions, 5–8, 11, 12–134
Constitution of 1836, 5–8
Constitution of 1861, 8–9
Constitution of 1864, 9–11
Constitution of 1868, 11–13
Constitution of 1874, 13–16
Contracts, 40, 8, 113
Corporations, 99
Counsel, right to, 37
Counties, County Seats and County Lines, 105–06
Counties
- interpretation of powers of, 218
- representation of, 218

Court system
- schedule for, 123
- Supreme Court power over, 71. *See also* Judicial Department

Credit
- of local government, 103
- of state, 103, 226

Crime, rights of persons accused of, 37–38

Criminal cases, right to jury trial in, 36
Criminal offenses, determination of, 36–37
Cruel and unusual punishment, 37

Death penalty, 37
Debt, imprisonment for, 40
Debt limits
  local government, 103
  state appropriations, 59, 149
Declaration of Rights, 33–44
Declaratory judgment, 52
Defendants
  presentment or indictment of
    grand jury, 36
  rights when accused of crime, 36
Departments, 49–50
Distribution of powers of government.
    See Executive Department;
    See Judicial Department; *See*
    Legislative
Double jeopardy, 36, 55
Dual officeholding, limitations on, 117
Due process of law, 36

Education, 99–100
Election(s)
  to fill unexpired terms, 176–77
  general, 63
  of governor, 61–62
  legislative, 51, 129–20
  schedule for, 135
  submission of amendment at, 145
Eligibility requirements
  for governor, 64
  for state legislative seats, 55
  for Supreme Court justices, 71–72
Eminent domain, power of. *See* Power of
    eminent domain
Employees' rights, 168
Equal protection of law, 45
Evidence
  search warrant and, 39
  self-incrimination doctrine and, 37
Excessive bail or fines, 37
Executive Department, 63–70
  executive branch, 68, 131, 222
  executive clemency and parole
    system, 54, 68
  governor, 65
  militia, provision for, 66, 97
Exemptions, 91–94

Fees, 112
Finance
  appropriations, debt
    limit on, 59–60, 151
  local indebtedness, 103, 159, 160
  public schools, 107–08. *See also* Taxation
Finance and Taxation, 111–15
Fines, 37
Franchise and Elections, 45–48
Freedoms. *See* Declaration of Rights

Gambling provision, 125
General Assembly, 52–53
  amendment proposal in, 57, 120
  compensation of members of, 59
  election to, 52–53, 189
  impeachment by, 59, 109
General elections, 47
Government
  distribution of powers of, 51
  structure of, 51
Governor
  appointment of executive officers, 69
  appointment of judges, 72
  election of, 64, 211, 212
  eligibility requirements, 65
  impeachment of, 66, 109
  powers and duties of, 120
  salary of, 112, 198
  special session of legislature and, 69
  supervision of executive branch, 68
  term of office, 63, 173, 220
  vacancy in office of, 66, 137
  veto power, 67, 154. *See also* Executive
    Department
Grand jury, presentment or
    indictment of, 36–37

Habeas corpus, 38
History, constitutional, 5–25
Horticultural property, taxation on, 101

Impartial jury, right to, 37
Impeachment
  of public officers and employees, 128
  of Supreme Court justices and other
    judges, 128
Impeachment and Address, 109–10
Imprisonment for debt, 40
Indictment of grand jury, 36, 37
Indictments, 86

Initiative process, 150
Item veto, 68, 167

Judges, 71–72, 74–75, 84
Judicial Circuits, 123
Judicial Department, 71–98
  appeals, 72
  chief justice, 71
  circuit courts, 74–76, 77–78
  corporation courts, 74–75
  county courts, 74–75, 79, 80
  court of common pleas, 74–75
  court system, 71
  justices and judges, 71, 77, 79–80, 81
Judicial power, 71
Judiciary, 71–87
Jurisdiction
  of county prosecutors, 79
  original, 74
Jury
  grand, presentment or indictment of, 36–37
  impartial, 37–38
  province of, 37–38
Jury trial right, 35, 164
"Just compensation," notion of, 42
Justices of Supreme Court, 75

Labor relations, employees' rights and, 182–83
Laws
  governor's power and duty to execute, 62
  local, 58
  special, 58
Legal profession. Supreme Court, 156
  jurisdiction over, 153
Legislative, 51–62
  appointment in Senate and General Assembly, 51
  legislative powers, 51
  limitations on law-making, 52
  limitations on legislators, 52
  oath of office, 131
  structure of legislature, 51
Legislative procedure, rules of, 54
Legislators
  compensation for, 184
  ineligibility for, 53
  limitations on dual officeholding, 52
  oath or affirmation of office, 131
  protection from litigation, 93

Legislature
  adjournment of houses, 57
  bicameral, 51
  eligibility requirements for holding seat in, 51, 52
  journal of proceedings, 53
  organization of executive branch and, 68–69
  power to judge qualifications of own members, 53, 67
  quorum in, 52
  regulation of elections, 48
  schedule for, 51
  special sessions of, 69
  vacancies, 52
Libel, 35
Liberties. *See* Declaration of Rights
Local government indebtedness, 103
Local laws, 58
Lotteries, 129

Military, the
  quartering of soldiers, 44
  subordination to civil power, 98
  voting rights of personnel in, 185
Militia, 97–98
Miscellaneous Provisions, 125–33
Municipal and Private Corporations, 99–103
Municipal corporations, interpretation of powers of, 99
Municipalities, power to grant tax exemptions, 93

Oath of office
  for legislators, 131
  for officers of legislature, 131
  for state officers, 131
Organize, right to, 176
Original jurisdiction, 72, 80, 84, 106

Pardons, governor's power to grant, 41, 68
Petition, right of, 34
Power
  distribution of government of, 49
  gubernatorial, 64
  judicial, 71
  legislative, 51
Power of eminent domain
  private property taken through, 42
  urban redevelopment and, 42

Practice and procedure, Supreme Court, 73, 74
Preamble, 29
President of Senate, 56, 66–67
Press, freedom of the, 35
Private property for public use, 42
Privileges. *See* Declaration of Rights
"Probable cause," issuance of warrant and, 39
Property, private, for public use, 42
Prosecutors, county, 79
Public notice, of administrative rules and regulations, 136
Public office, religious or racial test for, 13
Public officers and employees
  county, 213
  impeachment of, 109–10
"Public purpose" doctrine, private property for public use, 42
Public school system, free, 107
Public trial, right to, 37
Punishment, cruel and unusual, 37

Quartering of soldiers, 44
Quorum
  in legislature, 54, 217–18
  Supreme Court, 71

Railroads, Canals and Turnpikes, 113–14
Referenda, voting on, 149
Religious freedom, 43–44
Religious sect, ban on establishment of, 44
Reprieves, governor's power to grant, 68
Residence, voting rights and, 189
Retroactive laws, limits on legislature relating to, 41
Rights
  to appeal, 82
  education, 99
  voting. *See* Suffrage
Rulemaking power of Supreme Court, 77

Salaries
  of governor, 112, 127, 132, 198
  judicial, 71, 123, 175, 185. *See also* Compensation
Schedule Article, 135
  court system, 136
  executive, 135–36
  legislature, 53
  phase-in of laws, 135
School funds, 107, 168
Seal of State, 64, 132
Searches and seizures, freedom from unreasonable, 39
Secretary of State, 66, 67, 110, 127
Self-incrimination, right against, 51
Senate
  compensation of members of, 56, 184, 218
  election to, 52, 190
  governor's power to convene, 69
  impeachment trial in, 67
  term of office for senators, 52
Senate districts, 172, 181, 181
Separation of powers doctrine, 49. *See also* Executive Department; *See also* Judicial Department; *See also* Legislative
Sheriffs, 85
Soldiers, quartering of, 44
Speaker of (lower house of legislature), 56
Special laws, 59
Special session of legislature, 69
Speech, liberty of, 36
Speedy trial, right to, 35
State officers, 70
Succession in office of governor, 130
Suffrage, 45–48
  qualifications for, 141
Supreme Court, 71–74, 143
Supreme Court Rules, 71–72

Taxation
  exemptions, 91–92, 160, 208
  property, 41, 86, 87, 107, 215. *See also* Finance
Terms of office
  of governor, 73, 173–74
  of senators, 52
  of Supreme Court justices, 71
Treason, 39, 68
Trial
  public, right to, 37
  "speedy," right to, 37
Trial by jury, right to, 37, 164

Uniformity principle of property taxation, 42

About the Author

KAY COLLETT GOSS is Senior Assistant for Intergovernmental Relations, Office of the Governor, State of Arkansas.

www.ingramcontent.com/pod-product-compliance
Ingram Content Group UK Ltd.
Pitfield, Milton Keynes, MK11 3LW, UK
UKHW020848150926
475595UK00003B/72

9 780199 778966